Acclaim for Paula McLain's memoir

LIKE FAMILY

GROWING UP IN

OTHER PEOPLE'S HOUSES

"Astonishing. . . . With her poetic gift for language, an extraordinary frankness, and narrative generosity, McLain demonstrates through the impenetrable bond with her sisters the true meaning of family." — Kera Bolonik, *Chicago Tribune*

"A powerful and haunting memoir."
— Anne Martiro, *Ann Arbor News*

"If every memoir were like Paula McLain's *Like Family,* there would be far fewer accusations of navel-gazing made against the genre. That's because McLain, who writes about the years she and her two sisters spent bouncing around the foster-care system in the early seventies, is sharing something much more illuminating than a string of bad relationships or a substance abuse problem. McLain's voice is deft and often humorous as she limns the profound moments of sadness and strange exhilarations of her rootless youth. While the subject matter pierces your heart, McLain refuses ever to play the pity card, and her clear-eyed approach opens our eyes to the strange subculture of 'lost' children. A sometimes startling, always engaging view of the hidden world in our own backyard."
— *Elle*

"McLain displays her poetic inclinations with florid descriptions. . . . A brave account."   — *Publishers Weekly*

"What makes *Like Family* so remarkable are not the peculiar circumstances of Paula McLain's childhood but the depth of understanding that she brings to those circumstances, and the beautiful prose in which she renders that understanding. Seldom have I seen so vividly evoked the need to belong to some, any, kind of family and the painful negotiations that time brings to even our closest intimacies."

— Margot Livesey, author of *Eva Moves the Furniture*

"The first thing that strikes the reader about *Like Family* is that the author has chosen her words very carefully, fastening her story to a spectacularly stark but beautifully resonant prose. . . . McLain reveals in waves of childhood memory what it was like to grow up in foster homes, buffeted from family to family, never quite feeling at home. . . . It is the mixture of sweet nostalgia for growing up, combined with the harsh emotional scars of neglect and abuse, that make this book remarkable. McLain leaves the reader knowing that a child is not the sum total of the abuse she experienced at the hands of others, but somewhere, between the neglect and the mistreatment, a child is able to create a space and a life that is her very own."   — Kathleen O'Grady, *Bust*

"This book has a power of its own — the raw force of a memorable and well-told story of children who overcome the injustice of their abandoned state and grow up to fashion some sort of reasonable adulthood for themselves. You're likely to have a lump in your throat by the end of this gutsy and honest tale."

— Pat MacEnulty, *Fort Lauderdale Sun-Sentinel*

Also by Paula McLain

Less of Her

LIKE FAMILY

GROWING UP IN
OTHER PEOPLE'S HOUSES

A Memoir

PAULA McLAIN

BACK BAY BOOKS
LITTLE, BROWN AND COMPANY
NEW YORK BOSTON LONDON

Back Bay Books / Little, Brown and Company

Hachette Book Group

1290 Avenue of the Americas New York, NY 10104

littlebrown.com

Originally published in hardcover by Little, Brown and Company, March 2003

First Back Bay trade paperback edition, May 2004

Reissued, August 2013

Author's Note: This is a work of nonfiction. The events and experiences detailed here are factual and represented as faithfully as possible according to my memory. In many cases, time frame and place-names have been altered, and virtually all names of individuals — aside from my own and those of my sisters — have been changed in order to protect their privacy.

The author is grateful for permission to use the following: "Without Rings" by Neil Young, © 1998 Silver Fiddle, all rights reserved. Used by permission. Warner Bros. Publications U.S. Inc., Miami, FL 33014. The poem by Emily Dickinson on page ix was reprinted by permission of the publishers and the Trustees of Amherst College from *The Poems of Emily Dickinson,* Thomas H. Johnson, ed., Cambridge, Mass.: The Belknap Press of Harvard University Press, Copyright © 1951, 1955, 1979 by the President and Fellows of Harvard College.

Library of Congress Cataloging-in-Publication Data

McLain, Paula.
   Like family : growing up in other people's houses : a memoir / Paula McLain. —1st ed.
     p. cm.
   ISBN 978-0-316-59742-5 (hc) / 978-0-316-90909-9 (pb) /978-0-316-40060-2 (reissue)
   1. McLain, Paula — Childhood and youth. 2. Foster children — California — Biography. 3. Women poets, American — Biography. I. Title.
HV883.C2 M35 2003
362.73'3'092 — dc21
[B]   2002073060

10 9 8 7 6

LSC-H

Text design by Meryl Sussman Levavi/Digitext

Printed in the United States of America

For my sisters
and
for Connor

What fortitude the soul contains,

That it can so endure

The accent of a coming foot,

The opening of a door!

— *Emily Dickinson*

I'm picking something up.

I'm letting something go.

Like a dog, I'm fetching this

to you.

— *Neil Young*

LIKE FAMILY

DOGS ARE EASY. IF their tails are up and their eyes are soft, you're in. Sometimes they need to smell your hands, your shoes, between your legs. Sometimes they just throw themselves full tilt, all of them at all of you — like the Lindberghs' dogs. They were what we saw first, a happy blur along the fencing as our social worker, Mrs. O'Rourke, slowed the car and stopped in front of a whitewashed wooden gate. Teresa got out to open it, her sneakers sending dust. With one hand on the metal latch, she pointed to a sign that hung from the center of the gate and spelled out, in blocky white letters, LINDBERGH ACRES. She grinned, flashing her chipped front tooth, and ran back to the car. "They named it," she said, crawling in beside me. "Just like Big Valley."

The brown ranch house squatted on a low hill. Dry grass stretched to every side and looked, from the car, like giant slices of toast. How different it all was from the Spinozas' boxy row house in central Fresno; the Clapps' well-groomed lawn and portico with a blinding-white Cadillac; the Fredricksons' Palo Verde tract home. The driveway here wasn't concrete but dirt, with deep potholes and stones. To the left stood a large pasture where several horses lumbered behind an electric fence. *Horses!* To the right, fields and fields, mushrooming fig trees.

The Lindberghs' house was ringed by an oval of split-rail fencing and a lawn that looked determinedly untamed: crisp brown around the edges with crabgrass and clover erupting every few feet like acne. It was late afternoon, and the family had come out onto the lawn to greet us. Bub and Hilde both wore new dark-blue jeans, cowboy boots and dress-plaid Western shirts with pearly snap buttons. Their seven-year-old daughter, Tina, did an anxious series of little hops forward and back, looking, with her cap of straw-colored hair, her yellow shorts set and bare feet, like a round yellow bird. She was getting sisters. We had been promised to her, and here we were.

If there's anything odder than being introduced to your new family of complete strangers, I don't know what that might be. The social worker sticks around for a while, trying to break the ice, but when she leaves, it's just you and your questions, popping like flashbulbs, and these people who will sit you down and feed you dinner and show you to your room. In that way it's like a hotel because nothing belongs to you. It's all being lent, like library books: the bed, the toothbrush, the bathwater, the night-light under the medicine cabinet that will help you recognize your own face at 2 A.M. when you get up to pee.

As I stood on the Lindberghs' lawn next to my sisters, it occurred to me — for the first time — that the families who took us in were being introduced to absolute strangers too. The big dogs danced and squirmed, gleeful with new smells, but Bub and Hilde held as tight and still as a pair of garden gnomes. They didn't know what would happen; they didn't know the first thing about my sisters or me — what we'd say or do, if we'd stay for a month or a year or three. And us, we'd seen the backseat of Mrs. O'Rourke's car too many times, our clothes in garbage bags on the floorboard. If we felt any hope that this new situation would be different, then it was the stowaway version, small and pinching as pea gravel in a shoe. Bub and Hilde seemed nice enough, but didn't everybody at first?

Mrs. O'Rourke's car wambled down the drive, tires falling into every third pothole. We watched until she was out of sight and then watched the empty road. Finally, there was nothing to do but turn toward the Lindberghs. We stood, the three of them and the three of us, on the grass dry as cereal, and the noises all around — the snuffling dogs and the buzz of the air conditioner and the sprinkler pelting a row of yellow roses — seemed to be saying, *Now what? Now what? Now.*

⸺⸺

THE LINDBERGHS LIVED WAY out of town in Ashland, California, which is right next-door to Fresno in the San Joaquin Valley. You've probably heard of Fresno, it being one of the likeliest places to get shot in the head in a dark alley and also the raisin capital of the world. Penny and Teresa were born in Spokane, Washington, where our mother is from and where she went for help when our father ran off and left her midpregnancy, as was his habit. With my birth, she didn't have to go to Spokane because her mother came to her, and so I was the one delivered in a Fresno vineyard — or rather in a hospital wedged between vineyards. The place was tiny, and since no rooms were available when my mother's time came, she labored in a hallway next to the washer and dryer, panting and contracting while a load of sheets twisted and filled with sudsy, grayish water, shutting her eyes against nausea when her mother offered her quaking cubes of strawberry Jell-O. This was in October, past the drying season, but I'll bet the air around the vineyards still hung with the sickly sweet smell of grape funerals. It's all the juice that does it, sugar collapsing on itself as the grapes shrivel into shrunken little heads. It stays and stays, that smell. You keep thinking you can blink it away or swallow it down, but you can't.

I was eight years old the day our social worker brought us to the Lindberghs'; Penny was eight too, being only eleven months my junior, and Teresa was ten. It was late September 1974, and still quite hot. Mrs. O'Rourke's yellow station wagon didn't have air-conditioning, so the windows were down, funneling a furnace-blast of air through the front and out the back. We drove and drove. I looked out my window, Teresa looked out hers, and Penny sat in the middle, her feet on the hump, hugging the Barbie camper she'd just gotten as a birthday present from the Fredricksons, our last set of parents. Penny stroked the pink-decal striping as if it were puppy fur, her head bowed so that her red-brown hair fell forward. The cut was so severe it looked to be all bangs, the first tier falling to right above her gray eyes, the second touching her shoulders. With the way she was sitting, balled up like a hedgehog, I couldn't see her small, square face with its dusting of rust-colored freckles.

"All right," Teresa said, turning to me, "I've thought about this, and what I think is *you* should be the one to share a room with the new girl. You're the friendliest. You'll make the best impression." Penny looked up from her camper long enough to give her approval, and it was done. Frankly, I felt like a sacrifice, but what was I to say? *No, I'm not friendly? I'm a real pill?* Besides, as the oldest, Teresa always decided official business. Penny's and my job was to nod.

"Okay," I said, and went back to my window, to the Jekyll-and-Hyde landscape whooshing by: dry ditches and lush, leafy almond orchards; ravaged, abandoned lots and crops of soybeans greener than green.

OUR FIRST DINNER WITH the Lindbergh family was spaghetti. A big cauldron sat in the middle of the table, and we fished from it, eating with noisy slurps, tomato sauce everywhere. They were good eaters, the Lindberghs, with pie-plate faces, fingers like Vienna sausages, shoulders biscuity and broad and stooped. I watched Tina wield her fork as if it were a spear, stabbing a single fat bean like a javelina. She was hungry. They were all so very hungry.

"You're nothing but twigs," Bub said, pushing the plate of Wonder bread at us, the green beans, the gallon jug of milk. "Didn't anyone ever feed you girls?"

We were on the twiggy side, it's true, all elbows and shoulder blades with collarbones like miniature reservoirs. Penny and I both weighed fifty-six pounds, but since she was half-a-head shorter, she looked stockier and more square. She had always been the physical blip, the one-of-these-things-is-not-like-the-other sister. Her auburn hair was stick straight and fine; mine and Teresa's was unruly with thick dark curls. Her eyes were a watery gray; ours were brown. Her ears were small and close to her head; ours stuck out like jug handles, like car doors, like the Baby New Year's when he took off his big black hat. Although Teresa had chipped her right front tooth when she was seven, when she had her mouth closed we looked enough alike that we could make Penny feel positively alien and did, telling her she came from a goose egg, a spaceship, the moon. She'd stutter (which she did whenever she was nervous), sputter and deny it, her top lip pooching out like a nursing blister, the opposite of a pout, and we'd feel bad enough to stop for a while. Truth be told, she was probably the cutest of the lot, but why would we tell her that?

After dinner, we piled into the Lindberghs' beat-up blue truck. Following Tina's lead, we jumped in back and scooted to the front of the bed to sit in a row, backs pressed against the cab.

It was still fully light and warm, evening coming on slow and soft. The whir of the road under the truck made it too loud to talk, but it was nice just being there, watching our new neighborhood rush by, streaky and smeared. Tina sat next to me, her coarse blond hair blowing crazily, her plump legs straight out, scuffy tennis shoes pointed in at each other. She was sockless and had a scab the size of a pencil eraser on her left anklebone, ridged and scaly, ripe. Maybe she was the kind of kid who didn't pick scabs. Who knew? She was uncharted territory, this new sister, her own frontier.

Our destination was a huge furniture warehouse out by Highway 99. We were after bunk beds and got to help pick them out, climbing up and down the ladders of showroom models, bouncing a little on the mattresses like people in commercials. When we got back to the Lindberghs', everyone changed into pajamas and brushed teeth; then Bub called us all into the living room. I thought there was going to be a family prayer but then noticed he had set up a reel-to-reel recorder on the floor. He had us sit Indian-style in a circle while he fussed with the machine. "Testing, testing." The microphone looked as small and silver as a sardine in Bub's sun-toughened hand. He tapped the talking end several times, blew into it and then, when satisfied, began to play radio commentator, going around the circle, asking each of us our names and how old we were, and one thing we were happy about. In that way, it was a little like Thanksgiving. He started with Penny, and although she stared into her slippers, she said her name and age without stuttering a bit, then briefly described the wonders of her Barbie camper — the miniature Styrofoam ice chest, the lantern no bigger than a jelly bean.

I rubbed a section of my hair back and forth across my lips, my oldest habit. I was trying to think of the perfect thing to say, but when the mike came around to me, there was nothing but air in my mouth.

"Hey, have you forgotten who you are?" Bub teased.

I dropped my hands and flushed. "No. I'm Paula." My name came out with a dry croak, and I had to repeat it: "I'm Paula and I'm eight and I'm happy for . . . for. I'm just happy, I guess." I reached for my hair again and looked through my crossed legs at the carpet, a medium shag with blue-and-brown twists.

"Well, that's all right," Bub said. "That's a start."

When he got to Tina, she flung one plump arm around Teresa's neck, nearly knocking her over in the process. "I'm Tina Marie Lindbergh, and this is my new bestest buddy!"

Teresa grinned and nodded *yes, yes, yes,* her curls shaking excitedly. Pinned against Tina, she looked much younger than usual and completely uncomposed. Joyful.

Now wait just a minute, I thought, *I am Tina's roommate. I am the friendliest, so why is Teresa suddenly the bestest buddy? And what is a* bestest *buddy anyhow?*

Once the opening ceremonies had ended, we headed down the hall to bed. Tina's room was pretty and more feminine than I would have guessed, with pink walls, purple-flowered curtains and an industrial-size night-light with an eyelet shade and purple bulb. It wasn't at all dark in there, but I imagined that was the point. I watched Tina climb the wooden ladder to the top bunk and settled myself on the bottom. We lay there in silence for several minutes. *Shouldn't we say something?* I thought. *Even if it's just good night?* Then, quite spontaneously, I hopped out of bed and stood on the ladder to face her. "Here," I said, holding out my floppy beanbag toad. "This is Froggy. He's good to sleep with."

She thanked me and smiled sleepily, and I was glad I had done it for all of about five minutes, until I heard her fall into a deep, diesel-like breathing and realized I wasn't going to be able to sleep myself. Not only was the mattress new and crinkly, but the outside noises were all wrong. Instead of cars and sirens, there were crickets; a dog padding across the patio, shaking his collar; horses feeding with sharp tugs of grass that sounded like something perforated coming apart. Why had I given Froggy to Tina? She probably didn't even want him. The beans wouldn't stay in his left leg, and his bubble eyes had been rubbed clean of the black eyeball paint. He was a stupid toy. Stupid. I covered my face with my pillow and breathed in and out, in and out, then surfaced again. Deep, purple shadows fell over the horse posters thumbtacked to the wall and over the shelves with plastic horse figurines in different sizes, some with saddles and reins that looked to be real leather. Tina was lucky to have such nice things. It occurred to me that since I was there borrowing her room, her closet, half of the dresser pasted with Super Friends stickers, the nightstand and water glass, even her parents, sleeping right across the hall and snoring like a cave of bears, maybe I could borrow a little luck too. A thimbleful, a knuckle's worth, a smidge.

OUR REAL MOTHER HAD been gone since early in the fall of 1970. Up and gone, gone and went, winked out like a dead star. She went to the movies with Roger, the boyfriend, and never came back. I was four then; Penny was three, and Teresa was six. They took us to our grandmother's house in central Fresno and left us on the stoop.

"It might go late," Mom said to Granny, smoothing one hand over her bubble of brown hair. She wore a fitted blouse and a tan wool skirt with white threads woven through. The pattern was slanted, a spattering that looked like driving rain or like snow blowing across an open field, though I had never seen snow. She fished in her handbag for a cigarette and then held one, unlit, while she touched each of us lightly through the metal railing. "If it's late, we'll be back tomorrow. In the morning."

Granny just nodded and waved. She told us to wave too, and we did, none of us knowing Mom's movie would last just short of sixteen years. Perhaps not even she knew this as Roger adjusted his mirrors and guided the car into traffic on First Street, where the streetlamps were just coming up.

Granny, who was my father's mother, set us up a pallet on the living-room floor and let us sleep in our clothes. The next day was Saturday, and she promised waffles. When we woke up, our mother still hadn't come back for us, but there was the full, good day at Granny's. We walked to Radio Park and played on the swings, leaning back so our long hair swept the wood chips in the hollow under each. Days passed this way, but Granny didn't seem worried. Then Deedee — our aunt and Mom's best friend — came by to say that Mom and Roger had left the state. They were headed east for Montana or Wyoming, one of those states that's flat on the map but wide-open to the eye. We never got a post-card, so I don't know if they stayed in old motels with fluttering vacancy signs, if they stopped to see the Hoover Dam or the Grand Canyon or the world's largest frying pan. I don't even know if they got there, wherever *there* was, or if it eluded them, moving always just ahead of the car.

For the next few months, we stayed with Granny and waited for our dad to come and collect us, to make known how things would be. I imagine we were a handful for Granny, who near as I could tell was born old. She wore see-through-thin cotton dresses and cat's-eye glasses, heavy lace-up shoes and peach cotton stock-ings, an endless supply of which were curled in her bureau like sleeping gerbils. Granny had survived two husbands and was being courted by Mr. Dobbs, a heavyset mouth-breather who sold peanut brittle from a cart on Fulton Mall. Her little rat-dog, Tiny, wasted no time getting friendly with Mr. Dobbs. They napped together, Mr. Dobbs in the green-vinyl armchair in front of a silent baseball game, Tiny knotted up in the bib of Mr. Dobbs's overalls, entirely hidden but for the velvety tips of his long ears. We liked Mr. Dobbs too. One rainy afternoon, he cleared the lunch dishes from the table and showed us how to make an edible Christmas tree out of food-dyed Cheerios and marshmallow cream and a toilet-paper-roll holder. We used Red Hots as orna-ments, holding them in our cupped hands until Mr. Dobbs was ready for the delicate placement. After, our fingers were stained and sticky, lickable.

Sometimes Mr. Dobbs attended services with us at Granny's church, the Gospel Lighthouse, but more often he stayed home and snoozed with Tiny. We preferred this only because it left the front seat free and gave us complete control of the radio, which had buttons like piano keys that you pushed down instead of in. Granny was a serious Pentecostal who believed in original sin and the laying on of hands, and that some were moved by the Spirit to speak in tongues. As a girl, she was baptized in a white dress in a real river, her head shoved under by the preacher, who stood by her, waist-high in the water in his good suit. They didn't baptize like that anymore, at least not at the Gospel Lighthouse, where the baptismal font sat in its own room behind the pulpit and a screen of deep-blue curtains. It was sort of a little swimming pool, and shallow enough that the baptizee had to lean way back to get his or her head under, like limboing without the stick. When I made this observation to Granny, she shushed me, saying that Limbo was the dwelling place for the poor souls stuck between heaven and hell and that I'd best start paying attention.

If the devil was alive and well in the world, and I had every reason to believe he was, then the most likely place for him was the women's bathroom at the Gospel Lighthouse, which you could only get to by leaving the building and going clear around the side of the church where the Sunday-school classrooms met and where the preacher's voice, as you sat trying to pee, sounded like a yellow jacket smacking into stained glass. The bathroom floor was laid out in a pattern of cracked gray tile that sloped toward a drain hole the size of a baby's head. Somewhere under there, who knew how far down, the devil slept fitfully. I tiptoed around that hole in my patent-leather shoes to the stall where the door creak sounded human, then to the sink to wash my hands.

I'd have skipped that last step in a hot minute if it weren't for Granny, who always asked to sniff our palms after to see if she could smell soap.

One Sunday when we were still living with Granny, the preacher was hollering, doing his usual mad–string puppet routine, and Penny started hollering back. Within seconds, Teresa was crying too, and then I started in, all of us louder than the choir that had been humming "Shall We Gather at the River?" as background. Granny fastened us with a look that said she was about to drag us out by our ears and give us something to cry about, but then the preacher broke in with a "Praise the Lord!"

"Jesus is here," he said, throwing both arms up and out as if to catch something bigger than himself. "Here in this cursed room. It's His little finger that's reached out to touch these children, and with that touch they have been saved from a life of eternal damnation."

Granny started crying then, and people all around her in the pews reached out to pat her on the shoulder, saying how blessed our lives were going to be now that salvation was in the bag. The sermon was called short because of the miracle, and we had a party. Each of us got two frosted cupcakes, which we ate sitting on the church steps. Granny beamed and beamed, and it was easy to believe her face: we *were* Saved. This was the big time, the big top, Jesus' best hat trick. Our souls would be preserved, put up like peaches in a Mason jar, stowed safe until we needed them, until happy was an actual thing, as sound and solid as Granny's two hands on her Bible, as King James doing Jesus in red, as the cupcake that dropped frosting in my lap — something sweet for later.

BUB LINDBERGH WAS RAISED Protestant, Hilde was raised Catholic, but both converted to Mormonism soon after they were married. A team of missionaries had come to their door wearing sharp navy suits and name tags, and Bub, always eager to learn more about anything at all, had asked them in. The missionaries came every day for a week, giving their testimonies, and at the end of that time, Bub and Hilde were convinced of some things — that Joseph Smith had been visited by an angel in the form of a great white salamander, for one, and that he had somehow learned overnight to translate Hebrew, a shocking display of intelligence that was a sure sign of divine intervention. They agreed to be baptized again and married again too, in snowy white garments (think: underwear) in the Oakland Temple. By the time we came along, Bub was a deacon in the church, and Hilde ran the nursery on Sundays. They tithed 10 percent of their income; fasted sunup to sundown on the appropriate days; drank the prescribed Pero, an uncoffee that tasted like wheat germ; and filled their garage with barrels of flour and honey and lard for the scourge preceding the Second Coming. Every Monday night was Family Home Evening, a time set aside for family fellowship, meaning we played Twister or Spoon Golf after dinner instead of watching TV.

Hilde worked hard at being a good Mormon, though her faith was sprinkled with and confused by superstitions from her childhood in postwar Germany. She believed in signs and portents, that the dead speak to the living through dreams and that the devil knows us, each to each, all the way down to the sock lint between our toes.

"He will come to your window one night," Hilde promised once. She had come into the bathroom while I was brushing my teeth before bed, and moved around me as she talked, straightening the bath towel, closing the lid of the wicker hamper, rubbing water spots from the faucet with a wad of toilet paper. Her toffee-colored hair was frizzled from a recent perm and sprung out over her ears, looking as nervous as her hands. "He'll come to ask you a question, and you'd better know the answer."

"Why me?"

"Not just you. He comes to everyone at some point. You can't escape. No one can."

"Don't be a fence-sitter," Granny's preacher used to say, talking about the great war in heaven and about the angels who wouldn't choose between Satan and Jesus because they wanted to see who would win first. Those rooting for Jesus got to stay angels, those on Satan's side were damned to hell for all eternity, and those on the fence were sent to Earth, removed from God, to learn the wrongness of their ways. Here I was, the descendant of a fence-sitter, and here was the devil, no longer simply in the mouth of the preacher or somewhere way down under the drain hole in the women's bathroom at the Gospel Lighthouse, but on his way to my window. He had a plan. He knew my name. Thinking about this made my elbows sweat and my tongue feel like a tomato. It took real effort to ask Hilde, "What's the question?"

"I can't tell you that."

"What's the answer?"

"You'll just have to figure it out for yourself," she huffed. "What? Did you think you were extra bratwurst?"

To think you were extra bratwurst was to believe you were above it all, too big for your britches, a princess who wouldn't abide the pea. It must have been a German phrase. Hilde was a full-blooded German. She was born in Germany and lived there until Bub brought her back in 1957 as his GI bride. Everything was so new to her — she had never been in the States before — and he felt bad about leaving her home alone all day when he went off to work. So he started bringing her by his mother's in the morning and picking her up on his way home. They got along right away, Noreen and Hilde, cut from the same cloth, as they say, a phrase that more than suited them because they made all their own clothes on Noreen's rickety Singer using the same Butterick patterns: tent blouses with V necks and square patch pockets, polyester pants with sewn-in seams down the front.

Hilde said that what she liked best about America those first years was white bread. It was soft and sweet, like cake, not at all like German bread, which was brown and dense and bricklike. Hilde believed most American food was empty and fatty. She'd hold up a hunk of Velveeta cheese in its rectangular box and say, "This isn't cheese. It tastes like butter; it tastes like nothing." Real cheese, to Hilde, was Limburger, which Bub made her wrap in ten layers of Saran because he said it smelled like shit. It did too, as if it had been buried under a legion of cows and the cows under a pyramid of their own dung. I couldn't believe she ate it, or the knuckle-colored, spongy meats and pickled fishes that came in small hourglass-shaped jars. After the jars were empty, she washed them out and put them up on the windowsill above the sink. Some were filled with toothpicks or bobby pins or crusty pennies, but most floated avocado seeds in various stages of germination, white roots like hair swimming in slimy brown water, wormy shoots rising to poke the screen.

When Hilde wasn't dieting, the fridge fairly oozed with gross German food; when she was, there wasn't much but the prepackaged dinners from Weight Watchers that looked like they wouldn't satisfy a hamster. She always stuck to the diet at first, doing exercises in the kitchen, lifting cans of cling peaches over her head, grabbing onto a chair back to do leg lifts. Then, invariably, she'd fall off, forgetting to go to meetings or weigh-ins. It looked hard, losing weight, but my sisters and I had the opposite problem. Bub decided we'd been starved in our last foster home, and he started a weight-gaining contest to right this wrong. Whoever could gain ten pounds the fastest would get a new pair of pants. I don't think any of us considered that gaining ten pounds would probably mean we'd need a *bunch* of new clothes; we just started chowing in the spirit of competition. The morning the contest began, I ate a whole package of link sausages and four hard-boiled eggs. Penny took a big forkful of butter and swallowed it without chewing. We didn't even get sick, just kept eating: hero sandwiches as big as footballs, whole pizzas, ice-cream floats in the huge plastic cups they give you Coke in at 7-Eleven. The whole time, Bub looked on and smiled as if, when we were eating like that, he could nearly see us as his daughters.

⁖

JOSEPH LINDBERGH HAD BEEN called Bub ever since his little sister, Gloria, was learning to talk and couldn't say *brother*. "Bubber," she'd call out. "Bub." He looked like a Bub too, barrel-shaped on top with a round face and short neck cooked red-brown from long hot days digging ditches and fitting PVC pipe as a field foreman for Pacific Gas and Electric (PG&E). He earned twenty dollars an hour and never went to college. "Who needs a diploma?" he'd say. "I get to be outside all day, and if I get tired, I remind myself that in just three more minutes, I'll have earned another dollar."

Bub's people hailed from Oklahoma. They were religious when it suited them, gossipy as magpies and disapproving of various other relatives in a rigid and baffling system that resembled, to me, long division. The men wore overalls and chewed toothpicks into mush. The older women called each other "Aunt Sis," and anyone under thirty "missy" or "sister." "The kids" could mean anyone's children or grandchildren, but "you kids" was always a warning, hissed out with hands on hips: "Messin' and gommin', that's all you kids ever do" or "If you kids let any more heat in this house, I'm gonna lock your pretty little butts outside."

My sisters and I met Bub's mother, Noreen, very soon after we arrived at the Lindberghs', when she hosted a barbecue in our honor. She greeted us at her screen door in pink pants, a daisy-print cotton smock and house slippers. She wore wire-rimmed glasses and smelled of permanent solution.

"Well, now," Noreen said, looking us over, "have you been starving these girls, Bubby?"

"Hell no," he said, laughing. "They came that way."

"We'll fix that. Come on in, and don't bring any flies with you."

She ushered us past a dark front room and right back out again through a sliding glass door into the backyard, where other relatives huddled, the men around a grill smoking with meat, the women around a saggy wooden picnic table. Bub's sister, Gloria, came right over and introduced herself, shaking our hands as if we were grown-ups. She was tiny and muscular, her sandy hair cut in a Mrs. Partridge shag. Next to Bub and Hilde, she looked Lilliputian, as did her six-year-old daughter, Krista, who was cute in every way I thought a girl should be. Her eyes were jewel blue, her nose was a button and her shiny blond hair framed her heart-shaped face, flipping up at her shoulders. She wore a sassy tank top with shorts and flip-flops, all the color of Orange Crush. Next we met Vicky, Gloria's older daughter, who shuffled up in ground-dragging boys' jeans and a flannel shirt with the sleeves down and buttoned, even though it was eighty-some degrees. She must have been fourteen or fifteen, and she looked as if she found the whole family thing quite intolerable. After meeting us, she slunk away into Noreen's back bedroom and spent the rest of the afternoon listening to *Goodbye Yellow Brick Road* with the lights off.

For supper, the women had prepared peppery hamburgers with buns slathered in mayonnaise, toasted, then put into a paper grocery sack so they wouldn't dry out; there was corn bread baked thin and crispy as a cookie, seared mustard greens and a goulash simmering on the stove, smelling up the house with okra and onion and green tomato. Everyone ate outside — adults at the picnic table, kids hunkered down on the patio, our bare feet on the pricker-studded lawn. Every so often, Big Lenora or Uncle Jack would peer over at my sisters and me as if we were chimps in a zoo, as if it was fascinating, instructive even, to watch us eat potato chips and scratch our bug bites. At one point, Noreen's hunchbacked sister, Birdie, leaned over and hissed, to anyone at the table who was listening, "Imagine, Bub and Hilde taking those girls in just like they was their own."

I brought my plate up to hide my face but only succeeded in buttering the tips of my hair.

⌐

WE WEREN'T THEIR OWN. There was no question about that. Every time a woman in the checkout line at Continental Market got even remotely friendly with Hilde, she would be rewarded with the tragic details of our story. There followed the standard beaming and cooing at Hilde and Tina ("such *good* people"), the beatific smile at my sisters and me ("what *lucky* girls"). The only time we could even begin to forget who we were and would never be was when Bub came home from his long days at PG&E. He always had dirt in the rolled cuffs of his blue jeans and carried his big black lunch box and silver-handled thermos. When he sat down in his TV chair, my sisters and I ran to mob him, fighting over who got to tug off his steel-toed boots. Sometimes he did his Quasimodo routine, hunching over so his fingers skimmed the ground. He loped around after us, making little slurping noises and saying, "Quasi wants kisses. Come give Quasi a kiss."

When Bub fooled around this way, Hilde would stand at the mouth of the kitchen with her arms crossed and say, "You girls are getting too old for that." Maybe so, but when we were the right age to be rolling around with a dad, we didn't have a dad, not really, not one who would play with us and give us nicknames and teach us to shadowbox and Greco-Roman wrestle. I felt drunk when Bub picked me up and swung me around the living room, as if I were swimming in a washing machine, everything dizzying to blue. He tickled us under our scrawny arms and behind our knees and where our ribs stopped. We squirmed and laughed until tears came.

"There, that ought to last you a week," he'd say, but then before we were even into full whine, he was Quasi again, and we were Esmereldas. We were gypsies.

OUR REAL DAD'S NAME was Frank. He was a grill and short-order cook, sliding between restaurants like the Desert Inn and Sambos and Happy Steak, flashing the manager a killer smile when he'd screw up, showing up late or not at all, moving on when the smile stopped working. He was moody and shiftless, prone to smacking things or people around when he felt trapped or threatened or had been drinking too much. Although he was gone more than not and had, on more than one occasion, questioned whether my sisters and I were his at all, I remember his hank of red-gold hair and freckles and too-wide ultrawatt smile, the starburst of crinkles around his blue-gray eyes. I remember too the hop-shuffle in his walk as he crossed the parking lot of Sunset Liquor, as if he was listening to music that we couldn't hear, something with drums.

We always stopped at Sunset Liquor on the way to the drive-in, where we went pretty much every Saturday night when our dad was in town; we stopped and waited for him to shuffle in for his six-pack of Coors, his bourbon in brown paper. The lot was full of old-gum and spilled-soda-pop smells, broken glass in spirograph patterns. Moths pinged against the pink-and-yellow marquee, sizzled and stuck. My sisters and I sat in the backseat, already in our pajamas, while up front our mother was scooched all the way down with her feet on the dash. She was headless this way, but we could see part of her arm out the window — a hand, a thumb pressed to the filter of her cigarette as if she was saving a place for her mouth to go later.

Dad came out of the store, careful of his shiny black lace-ups. He was a little overdressed for the drive-in, wearing a starched open-collared shirt and creased slacks, overdressed in the same way Roger was when he came visiting, hair slicked darkly in place, piney aftershave preceding him by a good ten feet. They were both dapper, both tall and thin. Roger didn't have Dad's wild hair, though, and didn't have the odd mix of nerve and goofiness that was in evidence as Dad eased the Galaxy out of the liquor-store parking lot and gunned it, less for the speed than for the shriek he got from the backseat and the way our mother sat up then, grinning, and put her hand on his thigh.

The last movie we saw all together was *Butch Cassidy and the Sundance Kid.* From the speaker resting on my dad's half-open window came a strummy ukulele song about raindrops on your head; my sisters fought silently about who would shuttle the next beer from the ice chest up to the front; over by the snack bar a group of kids played on the swings, their feet throwing giant shadows over the hoods and hardtops like tentacles, like the Blob. Everything was monsters and stars in the Morse-code light.

"Look," I said, and poked Teresa. I pointed to our dad's head and showed her how to squint so that the red tips of his hair with more red flickering through looked like Mars on fire.

When I woke up, my foot was asleep, the pins coming on when I shifted. My sisters weren't moving, and the front seat was quiet. "Hey," I heard either Butch or Sundance say, "who are those guys?" I took Penny's pillow, put it under mine and dragged part of the blanket over to see stone buildings with arches, the

Bolivian sky. Butch and Sundance were lying on a floor looking bitten and bloody and terrible, and still Butch was talking about the next good thing, Australia this time, the vaults in the banks falling right open. When they made their big break, running out into the courtyard with cocked pistols, they didn't know that everyone but God was out there, waiting with rifles and enough ammunition to put a whole army down. There were rounds of gunfire, but Butch and Sundance didn't fall. Nothing fell because the screen was frozen.

"I don't believe it," said my dad. "They can't be dead. They were too lucky."

"Face it," Mom said. "They're Swiss cheese. Still, I won't be surprised if Hollywood finds a way to bring them back from the dead and make some more money off of them."

Dad snorted, an air-through-the-nose sound, and waggled his head. On the way home, we passed the liquor store and the Chevron station and the McDonald's with the clay Grimace sprouting from the flower bed like a purple shrub. At a traffic light, Mom flipped the visor down and checked her hair, tucking a few wayward strands behind her ears, fluffing the back with quick pushes of her hand.

"How much money do you think the drive-in takes in on a busy night like this one?" Dad asked.

"Hell, I don't know. How should I know?"

"There must have been two hundred cars tonight. Two hundred cars at three dollars a car. It'd be like picking an apple. That easy. There's just the one guy sitting by himself in the ticket booth, and he can't be more than eighteen."

She exhaled a mushroom of smoke, flipped the visor back up.

It was its own twilight, that moment. No click and pause, no "watch this," just dark getting on with its business. My dad couldn't stop what he was about to do any more than he could unthink a thought. He would go back to the drive-in with a butcher knife wrapped in newspaper to pick his apple — but since he wasn't Butch or Sundance, not fast or lucky or clever, nothing would go right. The police would catch him before he was even out of the drive-in, and he'd spend weeks in the Fresno County Jail, waiting for the trial, wearing an orange jumpsuit that looked like pajamas and eating, not hunks of stale bread, but regular food, things we had at home, like baloney sandwiches and pork 'n' beans and oatmeal. At the trial, the judge would give him the least-harsh sentence: two years at a work camp in New Mexico, where he was born. He'd be a slave for the state there, clearing brush, building roads and ditches. Given phone time, he'd call our mom to say in fourteen different ways that she'd better not be having an affair, by God, she'd better not be or he didn't know — "shit, please, baby, please" — what he'd do.

BEFORE THE LINDBERGHS, ALL of our placements were in the suburbs of Fresno or in town proper. To get to the Clapps', you had to drive *through* the country, but the Lindberghs' house *was* the country. Our bus stop at our neighbors', the Abels', mailbox lay beyond one barbed-wire fence and two electric ones. For the first few weeks of crawling under and through these, my sisters and I snagged T-shirts and felt the tingle — hot and icy at the same time — as electrified wire grazed one of our shoulder blades or the tops of our heads. Then, suddenly, we were naturals, stooping to the right level automatically, like knowing the steps of a dance not in your head but in your body, which doesn't forget.

The Abels raised cows and pigs for slaughter. Several barrels used for catching blood and entrails stood in their barn, and though they washed them out after every use, we could smell the barrels clear from the side of the road where we waited for bus number six to take us to Jefferson Elementary. I couldn't imagine the Lindberghs ever keeping animals like that, for food. Bub was too soft. You could hear it when he talked to the horses and our dogs, Bear and Badger, and even to the chipmunks that ran around on the woodpile. Baby talk, low and combed with honey. When the man came out to castrate our two male calves so they could be sold at auction for beef, Bub had to walk in a circle as soon as the first clamp went on. I felt a twinge too, when Twister started to bawl, but I watched everything — it was too weird and disgusting not to. The man obviously knew what he was doing and was quick with his knife, slitting the outer sack like the skin of a fig, then gripping the exposed testicle between his index and middle finger. It was as pink as a tongue.

Living on a ranch meant we had chores: a flake of hay for each of the horses, morning and night; fresh water in the stock tank; dry food in the dogs' big dish in the garage; water for the yarrow, the bug-bitten roses, the fruit trees lining the drive. I liked the work, liked even the word *chore,* which made me feel like a frontier girl, like Laura Ingalls on her prairie: *I'm going out to tend to the hens, Pa. How long till supper's on?*

Some six months after we came to live with the Lindberghs, Bub decided it was time for my sisters and me to have ponies of our own. Tina had a pony, a brown-and-white Welsh named Patches the Wonder Horse. Patches grew fatter by the year on English muffins smeared with peanut butter and jelly, fried squash, melon rinds — pretty much anything we'd give him — and was frankly more of a dog than a horse. We didn't even keep him corralled most of the time; he roamed wherever he wanted to, mowing the lawn, drinking out of the fishpond, lumbering into the garage to sample from the dogs' bowl. Once, he walked right through the front door and stood in the entrance hall, his big head swinging around so he could look into the kitchen, where we were eating dinner.

The livestock auction where we went to get the ponies was thrilling: animal smells and snorts and whinnies, folks swatting flies and throwing peanut shells into the sand at their feet, and above it all, the auctioneer singing about money. When it was over, we had Princess and Queenie for Penny and me, respectively, and

Velvet for Teresa. They were black, all three of them, with white stars on their foreheads, but differently shaped ones. Queenie's star was a moon. Her eyes were the softest, deepest black; her ears were furred like a bobcat's, alert and expressive.

The new ponies quickly became our pets. We braided their manes and tails, twisted dandelions into their forelocks. We played a vaulting game that Tina invented, where we ran up behind the ponies, jumped up by putting our hands on their big butts, scooted across their backs and slid down their necks. It's a wonder they didn't kick us in the head for this.

Bub and Tina taught us to ride. We practiced first in the corral, then in the field, and soon we were skilled enough to be turned loose on the neighborhood, which at that time was so scarcely populated that we could have ridden out to where the foothills began without running into so much as ten fences. On Saturday afternoons, we'd put bareback blankets on the ponies, pull canteens over our heads so they thumped against our hipbones and head out for the afternoon. We'd ride along the dry ditch or toward the orange orchards or over to Shaw, where Tina said developers had tried to get a golf course started, but no one came out to play. It was so grown over that we were surprised when we'd canter into a sand trap buried under switchgrass and foxtail, or trot onto the raised flat patch where the golfers were supposed to tee off. It was like *Planet of the Apes,* how we could see the fringe of one abandoned world buried beneath another.

No matter where we headed first, we always ended up at our favorite fig tree. Tying the ponies to low branches, we'd pull the blankets off to have something to sit on in the shade. We'd take long pulls from our canteens, though the water tasted like feet and tinfoil, and eat peanut-butter sandwiches, smushed and warm from being in their paper bag. Once, we all fell asleep like this, sprawled out under the fig tree. It was so hot that day that I felt as lumpy and heavy as a bale of hay. We each lay on our blankets, not talking, and looked up through the layers of leaves, which shifted and threw soft, spotty light on parts of the tree and the ground and our bodies. Penny leaned back against the trunk with her eyes closed. Circles of light moved in her hair. They looked like butterflies.

NEARLY EVERY DAY OF our time with the Lindberghs, Hilde was up by six-thirty and out on the lawn, standing bull's-eye in the circle of the big green garden hose, her thumb on the opening, drawing the water into small circles and figure eights. She was nuts about that lawn. We had a gunlike spray attachment and several rainbow sprinklers, but she never used them; she trusted the hose. During the school year, when we walked by her on the way to the bus, she rarely looked up she was so into it. In the summer, she started banging on the outside of our bedroom windows around eight. *"Aufstehen, aufstehen, Falle Leute,"* she yelled: "Get up, you lazy people." She came in panting while we sat at the table with our bowls of puffed rice, her hands fluttering at the hem of her blouse, a light sweat beading on her upper lip. "What's wrong with you girls? I've been working for hours."

By nine o'clock, whatever the day or season, Hilde was out the door and on her way to Noreen's house. She had breakfast and lunch there, stopped by Shop 'n' Bag or Continental Market for groceries, then raced home to have dinner on the table when Bub rolled up the drive at five-thirty. At first I thought it was a little kooky that she was always at Noreen's, but soon I understood: she was lonely. Who wouldn't be, hanging around the house all day? Once you did the dishes and vacuumed, what would there be to do? Soap operas would help, but she got those at Noreen's. They sat and crocheted and talked excitedly back to the TV when something good happened. *Days of Our Lives* was their favorite — "The Show," they called it, as in "Hurry up and get in here, Hilde, or you'll miss THE SHOW." God forbid.

The only thing Hilde loved more than her days with Noreen — yammering over tuna salad, keeping up with The Show, beginning another afghan, chair cover, toaster cozy — was her daughter. Trying to make Tina happy was perhaps Hilde's truest mission. She kept Tina's bottom dresser drawer filled with bar chocolate and diet cookies and boxes of Jell-O, which Tina liked to eat raw, late at night, dipping in a wet finger and licking off the powder. Tina had more new clothes and nicer ones than we did, and received double our allowance, but we weren't overly jealous. How could we be once we learned Tina was the reason we had come to the Lindberghs' in the first place? Bub and Hilde had planned to have several more children after Tina, and although they tried for years to conceive, these attempts were foiled by what Hilde mysteriously termed "female problems." They might have given up if not for Tina, who wanted siblings as much as she had ever wanted anything. We were the solution. Adoption was too permanent, but foster kids were like ponies bought at auction — you could always take them back. Bub called the Department of Welfare and settled on us because Mrs. O'Rourke insisted that if someone didn't offer to take us soon — three children together were so hard to place — we'd have to go to a group home. That could be rough, she counseled; who knew what would happen to us there. Bub convinced Hilde it was the right thing to do. They signed the papers, took the preparatory class. Everything was set until the week before we were to arrive, when Hilde found the thermostat in the hall had been messed with and the heat turned on — this, when temperatures outside were still in the nineties. They asked Tina if she'd tampered with it, and she lied.

"I know you did it," Bub said. "Just admit it, and everything will be fine."

"No," she said. "It wasn't me."

Bub told Tina she'd blown everything, that we weren't coming anymore because, as a liar, she didn't deserve sisters. He let her spend a tearful night reflecting on her wrongdoing, then changed his mind. That's the story of how we almost got sent to the group home, one Tina liked to tell when she was feeling particularly monarchical.

I wasn't sure she didn't have plans to rule the world, our Tina. Maybe it was an only-child thing. We never played a game of Monopoly in which she wasn't the banker and didn't get the car as her game piece. Even in pretend games she was tyrannical: her favorite person to be was this filthy rich rancher with ten thousand horses and a crop of cowboys who worked for her and had to call her "Ma'am," tipping their hats as they said it. She ordered us around, telling us who we were supposed to be — a cowhand or cook or Indian guide. She ordered her parents around too and was rewarded with a brand-new five-dollar bill or shiny red cowboy boots or a store-bought violin. If we had to borrow instruments from school, flat and black and smelling of other kids' hands, well then it was only right and fair. Tina was Bub and Hilde's real daughter.

Were we real to anyone? That was hard to say. Our father was who knows where, maybe in prison again. Our mother was so many years away that I had difficulty conjuring the smallest detail: the shape of her eyes, her smell, the way her hands moved in a gesture. And why would I want to think about her? If I allowed myself any image, it was a quick still of her as she must have been the day she left in Roger's car: her head back on the pale vinyl, eyes closed so she could feel it all, the Indian-summer sun, wind nuzzling her hand like a cat. With her eyes shut tight, she could be a passenger, just that, rocketing toward what was still possible.

How good it must have felt to let the road have its way, the dark line of it pulling hard enough to comfort.

⟿

TINA WAS FIERCELY COMMITTED to being a tomboy. She was thick through the torso and neck like her father and never gave a thought to her clothes or hair, or about harassing the neighbor kids by picking up dried horse turds and chucking them like dirt clods. Maybe this was why these kids weren't exactly amenable when my sisters and I tried to make friends with them — at least not at first. The Swensons, who lived directly across the street, had four children, a girl our age and three older boys. Two houses to their left were the Lindes, with a boy and a girl. Together, the six had built a sturdy-looking plywood fort set back on an empty property. They spent time there after school and on weekends, and one Saturday, my sisters and I got brave enough to go over and introduce ourselves. We even convinced Tina to come along. Maybe they had binoculars, or maybe they had just been waiting for our arrival, sure we'd come poking around sooner or later, but before we were even halfway through the field, the kids ran out, whooping and jeering. They carried spiny masses of uprooted star thistle as weapons, and we ran for all we were worth.

About twenty yards from our property, the kids gave up the chase, turning back toward the fort, and that's when I ran onto a nail with my full weight, piercing my sneaker and instep. When I got to the house, hobbling and howling, Bub pulled off my sneaker to reveal a deep pink hole speckled with flakes of rust. Some of the pieces he dug out with his pocketknife; others he flushed with alcohol. I screamed and squirmed until he pronounced me cured. Two days later, I was reading on the couch with my shoes off when Bub noticed the red line snaking over my ankle and up the side of my leg. I guess I had noticed it too, but thought it was part of the whole step-on-a-nail process. No, he said. This was serious. He took me to the doctor, who numbed my foot and poked around in the nail hole with a silver tool that looked like the thing you use to get at nut meat. It didn't take him long to root out a piece of rust Bub had missed. It was small, the size of a button on a doll's dress, but I felt I might throw up thinking about it. Not only was it in there without my knowing, but my body had oozed around it for days, festering.

"That red line," said the doctor, pointing, "was headed for your heart. That's what poison does."

I stared at the worm of the line as if it had menace, intention, had been digging its tunnel while I slept and played and thought I was A-OK. If it had made it all the way to my heart, I'd be dead — boom, just like that — and all because of a button, a baby tooth of rust.

UNLIKE OUR MOTHER ON her ghost road, our dad resurfaced every once in a while, especially in the beginning. We'd get a phone call, his voice husky with feeling, or a visit. When I was six and we were living with the Clapps, he brought presents, and two years before that, before we'd known any family that wasn't our own, he seemed to be bringing himself.

I don't know how many months passed between our mother's leaving and our dad's early release from the work camp. I only know that Dad called Granny when he was out to tell her he was headed back to Fresno to get us. On the day he was to arrive, Granny scrubbed us sore and lined us up on the couch in our best dresses. "Now you girls be nice to your daddy," she said. "He's been gone a long time. He's been away in the army."

This was the first we'd heard of any army, but we bought it, thinking he might swing through the door in uniform, holding one of those hats that look like pea-colored paper boats. It was so much nicer to think of him this way than as someone who'd been in prison, wearing an entirely different uniform and no hat whatsoever.

When he came, he looked bigger than before, and his face was red, though I couldn't tell if it was from sun or because he didn't know what to say to us or to Granny, who stood at the mantel, hip out and arms crossed tight. When he squatted in front of us, grinning wide enough to split something, Penny began to cry and didn't stop, even when Granny tried to bribe her with pudding and cold chicken.

Was he surprised to find Mom gone, or did he know already? Were we different than he remembered? Louder? More skittish? Quieter? More difficult? Maybe he thought he could care for us on his own, then reconsidered, or maybe he knew all along that this would be a business visit; in any case, the very next day, he drove us downtown to the Department of Welfare and talked to a series of social workers about getting us placed in a foster home. The three of us sat on a wooden bench out in the hall while this happened, swinging our legs, talking about what kind of treat we were fixing to get. At that time, the welfare building in Fresno was situated directly across from the fairgrounds and right next to a McDonald's; surely, we were in for a ride on the Ferris wheel or, at the very least, some French fries. What we got was a ride back to Granny's, where he dropped us off and said, "You girls be good, now. I'll be seeing you soon."

WHILE MY SISTERS AND I waited for our first foster-care placement, we stayed with our dad's sister Bonnie, a no-nonsense chain-smoker with a hive of red hair. In the evenings, she heated up cans of SpaghettiOs while we labored over card houses at her slick coffee table. We slept all together on Bonnie's foldout couch, which should have been more comfortable than our pallet at Granny's, but wasn't. It was new and squeaky, and the mattress smelled like rubber rain boots. At Granny's, everything felt right, smelled right, sounded right, even the winos calling out to one another at the gas station on the corner, the sirens hurtling by on their way to trouble. We would go back to Granny's for visits, sure, but would never live there again. She was too old. We couldn't stay with Bonnie for long either, because she wasn't a mom, she was a telephone operator.

"Now don't you worry," Bonnie told us over creamed corn and wieners. "Any day now a family is going to swoop you up and claim you for their own."

I wanted that day to come but wasn't sure how it could ever really happen. If our own family couldn't find a way to keep us and care for us, how could perfect strangers do the job? Still, I nodded and chewed, ate up what Bonnie served, slept on her squeaky, creaky couch, waited like my sisters waited for the family that was coming along shortly, any day now, any day.

Bonnie wasn't a bit like her mother, but she had Granny's habit of ending every third sentence with a small "Lord willing," and there was a lot of God at her AA meetings, where she dragged us some three nights a week. It wasn't unlike church, the way they sat in a circle of hard chairs, one person talking, the others nodding and saying, "Yes, yes." My sisters and I mostly played outside or on and around the stacks of folding tables at the back of the meeting hall. Bonnie said we didn't need to be hearing all those sad stories, but to me they were fascinating. Everyone there had hit rock bottom. They talked about it as if it were one very specific place, Rock Bottom, like Granny's Limbo. Wives had been lost there, and jobs. They talked about it as if they still knew the way.

Bonnie was a tired kind of pretty in her brown pantsuit and turtleneck, square-toed zip-up boots. Men were always trying to nuzzle up to her after meetings, but I never saw her do more than bum their cigarettes and pat them on the shoulder or knee with an even compassion. There were never any men in her apartment either, just us and the emptied cartons of Pall Malls and Patsy Cline on the turntable, falling, falling to pieces.

On long afternoons when Bonnie was away at work, we'd run around the half-mile or so of sidewalk that snaked through her apartment complex. There was a neighbor boy named Chip who liked to pretend he was Penny's pet monkey. He followed us everywhere, even into the laundry room, where we each folded ourselves into one of the front-loading washing machines, hiding from no one in particular. In my metal bubble, spaceship for one, I'd call, "Hellohellohello," and let the alien translation come back at me in galvanized pings.

The buildings in Bonnie's complex were green, and it struck me that every apartment we'd *ever* lived in had been green — olive, avocado, artichoke — and the kind of stucco that could take the skin off the back of your hand. We moved often when our mom and dad were together, but it didn't really matter since the buildings were so much alike and the days too, and none of them so different from our time with Bonnie.

At Bonnie's we waited for a family. When we still *had* a family, we waited for dinner, bath time, *Bonanza;* for our mother to wake up, for our father to come home from his latest "business trip." Sometimes we waited on the balcony outside our apartment while our mom visited with Roger, the quiet, lanky brother of her friend Lynette. Roger just started showing up one day, smelling of pine needles and wearing a pressed white shirt, and soon this came to mean we were out — out for the afternoon with the door locked behind us. In that building, we lived on the second floor. Below us, in a sad-looking courtyard, there was a patio table missing its umbrella, some shedding red oleander and a bone-dry, dirty swimming pool. From the shallow end of the pool all the way to the drain, a long brown crack ran and ran, as thick as my foot in some places and in others like a spider's thread, barely there. When we were outside, Teresa was the mom. Though only four or five then, she knew what was okay and what wasn't. We could peel the banister like a banana, letting strings of rubbery paint slither to the cement. We could spit down into the courtyard, but we couldn't go there or play in the empty pool; we couldn't knock on our own door, even if we really wanted something, like a cookie, like shoes.

One day, the lady next-door was having a birthday party. She came outside with three pieces of cake — white with white frosting — stacked on a paper napkin. "You poor things," she said, the words coming in high whiny puffs, the way people talk to kittens in cardboard boxes in front of the Safeway. She must have thought we were starving. We played prisoner with the cake, scooting to hang our legs all the way through the iron rods of the balcony. We stuck our arms out too so that we had to reach back through to eat. We *were* starving, we decided; the cake wasn't cake but bread, and the only thing we were going to get all day, or for a long time anyway, and it was good that way, better.

Through the door to our apartment we could hear the vacuum running. It made one noise, pitched up and spinning, because it wasn't moving on the carpet; it wasn't cleaning anything. Teresa said Mom turned it on because she didn't want us to hear her with Roger. Sometimes her gravelly laugh came through the door too, but mostly there was just the vacuum, pulling air in that same spot. If our dad had come home right then, Mom and Roger would have been in big trouble, but we knew he wouldn't. When he was there, he was there, and then not — going the way a good day went, so that we didn't know if we'd see it again, that white cake, the sky with clouds pushed into meringue and the voices next-door singing Happy Birthday to dear Anna.

When our dad *was* around, a lot of napping happened, theirs and ours. The apartment was a cave then, with all the bedroom doors closed and the shades drawn so it was hard to know just how long any afternoon was or would be. As the oldest by seventeen months, Teresa had her own bedroom, but Penny and I shared a double bed and a view of the ceiling, which was flecked with glitter meant to look like stars. Sometimes we actually slept, but mostly we had staring contests, kicked at each other under the blue sheet, or raided our own dressers to put leotards on our heads and socks on our hands. We dropped to the floor and crawled through the house. If our mom was asleep on the couch, we'd watch her — her hair squashed like a nest, her arms like cooked spaghetti — and silently dare each other to touch her, an earring or toenail or the pocket of her bathrobe where she kept cigarettes and safety pins and tissues balled like baby animals.

On one of those afternoons, there was a fire in the ditch behind our apartment complex. Penny and I were in bed but awake, and I watched her gray eyes widen as the fire engine drew nearer and nearer, its siren like a yo-yo, climbing and sliding. When it couldn't get any louder, the sound stopped. We stood on our pillows and opened the curtains to see the truck, shiny and close, and the firefighters in yellow slickers and knee-high boots. Even with the window closed, we could hear them shouting at one another and the sound the hose made as it came off the truck and folded out of itself. The fire was mostly hidden from us by a length of fence, but we could see smoke rush up in plumes and hear the flames snapping through dry grass and whooshing a little as the fire line leaped ahead. There was another sound too, as if the blaze were chewing, spitting out what it couldn't swallow.

Penny said we should sneak out the window, but I said no. I took her hand, and we walked right through the front door in our bare feet, believing we couldn't possibly get in trouble. This was a fire, after all, and as close as it could get without really happening *to* us. Many of our neighbors had come out too, and we all stood in a line on the sidewalk, the way people watch a parade. When it was over, the ditch was steaming and wet; black patches pawed up the sides. The firemen retreated, and the neighbors and Penny and I walked back the long way.

Inside, it was still nap time. A fan in the living room blew into a set of blinds so that they ticked in a rhythm like typing. Other than that, the apartment was quiet. I tiptoed to my parents' room and cracked their door. They'd tucked a blanket over the window shade to block all light. It might have been the middle of the night in that room; it might have been any time at all. Mom's side of the bed was nearest, and I could make out her nightstand, the cut-glass ashtray full of butts and used matches and rock-hard wads of spit-out gum. Beyond that she was sprawled, rumpled as the sheet, her yellow slip yanked down and sideways. My dad was the lump to her right. One of them was grinding their teeth a little.

Back in our room, Penny had climbed into bed, so I did too, though I felt seeing the fire had made us too old for naps. We pulled the sheet over our heads and played parachute with it, kicking the blue up as far as it would go.

I DON'T KNOW HOW long we stayed with Bonnie — a few weeks? a month? — before the phone rang one morning as we were all eating breakfast. It was the social worker. I watched Bonnie's face as she talked, letting my Rice Chex sog up. She nodded yes and yes again, and then hung up, flashing us a smile. This was good news. A family had seen our school pictures and wanted us. Mrs. O'Rourke would be over in a few hours, so we'd better get hopping. Bonnie put us in the bath and washed our hair — not with the Johnson's baby shampoo but with her own that smelled like melon. We wrestled on dresses and tights, and Bonnie fixed butterfly barrettes in our hair. Then, sure we'd get dirty if we went outside, she made us sit, trapped on the couch with nothing to do but smack the heels of our good shoes together, pig poke and elbow one another until she had to put the couch cushions between us.

This was the second time we'd met Mrs. O'Rourke, the first being the day our dad drove us down to the Department of Welfare. She came to the door in a nice skirt-and-sweater set. Even her hair looked hopeful, teased up in back to a kind of soufflé, a sweep of frosted bangs in front, left to right. Bonnie had put what clothes we had in green garbage bags with twist ties, and Mrs. O'Rourke helped us carry them down to the parking lot. It was early afternoon, and the apartment complex was empty. Chip was off at school with all the other kids whose lives weren't starting over that day. The only one to say good-bye to was Bonnie, who stood in her doorway in a terry-cloth robe and knee-high stockings. As we pulled out of the lot, she waved with the hand that held her cigarette, sending up smoke ribbons, snaking and frayed. It was hard to know what to feel. I would miss Bonnie, but she could only ever be our aunt. Up ahead somewhere was a family, a mother, a place not to wait but to stay.

LIKE GRANNY, THE SPINOZAS lived in central Fresno, where donut shops and check-cashing places bloomed under freeways, where the *taquerias,* their menus painted in chunky red letters on the windows, locked and barred their doors at first dark. Off of busier streets like Clinton and Olive were avenues and lanes, drives and circles, some ending in cul-de-sacs, some butting up against flood controls or supermarket parking lots. Along these, small boxy houses were strung along the sidewalk like lines on a ruler. A few had gardens with trolls or plastic flamingos, but most of the yards were sad: dog-chewed, dandelion-blown, flecked with trash. The Spinozas' house was sided white, with a window to each side of the door, like cartoon eyes with *x*'s. The TV screamed as we came up the walk, sirens and a car chase, cops on a megaphone: *Surrender your weapons.* Through the screen door, Mr. Spinoza filled most of a fat recliner, his face washed yellow with TV light. Hearing the doorbell, he stood up, yanking on the waistband of his work pants. He shook Mrs. O'Rourke's hand, ushered us in and hollered for his wife, who appeared suddenly from the dark back of the house.

Mrs. Spinoza's puckered face was framed by tight gray braids, crisscrossed and fastened flat with pins. She wore a shapeless housedress and blunt shoes. She was ancient. I looked from her to the photos along the back wall showing the Spinozas' children, lots of them, all grown. This wasn't at all what I had expected. Why would someone like Mrs. Spinoza — who was at least as old as Granny, who had clearly spent all her mothering on her own long-gone kids — want to be a mother again? *Did she?* Mrs. O'Rourke said the Spinozas had seen our pictures and wanted us. That's what she told Bonnie on the phone. If they didn't want more kids, we wouldn't be there, right? *Right?*

When it came time for our social worker to leave, the three of us followed her to the door, and Penny reached out to touch her nylons, petting a little, the way I'd seen her do with Bonnie. I thought Penny might latch on and ask Mrs. O'Rourke not to go, or even cry. She didn't, though. None of us did, but when we turned around, the distance between the door and the couch seemed vast and unnavigable, like the distance between *Adam 12* and dinner, evening and morning, tomorrow and next week. We sat down.

While Mrs. Spinoza bustled in the kitchen getting dinner, there was a long spell of watching Mr. Spinoza watch the shifting screen. Then we heard a baboonlike whooping, and out ran a boy fresh from his bath. His hair was wet and black, and as he weaved through the room — around the fat recliner, over an ottoman — water droplets spattered in a fan. He hadn't even begun to dry off because his towel wasn't a towel; it was a cape, long and knotted around his neck so that it whooshed out behind him at high speeds. Naked Superman. He didn't stop whizzing long enough to look at us, but it was most certainly *for* us. Mr. Spinoza fully ignored the boy, and it seemed he'd go on and on, spinning like a wet top, until he tripped, falling into the end table with a thump, threatening a lamp.

"Dammit, Bobby!" Mrs. Spinoza yelled from the kitchen. She came to the doorway holding a pink bowl loaded up with yams. "Get to your room and put some clothes on right now or I'll tell your momma."

His momma? Wasn't *she* his momma?

Just then, the screen door opened with a squawk and in walked Louise. *Walk* isn't even the right word. She poured in like warm water through a flue. Her whole self, from shoe toe to hairline, seemed about to push free of what held her. The zipper on her tight skirt was half down and strained at its teeth; strands of her damp hair had escaped her haphazard updo and hung damply around her face and down her back. Before she was even fully through the door, she had her shoes off.

"Hey," she said, bending to rub where her toes were pink and creased-looking, "is this them?"

"Yeah," answered Mr. Spinoza, but he didn't turn to look at her. Good thing too, because she tugged her zipper the rest of the way down and stepped out of her skirt, right there in the living room. She stood looking at us for a minute, holding her balled-up skirt in one hand while she worked at the buttons of her blouse with the other. "How you doing?" she said, then headed down the hall, pulling her arms free.

It didn't take us long to figure out who Louise was — Bobby's unmarried mother and the Spinozas' youngest daughter; more complicated was how she fit into the family. Although Bobby called Louise "Momma," Mrs. Spinoza was the one who called him in for dinner, drew his bath, tisked over his mosquito bites. Louise worked as a cocktail waitress at a bar downtown. She was out late even on her nights off and slept until noon or beyond to make up for this, leaving it to her mother to get Bobby dressed and fed and on the bus to Grover Cleveland Elementary. Louise was forever tired. Some days she'd get out of bed and only make it as far as the sofa before she had to lie down again, calling to her mother to bring her hot tea with honey. Even her talk dragged, slow as a train climbing a hill.

Every day after school, we all played in the yard until dinnertime. If Louise was in town on errands, I'd keep one eye on the corner, waiting for the city bus to drop her off. I loved to watch Louise walk. The bus would rattle to a stop, burping black smoke, and out she'd come in her skirt and open-toed shoes, her purse swinging from one hand, strolling. She moved as if she were pushing through steam or a forest of warm, wet leaves. We'd say, "Hey," and she'd answer back, but there was something about Louise that made me think she never really heard us. Once in the door, she'd sit down in her father's big chair and start to shuck her street clothes as if this were the most natural thing in the world. Underneath she wore full slips in beige and champagne, tones so close to the color of her skin you'd have to look twice to see if she wasn't naked. She'd put on a robe but leave it open, the tie trailing off to one side like a tail. She'd go to the dinner table that way. At night she'd disappear.

Since Louise couldn't really be Bobby's mother, Mrs. Spinoza picked up the slack. It was an odd arrangement, but somehow it worked. The family went on. I couldn't help thinking that if our mother had had someone to do the mothering *for* her, like Louise had Mrs. Spinoza, she might have been able to stay. She wouldn't have had to be the grown-up then. She could have smoked her cigarettes and gone to her parties and let her moods take her where they might. Then, like Louise, she wouldn't have had to go to be gone.

I had a slew of questions about how my sisters and I might fit into the Spinozas' unusual family, but none of them got answered. There wasn't time. We only stayed with them through one hot spring, three months all together, then Teresa was accused of stealing seven dollars in change from a jelly jar that sat on Mrs. Spinoza's dresser. Teresa swore it was Bobby who did it, but only Penny and I believed her, and we didn't count.

Bobby was a pain from the beginning. He was seven, Teresa's age, but didn't act it. It was a while before I was sure he could even talk. Whenever we were in a room, Bobby would run and duck through, smacking the walls and doorjambs with his hands as if the house were a big drum and his to play. Other times he'd pretend to fall down over and over, watching us to make sure we were watching him.

One night, Bobby came into the bedroom my sisters and I shared and ripped the legs off of Teresa's Malibu Barbie. He was naked except for his towel-cape, and Barbie was naked too. He rubbed the hard little knots of her boobs and the blank space between her legs, making ugly grunting noises. Penny started to cry sputteringly, her top lip doing its baby poke. I sat like a statue on the bed, as if I'd been zapped with a phaser set on stun, but Teresa jumped up. In one move she was off the bed and had hit Bobby hard across the face. The slap made a comic-book *thup* that I replayed again and again in my head after he'd run off whimpering.

The very next day, Bobby came to the dinner table saying he'd seen Teresa steal the jelly-jar money. Two days after that, we were back in Mrs. O'Rourke's car. I'm not saying that I would have wanted to stay with the Spinozas forever, but I hated leaving the way we did, as if we were no-good and dirty, so much trash in the yard. I hated Bobby too. Maybe he couldn't help being mean to us. He didn't have a dad, and maybe he didn't really have a mother either, but try as I might, I couldn't feel sorry for him: his stupid towel, his monkey noises. At least we'd never have to see him again.

When we left the Spinozas' neighborhood, Mrs. O'Rourke turned left on Blackstone, and we drove and drove, past the community college and Mayfair Market, past strip malls and subdivisions. Town fell away to farmland: drainage ditches and turned-up fields and pastures dotted with cattle. I liked the way it smelled so far out, like wet dirt and the world carrying on. There wasn't another car on the road. Mrs. O'Rourke flipped the radio off to tell us a little about the Clapps, our next placement. Like the Spinozas, they were an older couple with grown children, but they had taken in foster kids before. In fact, they had another foster daughter right then, a little girl our age and wouldn't that be nice? She quieted then, and with the windows down and the music off, I realized I could hear insects in the vineyards and alfalfa fields. I found a favorite chunk of hair to rub across my closed lips and listened. There must have been millions of bugs out that evening, trillions even, but they made one sound, a whir that lifted and quivered and pulsed and was never a question.

IF OUR SECOND FOSTER mother, Helen Clapp, loved anything at all it was the color purple. Her bedroom was a shrine to
it: lavender carpet and duvet and dressing table, sausage pillows
in plum, deep-grape swags at the windows. She had purple pant-
suits and handbags and pumps. Although Mrs. Clapp was a
broad-shouldered, thick-waisted woman, she always looked
pulled together and spent no small amount of time in front of the
mirror to ensure this. When we went out, even to the grocery
store, she ratted her hair to an impossible height, shellacked it
with a big can of hair spray and applied face powder, spidery false
eyelashes and two neat coats of mulberry lipstick.

   With trips to town, as with most elements of daily life at the
Clapps', nothing varied. At T minus five we lined up at the door,
the three of us plus Becky Bodette, the other foster girl the Clapps
had taken in. We filed to the car, a sleek white Cadillac with white
vinyl seats. Once settled, we folded our hands in our laps and
stayed that way, per Mrs. Clapp, who scowled into the rearview
every two seconds to make sure our grubby little hands stayed off
the upholstery. Fine things weren't worth having if you couldn't
keep them that way.

   Like the other houses in the neighborhood — a nouveau
riche suburb with enough room for everyone to have several acres

of lawn and a Fresno zip code without Fresno's crime problem — the Clapps' house was substantial. Single-story and brick with white shutters, it had a huge side yard with trees older than the house, and a pool with a diving board behind chain-link fencing. There was a small red barn and a corral that held a dusky brown Shetland. A previous owner had named the pony Coffee, but Mrs. Clapp decided Cocoa suited her better, colorwise. So as not to confuse the pony about who she was, we were supposed to use both names for a while, then when Mrs. Clapp gave the okay, switch to Cocoa-Coffee, and then, in time, to Cocoa outright. I remember standing at the railing, offering sugar cubes with my hand out flat as I'd been shown. "Here, Coffee-Cocoa," I called, feeling heat climb my neck. The pony had black, bottomless eyes and fixed me with a look that said, *You people are plumb nuts.*

Mrs. Clapp had a great many strange ideas, which I attributed to the fact that she was rich. I had never known a rich person before, so it seemed as likely as anything that money was the reason we weren't to touch anything that wasn't triple-wrapped in plastic, why we couldn't go inside or outside, poop or burp or cough without asking permission. Becky Bodette had the rules down and rarely got in trouble. When we arrived, she'd already been there six months and no longer seemed to notice the child-proofing that made me feel as though we were living on a space station: sheaths of plastic over the living-room sofa and armchairs, rubber mats running door to door in every carpeted room, rubber disks in front of the TV so we could sit and watch *Bewitched* or *Family Affair* without leaving — what? our butt prints? — on the hi-low carpet. There was a den at the back of the house that wasn't plastified, and most of the time we played there. On nice days, we could ask to go outside, and if it was okay, Mrs. Clapp opened the door herself and locked it after us. When we wanted to come back inside, we had to knock and ask please. You were flat out of luck if you needed to pee, because if she had the dishwasher running or one of her soap operas on, she wouldn't hear the door and you could die trying to cross your legs and hold it.

Other than the pee problem, outside was nice. Brick planters surrounded the back patio and formed a kind of kennel for Mrs. Clapp's toy poodles. The black one was Gee Gee and wore a white collar; the white one was Gia and wore a black collar. They were indoor dogs, but Mrs. Clapp let them take in the air when we played outside. *Click click click* went their little toenails on the brick. They paced, patrolling us. It occurred to me that they might be watchdogs, disapproving sentries sending telepathic messages to Mrs. Clapp. *Dirty girl,* thought Gia. *Too loud,* Gee Gee added with a dry sneeze. The dogs were Mrs. Clapp's, no question, and the turtles in the pen at the back of the yard belonged to Mr. Clapp, which was why they hadn't been named. There he drew the line: "They're turtles, Helen," he said. "They don't come, and they don't sit."

"The names help you tell them apart," she countered, as if they were talking about identical twins.

"Rocks all look alike, and we don't name *them,*" he said, sniffing, and flipped up his newspaper like a heat shield.

Mr. Clapp was old. I suppose they both were, but Mrs. Clapp dyed her hair a hostile inky black, whereas Mr. Clapp didn't have much hair at all, just a half-circle ear to ear in the back, as white and fine as pulled cotton. His forehead was high and lined, and there were also lines running parallel to his big ears and along the sides of his nose so that it seemed his face was sliding steadily toward its center. Except for occasionally barking back to his wife, Mr. Clapp didn't have much to say. He left for work before we got up in the morning, and when he came home at six, he washed his hands, took out his *Fresno Bee* and vanished behind it in his recliner until Mrs. Clapp called us all to the table. His chair was camel-colored and velvety and didn't need to be covered in plastic since no one would dare sit there but him. Below the newspaper were his gray gabardine slacks, thin black socks, shined shoes. Above, just the curve of his forehead looking oddly undressed.

Mr. Clapp could have been my grandfather, but he wasn't. I didn't think of him as my father either, not that I was supposed to. It was a puzzle just what we were to one another, all of us. Take Becky Bodette. She did everything we did — ate the same food, played with the same toys, knocked at the same door to come in. She took baths with us and shared a bedroom with Teresa, and yet I never thought of her as my sister. She was "the other girl," and I didn't much like her. Although Becky was between Teresa and me in age, she seemed older, harder, meaner. When Penny stuttered during a game of Candy Land, her lips stuck on a percussive *b* or *p*, Becky would either mimic her or call her Porky Pig or both. Like Bobby Spinoza, Becky liked to get other people in trouble, if only to remind herself she could. One day when we were in the playroom, she challenged me to a reading contest. "I'll bet you can't even read that," she said, pointing to a box in the calendar pinned to the dark paneling. *Yom Kippur*. Was it English? I didn't know, and so I spelled it out first, *y-o-m*. When I got to the *p-p* part, she screamed out for Mrs. Clapp. "Paula just said *pee-pee*. She did. I heard her."

Mrs. Clapp sent me to my room, where I was to sit on my bed for two hours with no one to talk to and nothing to look at but my own toes. At dinner, I stared across the table at Becky, at her pixie haircut and striped turtleneck, her fingers curled on the spoon full of canned peas, and tried to unriddle her. Her eyes were dark brown, like Teresa's, but smaller and polished-looking, like rocks at the bottom of a fish tank. Her face was a hard little nut, showing no hint of a flinch when Mrs. Clapp barked at her for spilling milk on the tablecloth.

I wasn't certain Becky was even afraid of Mrs. Clapp. When a new rule came down, Becky was blank about it, blinking a slow okay — even the No Water After Five rule, which Mrs. Clapp began enforcing after she learned my sisters and I had a bed-wetting problem. She tried yelling at us and not yelling at us, making us go several times before bed, whether we thought we had to or not, but nothing worked. Finally, she devised that if she gave us nothing to drink, there wouldn't be anything to pee out. A good theory, but even that failed. We were bed-wetters, plain and simple, and now we were bed-wetters who thought about nothing so much as water, personal and plenty: magically refilling wells, Dixie cups that grew as rapidly as Jack's beanstalk until they could support a shoreline and tide, shells roaring with the world's earliest noises. And drowning dreams were better than flying dreams.

MONDAYS AT THE CLAPPS' meant sitting on the dinette stool with my eyes pinched while Mrs. Clapp brushed and yanked my thick hair into blue yarn ribbons. Teresa waited her turn at the periphery. Even when I couldn't see her, I knew she was holding her hands to her cheeks, pulling until her eyes were China-man slits. This was how I looked. When it was Teresa's turn to sit under the brush, Penny did the Chinaman, and it was funny every time.

Sunday was bath night, then an hour of *The Lawrence Welk Show* before bed. On Saturdays, we stretched out on the cool tile next to the kitchen sink while Mrs. Clapp washed our hair with the yellow baby shampoo in its tear-shaped bottle. Fridays we shopped for groceries at Mayfair Market. We held on to the cart while Mrs. Clapp steered and stopped and ticked items off her list with a purple pen. If we each stayed tethered, resisting the glossy wall of Apple Jacks boxes, racks of coloring books and Fruit Stripe gum, we got McDonald's on the way home. A hamburger and a Coke, no fries, which Mrs. Clapp swore they burned on purpose. When handed my bag, I put my face to the neck, inhaling ketchup, pickles, the sweet reconstituted onions.

Every day was named and numbered and certain — but sometimes a Monday was also Columbus Day or a Thursday was Halloween. On Valentine's Day 1972, rain fell so hard and fast that the water had nowhere to go. When Mrs. Clapp came to school to pick us up, we ran to the car through water as deep as the top of our rubber boots. The sack of valentines I held was as soggy as a strawberry, my name unreadable on the scalloped paper heart glued to the bag. Just as we got to the Cadillac, the sky started to drop hail like frozen BBs. Mrs. Clapp sat behind the wheel in her lavender rabbit-fur coat, her dry fingers toying with the door lock as though it were a chess piece, deciding whether she would let us into the car. We'd ruin it, we would.

Valentine's Day meant we'd been at the Clapps' for almost a year. That's longer than we stayed with Granny or Aunt Bonnie, longer than our mom and dad ever lived in the same house together without one of them running off. Did that mean we belonged with the Clapps more than with Aunt Bonnie or the Spinozas? Would we stay another week or year, or leave as suddenly as Becky Bodette, who one day climbed into her social worker's car and was never heard from again?

Mrs. Clapp explained that Becky had gone to live with her dad and his new wife, and that we should be happy for her. We knew about the father. Once a month or so, we would go with Mrs. Clapp when she took Becky to visit him. His apartment was at the top of a rickety set of stairs behind a garage where he worked on cars. We'd sit in the white Cadillac, watching their reunion through the rounded windshield. Becky's daddy was always filthy, his hands green-black with engine grease, his coveralls crazy with stains. When he'd bend down to pick Becky up, Mrs. Clapp would make a little clucking noise with her tongue. I couldn't help thinking about the noise that would come out of Mrs. Clapp if she knew our dad had been in prison. But maybe she *did* know. Maybe the social worker had given her a full account of us before we came, opening her thick manila file on the dining-room table, letting the pages spill out and tell.

BEING AT THE CLAPPS' house wasn't more lonely with Becky Bodette gone, nor was it less so. Would another girl come to take her place at the table? We didn't know. Would my sisters and I continue to be offered a place there? That was just as foggy. Mrs. Clapp had worked us into her routine, but she could just as easily work us out, or replace us with cleaner, more trainable girls, ones who didn't pee the bed, barf milkshake onto the Cadillac's white leather, cry out at shadows in the night.

One Sunday afternoon shortly after Becky had left, we all went to a birthday party for the Clapps' youngest grandchild, Trevor. He was turning two, and as we sang to him at the long table covered with presents and a flat cake with butter-cream roses, he cried, startled by the candles. Mr. Clapp sat on one end of the table, quiet but present for once. Mrs. Clapp held court at the other end in an eggplant-colored skirt set with a white silk blouse and fat, glossy pearls. Her hair, double-teased and double-sprayed for the occasion, looked like a ferocious wad of black cotton candy. Although she cooed loudly as Trevor tore through his gifts, I noticed she kept her manicured hands well off the table-cloth, which was smeared with chocolate and blue frosting.

Each of the Clapps' three children had big houses, but this one was spectacular with a ballroom-size formal dining room and gables and a guest house. A sweeping staircase connected the three floors, but there was an elevator as well, the old kind with a door that accordioned sideways. We weren't supposed to play on it, but we did, of course, me and my sisters and Rachel and Beth Ann, two of the Clapps' granddaughters who had our approval because they sang loudly into their hairbrushes when we came to visit: "Big Girls Don't Cry" and "Here he c-uh-uh-uh-uh-uhms, that's Cathy's clown." As the elevator creaked and climbed, we jumped up and down and rocked against the walls in a manner we hoped was terribly dangerous.

We stepped out on the third floor and started a game of hide-and-seek. Teresa was "it" first and leaned her forehead against the door of a closet, counting faster and faster as we scattered. I ran down a hallway and opened the first door I came to. It was a bedroom, or used to be. Now there were old dolls posed on shelves and spindly tables. On a large couch, twenty or thirty dolls were stacked in a pyramid with the smallest, most delicate dolls on top. Some were the size of squirrels, others like big fat babies, but none were at all real-looking. Their heads weren't rubber or plastic like the dolls I'd seen in stores and on commercials, but hard, like dishes. Some had half-closed lidded eyes fringed with lashes; others were made-up with perfect circles of pink on their cheeks, shell-pink lipstick on the tiny bows of their mouths. *Babies with lipstick?* All of the dolls in the front row wore long white dresses with lace collars at the neck and appeared to have no bodies underneath. I felt them staring at me, the empty dead babies, and was suddenly terrified that they might spill over to fall on me, their heads cracking open like eggs. I spun and ran, smacking right into Teresa, who sneered and said, "*You* tagged *me,* you retard."

That night I had a dream about the dolls. One was a vampire, its bat wings shuttling open and closed like a fan under the gown. It flew around the room, making swooping passes at me while the other dolls watched, blinking slowly. The lids were so thin I could see through them to the veins, violet and spidery. When I woke up sweaty, my heart knocking like a kettledrum, I felt grateful not to be alone. Penny was there in her bed, fast asleep and turned, her natty hair sprouting out of the quilt. She was only five and couldn't make anything stop or go away, but she was there, rubbing her feet the way she'd done since she was a baby, making her puppy noises: my sister.

ON MY SIXTH BIRTHDAY our dad came to visit us at the Clapps'. He had presents for me, a huge stuffed psychedelic turtle I named Charlotte, after E. B. White's book, and a copy of *Peter Pan*. He read it to us right then, Lost Boys and pixie dust, alligators with attitude. He didn't take us anywhere but stayed for a few hours. We showed him the pony and the pool behind its metal fence, the big tree that dropped walnuts we could stomp open and eat like real food. It was a good day. As he left, he told us he'd gotten married again, to Donna, our old baby-sitter. He asked if we remembered her. We did. She lived next door to us in one of the green apartment buildings. She must have been fifteen then, with a shaggy shag and corduroy jeans that swallowed her shoes. One night, she offered me a puff of her cigarette. Now she was married to our dad and about to have a baby.

"Once we get really settled," he said, "we're gonna come and get you. I mean it."

October passed without other incident, and then, in November, the Clapps threw a party with a luau theme, tikki lamps and pineapples and meat on sticks. For this, the pool was opened and cleaned, though no one would swim. It wasn't that kind of party. My sisters and I watched the festivities from the window of

Teresa's room at the back of the house. Becky Bodette's bed was still there, the spread so neat and tight it looked like a present we'd get our hands slapped for touching. We perched on Teresa's bed instead and sighed. It was all so lovely, the colored lights and the colored dresses. Women we didn't know threw their heads back and laughed, showing big white teeth. The men stood in herds of three and four, holding their martini glasses close to their bodies, even when empty.

"I'm going to run away," Teresa said. "I can't stand it here."

I can't stand it was one of Mrs. Clapp's phrases, but it sounded right in Teresa's mouth. She was eight, and we believed her almost all of the time — so we took out lined paper and the chunky pencils they give you in first grade and started on the note. My handwriting was better, so Teresa dictated while I wrote. The letter began well. We skipped the *dears* and plowed right into *Good-bye. I am never coming back.* Then we were stuck. We argued about how to spell *terrible* and whether or not she should use the word *hell*. Penny and I would still be there, after all, and could get in trouble for her swearing. Stumped, we gave in and played Pick-Up Sticks instead, though we agreed the running away had been a good idea.

The next day was Saturday, sunny and hot. By 10 A.M. the outdoor thermometer read 88 degrees, and Mrs. Clapp started filling the plastic pool. It was a baby pool with a pattern of fat, happy goldfish, but we didn't care. We fetched the buckets and shovels and beach balls from the garage and snapped on our suits with the pink flowers, though they were much too small for us now. The poodles were out, clicking and sniffing, but we ignored them and looked, instead, to the few bright reminders of the night before, mango-colored lanterns and paper umbrellas. We squinted into the pinwheel sun, easily forgetting the runaway note and Mrs. Clapp clucking her way through our dirty laundry behind the locked door.

When Teresa climbed out of the pool and started chasing Penny with a bucket full of pool water, even the dogs got into it, yip-yipping and hopping up on their narrow hind legs. They ran around and around one of the brick planters, the dogs chasing Teresa chasing Penny. It was like a cartoon until Teresa slipped on the water-slick cement, smashing face first into the planter. She started screaming like it wasn't okay, and when she stood up there was blood streaking her chin and bathing suit. Her front tooth had broken in half; the missing piece lay on the cement by her foot like a piece of seashell.

On Monday Mrs. Clapp took Teresa to the dentist, but he said there was nothing to be done. He could cap it, but her teeth were still growing. She'd push right out of it, and that would get expensive. The dentist said to bring her back when she was six-teen or seventeen. Two things were clear, however, and the first we could see on Mrs. Clapp's face: we'd be long gone by then. The second was that Teresa's tooth would stay broken for eight or nine more years.

At first, I couldn't stop seeing that jagged, snaggly tooth, but soon it *was* Teresa, as much a part of her face as her thick eye-brows, the Kirk Douglas dimple in her chin. We also had solidar-ity after the fall, Teresa with her tooth, me with the cotton patch I wore under my glasses after the eye doctor told Mrs. Clapp my left eye was "lazy." (Wouldn't you know it, even my eye was lazy.) When we played Peter Pan, we had props. My pirate eye made me a natural for Hook, Teresa was the crocodile and Penny was Tinker Bell because she was the littlest, and because she whined if she didn't get her way.

We clapped to show we believed in Peter Pan but forgot to believe our dad was coming back for us. And then, one day, there he was, parking his sporty new Ford in the shade of one of the looming oaks. He got out and stood leaning against it, feet crossed, hands in his pockets, posing. In his black-twill dress pants and stiff-collared shirt, he looked younger than his twenty-eight years, younger, even, than the last time we'd seen him. He looked like a movie star, like a photograph of a movie star playing a father. He was waiting for us.

THINKING BACK TO THAT day, I often wish I had stood at the Clapps' picture window awhile longer just watching him, drawing the moment out. If my sisters and I had walked to him instead of run, whispered instead of yelped with joy, perhaps time would have shifted just enough to let us keep each other.

We had three months with Dad and Donna. Three months and then we drove home from dinner out one night to find a police cruiser parked in our front yard. We'd been spared the sirens, but the lights were on, red and blue staining the lawn as well as the neighbors who had stepped out to see what all the fuss was over. Once inside, we saw two cops standing in our living room, crisp and blue with badges and guns and walkie-talkies, big belts with lots of snapping compartments — the whole shebang. They were looking around at the TV sets. Some were still in their boxes; others sat with dead screens and coiled black electrical cords. They were everywhere — under the kitchen table, stacked against the back door, hugging the sofa like end tables. One cop elbowed another in the ribs and said, "I guess they watch a lot of television."

I thought the sets, like the stereo equipment that rotated in and out of our apartment, meant we were rich. We had a lot. That's why our dad just stood in the center of the room, shrugging a little as the cops asked their questions. He wasn't making a break out the window, *Dragnet*-style. Any second he was going to explain the whole thing, and the cops would leave, shooing the neighbors back into their houses. But it was my sisters and me who got shooed, herded by Donna down the hall toward the bedrooms. The new baby, April, was asleep over her shoulder, and Donna made a big production of asking for our help to put her down. There were the tiny nylon socks to pull off, and her diaper needed changing. Teresa found the sack sleeper in a drawer, and the three of us stood around the bassinet to watch Donna pull April's little arms up and the cotton sleeper down.

In the living room, Dad was being asked to put his hands behind his back, but he already knew how it was done — thumbs together, palms flat. We didn't see or hear any of this, because we weren't supposed to. Instead, we watched Donna's fingertips graze April's delicate head with such fascination you'd think scenes from Martian home-life were being piped in by satellite. "Good night," we said to her powdery smell, her quick, soft breath. "Good night, little baby."

෴

WHEN OUR CASEWORKER CAME to pick us up, we cried and whined to please stay, but Mrs. O'Rourke couldn't help this or anything. Neither could Donna, who was crying so hard she had to go back into the house before we were even out of the drive. As much as we wanted it, Donna wasn't our mother — wasn't even our baby-sitter anymore. Besides, she already had her hands full with April and Frank Jr., who was two and into everything. If he wasn't safely in his playpen, he had a mouth full of cat litter or was trying to pull the toaster down on his head by the dangling cord.

Our dad was Frank Jr.'s father too, which could only mean he and Donna were having sex when he was still married to our mom. We never got mad at either of them for this, mostly because

Donna was so nice. Whenever we'd help set the table with Chinet plates and blue paper napkins, or try to sort the mountain of socks in the laundry basket, Donna would say, "You girls are such a big help." And sometimes, for no reason at all, she'd say that we were good and sweet, that she was glad we were around. Hearing that, we'd perk up, our souls wagging.

WHY THE CLAPPS AGREED to take us back was a mystery. Surely, we'd proven we were too much trouble. We tracked dirt, left fingerprints, couldn't seem to stop wetting the bed. I was the worst, and it didn't matter that Mrs. Clapp still enforced the No Water After Five rule. I had accidents anyway, even when I was so parched that I had the dream where my very own water fountain bubbled as soft as a voice next to my bed. I might not have a drop to drink after my glass of milk at lunch, but I peed anyway — because of the other dream, the one where I was outside, running to get to the toilet and finding the door to the house locked. Just when I thought I was going to explode, I would find a bathroom outside, a room I had never seen before attached to the garage. I'd sit down, feeling nothing if not blessed by the miraculous toilet, and let the pee go. In the morning, I'd wake up in the cold puddle of my nightgown, and Mrs. Clapp would throw me right into the tub, whether it was a Sunday or not, shucking the soiled sheets in to-the-elbow rubber gloves.

"That's it," she'd mutter, and I'd think, *She's going to call Mrs. O'Rourke to take us away*. But it didn't happen.

It kept not happening.

Everything was just as it was before we went to Dad and Donna's: shopping and McDonald's, the weekly hour with

Lawrence Welk that ended with him singing, *Good night, sleep tight, until we meet again.* He'd dance with all the beautiful women, one at a time, their pastel gowns flipping up to stir the bubbles that fell around them like a snow made of champagne.

The only real change was that I had been promoted to second grade. My pirate eye patch had come off, and I had a best friend, Olivia Alvarez. When I said her name, I said the whole beautiful thing, all those vowels making my mouth feel bigger than before, open enough to hold the name of a best friend. She was in the other second-grade class with Mrs. Norris, but we had recess and lunch together, running to meet each other at the Cyclone fence. In one place, there was a hollow carved out from kids sliding under. It was just deep and wide enough for me and Olivia to lie side by side in it, the metal hovering so near our chests that if we breathed deeply, the sharp edges poked down like the tines of a giant fork.

The two of us fit just so under the fence. We were also preserved there from the loogies of Rondo Begwits, who was quiet except for recesses, when he ripped petals from the rosebushes near the flag. He dribbled a measure of spit into the dented center of each petal, then chased girls around the jungle gym, chucking one when he got close. They were the perfect missiles, really, and perfectly gross: heavy enough to fly, slimy enough to stick.

Sixth-graders walked by our hollow in clumps. They wore hip-huggers and macramé belts, T-shirts that said *Hang Ten* and *Keep on Truckin'*. We wondered aloud how the couples stayed upright, slouched the way they were, arms threaded, each with a hand in the other's back pocket. Through the screen of the fence, we watched recess, games of foursquare and kick ball, kids waiting in line for the slide. From that far away, their heads were bug-size, squashable between our fingers. Everything was small and squinty except for Olivia and me, lying so close I'd forget which of us had what flavored gum.

THROUGHOUT OUR TIME WITH the Clapps, we spent at
least one weekend a month at Granny's. Mrs. Clapp would drive
us over after school on Friday so we could have dinner there —
canned corn and pork chops and applesauce tinted pink, whole
milk in jelly jars. Sometimes we had Granny's version of tacos:
cold flour tortillas stuffed with oily ground beef, shredded lettuce
and American cheese slices, ketchup drizzled over the works. As
we ate and talked, Tiny yipped at our ankles until Mr. Dobbs
picked him up and tucked him into the bib of his overalls. I loved
how Tiny was so happy he couldn't stop shivering, how the full
length of the denim pouch, from Mr. Dobbs's thick waist to the
metal fasteners, quaked over the invisible dog.

On many of these weekends, our cousins Keith and Tanya
spent time at Granny's too. Their mother, Deedee, was our
mother's best friend before she left; their father, Lonny, was our
father's older brother. When our parents were still married, the
two couples spent a lot of time together — separately, that is. The
mothers jawed afternoons away in our kitchen or theirs, gesturing
with their cigarettes over skillets hissing with Rice-a-Roni or
sloppy-joe mix, rum-and-Cokes melting in tumblers on a countertop. The only time they'd quiet was when they were listening for
us kids, trying to determine from the thumps and shrieks and
double-dog dares just what kind of trouble we were getting ourselves into. The fathers generally stuck around long enough to finish a six-pack of Coors on the sofa in front of whatever sporting
event was on: baseball, world-class bowling, tractor pulls. The
second six they would take to the car, seeing how sharp a peal
they could milk from the tires getting out of the drive.

After Uncle Lonny ran off to who knows where, Aunt
Deedee lived in the same house as before, but with her mother,

Vera, who kept house and minded the kids so Deedee could work as a secretary for an insurance company downtown. Vera wasn't at all like Granny. She wore slacks, for one, and wide-collared shirts, with dark shoes that looked like a man's slippers. Unlike Granny, Vera never remarried after her husband passed: "What," she liked to say, "would I do with a *man?* He'd only get under my feet." Since Vera wore size tens, this was, I thought, a safe prediction.

For the longest time, Tanya was a baby and out of sight if not earshot, in her crib or her swing or in the walker under the table, latched onto her mother's leg with a slobbery fist. Then boom, she was four and even more forgettable. We let her tag along with us because Granny would tan our hides if we didn't, but we groused about it. Although Keith was only a year older than Teresa, he was deferred to absolutely. He decided whether we played superheroes or kick ball, who was in, who was out, who was Robin to his Batman. Even if Keith weren't the oldest, we'd have listened to him. Long-bodied and tan with white-blond hair falling into his eyes, he was beautiful. I couldn't remember a time when I didn't love him utterly, when I wasn't chicken-scratching with my sisters for his attention. If I couldn't be Robin, I'd take Catwoman. If I couldn't be Catwoman, I might as well just die.

The other thing was that Keith could sing. His voice was bound to change soon, but right then it was high and strong. In Granny's car on the way to the Gospel Lighthouse, we'd do "I'm a trampin', trampin', tryin' to make heaven my home" and "This Little Light of Mine." Keith instructed us on the harmony, how to find our note and stick to it, even if we had to hold our hands over our ears like the hear-no-evil monkey, looking stupid and whacking each other in the chin with our elbows.

Stupid-looking or not, we were getting better and gave several performances at church. People were always asking Granny when we were going to sing again and wouldn't it be cute if we had matching outfits, maybe with a country-western theme? One Sunday, just as Penny and I were about to do a car-rehearsed "Jesus Loves Me" for the congregation, the choir leader said he was going to tape-record it. He knew a missionary family in Korea he wanted to send it to so children in his host village could hear us. I thought about my voice being heard by people so far away and so different that they had their own calendar, their own words for mountains and the moon, for everything. The preacher said Korea had been in a war, and though it was years before, a country after war needed the Lord more than food or water. Our song, then, was a way of getting Jesus there, all the way there, up on the jet stream, down like rain. I sang loud that day.

ALTHOUGH GRANNY'S HOUSE HAD a small front room, she always arranged the furniture on these weekends so that Keith had his own pallet, barricaded from ours by the lumpy brown couch. Boys were boys, girls were girls, and both needed to keep their hands and their "business" to themselves. When we flapped around in the wading pool at Radio Park or sat on Granny's stoop and took turns running the hose on one another, Keith always wore his swim trunks, and we wore our matching suits with the pink hibiscus flowers as big as cabbages. There was no flashing, no running naked through the sprinkler, no coed baths.

Mr. Dobbs, whom Granny had married shortly after we went to stay with Bonnie, didn't seem to present the smallest obstacle in Granny's pursuit of a life without sin. On the afternoon he moved into Granny's house, Mr. Dobbs opened his suitcase on the bed in the spare room and started lining up his things along the mirrored back of the dresser — a set of bristled hairbrushes without handles, the heavy shaving mug with its cake of soap at the bottom. After a time, the room began to smell like him, but since he kept the door closed, the rest of the house was Granny's: Juicy Fruit and White Shoulders perfume, biscuits and peppered gravy and floor wax, the smell of lace breaking down. At bedtime, they pecked each other on the cheek and parted in the hall.

Granny's room was a chenille cave, her bedspread flat and symmetrical, the runner of fringe at its edge hanging just above the wood floor like perfectly cut bangs. When her door closed for the night, the first creak of springs meant her heavy shoes were in the closet, laces tucked into the mouths, and that she now sat on the edge of her bed, rolling the thick cotton stockings down, thigh to toe. At the second creak, she was up again, unpinning her braids, placing her dentures in the pink cup. After Mr. Dobbs came, I started listening for him too, his snores and foot-rubbings. When I asked Granny why she and Mr. Dobbs didn't share a bed, she said he kicked his way through his dreams like a dog. That must have been why her dog, Tiny, preferred Mr. Dobbs, why Tiny slept nightly in a tight curl on Mr. Dobbs's second pillow, like a head without a body. From our pallet on the living-room floor, my sisters pressed against me, one on each side, I wondered if Tiny and Mr. Dobbs dreamed as one dog, twitching a little as they chased rabbits through a sweet, damp field.

The one time I remember Granny permitting Mr. Dobbs in her room was when Aunt Darla came to visit. Darla was Granny's youngest daughter and a great favorite with my sisters and me. Like our dad, Aunt Darla had pale skin and freckles unnumbered, but her hair was a deep brown, not red-gold. She had a sweet face, round as a button, and I thought her altogether wonderful. When Darla married, she chose me over Penny and Teresa to be the flower girl in her wedding, solidly fixing my crush on her. I adored my dress with its skirt stiff as a bell and the black patent shoes with a rosette on each ankle strap, but was stilled midprance when I saw Darla step out of the anteroom on Uncle Bill's arm. She was the real thing, quietly glamorous, a shining slice of the moon. I couldn't stop staring at her small sandled feet, at the glint of pink polish under her net gloves.

After the honeymoon, Darla and her husband, Mike, moved to San Clemente, where he worked as a welder, but they came for a long weekend, promising Granny they'd go to both services at the Gospel Lighthouse on Sunday. Saturday was all theirs, however, and they slept late. My sisters and I waited with ants in our pants until noon and then couldn't help ourselves. Teresa knocked once on the door, and then the three of us piled in and onto the foot of the low bed, waiting to be either entertained or told to shoo.

The newlyweds were surprisingly agreeable about being woken up. Mike stretched and scritched and started digging in the wad of clothes on the nightstand for cigarettes. His V-neck T-shirt was on inside out, and as he leaned over I could see the stains under the armholes, yellow-white with raggedy borders. He always looked like this, sleepy and rumpled, bits of his hair jutting impressively. He held up a pair of his own Jockey shorts, studied them for a short minute, threw them back.

"Damn, baby, where are my smokes?"

Darla made a little snorting sound, one of her laughs, then got up, straightening her bathrobe around her. It was a kimono, short and thin, with a print of cattails, their edges as soft as sticks of butter. She shuffled over to the windowsill where the red box of Pall Malls sat clear as day, snorted again, then lit one for them to share. Where she had been lying, the bottom sheet was dabbed with brown stains.

"What's that?" I asked, my finger edging up on a spot shaped like a Mr. Potato Head, ears and all.

"Well," said Darla, "we had chocolate milkshakes last night. I guess we spilled some."

This was fast thinking, but the wrong answer. Where did they get the milkshakes? Was there any left? Could we have some? Darla looked at Mike, who simply threw up his hands: *Don't shoot*. She stalled, plucking an invisible flake of tobacco off of her tongue, then busted out with it, the whole thing. She told us about the womb shaped like a pear that remade itself every month. That blood was food for a baby; that the penis got the whole business started. She used the word *vagina* repeatedly while my sisters and I sat silent. Penny had an edge of the pink chenille bedspread and was rubbing the plush between her thumb and forefinger. Teresa and I kept sneaking looks at each other that said, *Can this be happening?* We didn't want Darla to stop talking, not ever.

"The coolest part is if you love each other, it's not a sin." Darla leaned back into the headboard, wrapping and unwrapping her hand with the satiny tie of her robe. "In fact, if you love each other, it's your duty. Go forth and multiply. You can even ask Momma."

"Yesiree, we have to cleave to one another," Mike piped in.

I suddenly had a clear image of Mr. Clapp's turtles in their wire pen. I had never thought of them as male and female before, but now I understood why the bigger one sometimes crawled up on the littler one's back, claws swimming in the air. "I think I've seen cleaving," I said happily to Darla, and they both erupted into giggles, Darla giving Mike a little shove on the thigh with her bare foot. It didn't matter that they were laughing at me; I was thrilled to be sitting on the bed between them as they passed the Pall Mall with its wobbly head of ash. And when they finally did shoo us out, I didn't half mind. We'd been let in on the business of sex. We didn't sit and giggle about it, didn't talk about it at all, in fact. Teresa went directly outside, and we followed, taking the dirt path in back through the hole in the fence and up the alley toward

the corner store for snow cones. I dug into the pocket of my jeans
for the dime I knew was there and held it the rest of the way like a
small, sweaty promise.

⁓

IT WAS HARD GOING back to the Clapps' after a weekend at
Granny's, and the first night was especially so, endless and rigid,
muffled by purple and various plastics. We forgot about the No
Talking in the Bathtub rule, or maybe we didn't forget. Teresa
made us laugh on purpose, sculpting a long beard for herself out
of bubble bath. She crossed her eyes and stuck out her tongue,
and we laughed so maniacally you'd think we hadn't seen her do it
a hundred times at Granny's. We were all working on beards
when Mrs. Clapp came in and pulled the plug with a grimace. She
sent us to bed without *The Lawrence Welk Show,* which wasn't as
much a punishment as it was supposed to be since we'd been
watching TV all weekend at Granny's. There, we didn't have to
settle for tap-dancing twins or four brunettes in pink ball gowns
crooning "What the World Needs Now" in unison. Granny let us
watch whatever was on, *The Dating Game* or *Petticoat Junction,*
Laugh-In or *Hollywood Squares* or *Love, American Style.*

At Granny's I could stand in the doorframe with one foot in
and one foot out, like Paul Bunyan straddling the Continental
Divide, and she wouldn't do more than holler that I'd better get
busy with the fly swatter. She might say, "In or out, miss," but
she'd never lock me on one side or the other. We didn't have to be
dead clean and quiet all the time either. Granny made us take a
bath every other day, but she didn't care how filthy we were when
we got in it. One weekend, we all caught lice, even Keith and
Tanya. Granny said the bugs must have been living in the wood
chips on the playground at Radio Park. She told us to get into

our swimsuits and then put us all in the tub together, where we suffered the treatment, a foul-smelling shampoo that she administered with long gloves and a threat to fix our noses with clothespins if we couldn't stand it. We could. In fact, nasty bugs and nits aside, there was something about the ordeal that made me happy to be there, dirty with my dirty family, Granny saying we were as bad as orangutans but not meaning it, Keith making jokes about the five of us being Louskateers.

Whenever Mrs. Clapp came to pick us up, my sisters and I hid in Granny's closet or behind the big trumpet creeper at the side of her house, wishing ourselves invisible or immovable, part of the foundation or the furniture. As I hid, I thought, *This time, Granny's going to tell Mrs. Clapp to go on without us, that she's decided to keep us for good.* But it never happened that way.

Granny opened doors and hollered until she found us, then hand-delivered us to Mrs. Clapp, saying, "I'll see you girls in a few weeks. You be sweet, now, and remember to say your prayers."

I hated being in the car with Mrs. Clapp. Trips to and from Granny's or the grocery store, or daylong Saturday errands in Fresno were silent, stifled, torturous. I couldn't talk to my sisters, even to point out things like the mural of a man pushing a giant potato in a wheelbarrow that was painted on the side of a grocery store. I swore I could hear my own blood crawling toward my brain and away, a train chugging to the top of a hill, then dragged back by gravity to do it again. After Keith taught us to sing, though, I discovered the radio. Granny's car radio had been a piano to us, something to fuss with on the way to church, or background noise, as white as the sound of road ticking under tires. But now there was *music,* song after song unspooling like kite string in Mrs. Clapp's car. I heard everything, my new consciousness like an antenna straining for a clearer signal. It helped that this was 1972 and every other song seemed to be about somebody dying: "Fire and Rain" and "Mister Bo Jangles" and "In the Ghetto." There was "Honey" by Bobby Goldsboro and "(Bye Bye) American Pie," which wasn't just about people dying but about music itself. They were such weepers, these songs, and I couldn't get enough of them, of the way the sadness in them seemed to be finding mine, seeking it out, pulling it near. Loving it.

WHEN MRS. O'ROURKE CAME to check on us, we sat at the table, one at a time, so she could ask her questions. *Are you doing well in school? Do you need anything?* I answered the way I was supposed to, though I had begun to wish, when we went to the grocery store with Mrs. Clapp, that my sisters and I could simply walk away from her in the store and latch onto someone else's cart, changing mothers like brand names. I would look into the other carts, trying to gauge kindness by what kind of tissue a woman was buying, which cereal, which soup. Any other mother would do. I was nearly sure of it.

Before Mrs. O'Rourke left, she told us that Donna had contacted her, asking if we could spend a weekend with her and the kids. We were thrilled. Donna was a mother we'd actually choose. In fact, on the back of a picture I had of Donna and our dad on their wedding day, I wrote *Mom and Dad*. Penny got ahold of it sometime after we came back to the Clapps and scratched at the place where our dad's face was. After that, there were little copper squiggles over his eyes, but I could see Donna just fine, her lace jacket and full skirt, the hand she had raised in a toast.

When we went, we found Donna no longer lived in the apartment we had all shared, but in a trailer, the narrow kind with all the rooms stacked like train cars so that we couldn't get to the bathroom without walking through all the bedrooms, opening and closing one door at a time. April had gotten big. She crawled so fast it seemed she had wheels, and she could pull up on the coffee table, tottering on her sock feet. The last time we saw Frank Jr. he could say *bird* and *ball* and *hi;* now he never stopped talking. He tromped around in chunky black cowboy boots saying, "I gunned you, fall down" and "Who's gonna give me a cookie?"

Donna looked good, happy. She told us our dad was doing well, but didn't say where he was or when he'd be back. "He's thinking about you, though," she said. "He's always going to be your daddy, remember that."

I nodded but felt confused. Our mother was gone too, and there was no *always* attached. We had been always-less for some time, and because of that, I was ready to try anyone in the space her leaving left: Donna or the women in the grocery store, the mothers in line at McDonald's who said "Hush now" to their children in a way that made me think they didn't mean *Be quiet* as much as *There, there.*

Donna's trailer was near Villa Park, and she took us there every day of our visit so we could spin ourselves dizzy on the merry-go-round, point our toes at the hazy sky when the swings hung at the top of their arc. The park's best feature was a red rocket ship. From the cage at its narrow nose we could see the edge of town pushing out toward orange groves and vineyards and farther. This wasn't even Fresno anymore, but Ashland, GATEWAY TO THE SIERRAS, as the sign hanging over the main street downtown proclaimed in large snowcapped letters. Ashland and Fresno used to be two separate towns, but now there was no border whatsoever, just a subtle shift to newer, cleaner houses and supermarkets and schools. Ashland was safer; that's why Donna lived there. She said she slept better. I wanted to sleep better too, sometimes more than anything else I could name.

On our last night with her, Donna took us to Happy Steak and let us order vanilla milkshakes, salty steak fries and Happy

Dogs, which were regular hot dogs wrangled to fit on a round bun. We all sat around a big booth in the corner that was perched on a two-foot platform. The whole restaurant could see us up there, chewing with our mouths open, chucking cold fries at one another. We must have looked like a family.

BACK AT THE CLAPPS' it was dry dinner and dreams about my water fountain. I woke up sometime in the middle of the night with a thirst I was sure I wouldn't live through. It felt like all the dust from that scary room of dolls was balled up way back where my tongue began, where the piddly Dixie cup of Kool-Aid I got at snack time couldn't begin to reach. I climbed out of bed and shuttled to the bathroom with baby steps, afraid I'd wake the dogs, that they'd climb out of their matching fabric-covered beds in the Clapps' room and come sniff me down, yapping in alarm, but nothing happened. I made it to the bathroom safely, closed the door and crouched on the carpet, sucking a damp washcloth left to dry on the side of the tub. I'd done this before. My sisters did it too, I knew, because once I crept into the bathroom to find Teresa there. We just looked at each other; then she handed me the washcloth like she was done with it and went back to her room.

The day after, we didn't talk about it, but we never talked about anything really. How strange that sometimes I felt like we were all the same person, one nerve, one want, and other times that we were so separate that I couldn't find my sisters even when they were right next to me, couldn't find words even when my mouth was full of them. Somehow, though, even without sharing, we all found the same tricks, like squatting to pee behind the big shrub by the corral when Mrs. Clapp didn't hear us knocking to come inside; like holding a loose tooth in place with our tongues until nearly bedtime, then letting it fall out altogether, saying to

Mrs. Clapp that we needed to rinse because we tasted blood. Just the word *blood* made her shudder and look away, and we could sneak a whole glass of water easy.

I don't know why we never wet the bed at Granny's. She let us drink water anytime we wanted, soda too, which she let us pick out at the Pop Shoppe, big flats of root beer and black cherry and ginger ale in glass bottles that we took back when we were done so they could wash and refill them. Nightmares didn't follow me to Granny's either. Lying on our pallet in the living room, I was sometimes afraid that a burglar would come in and step on us, then shoot us for hollering. I heard noises, people on the street, cars screeching away from the intersection, but these were outside, distanced from me by a thick quilt, my sisters, the door and porch and sidewalk. Inside there was nothing to hurt me. I might have to put the pillow over my head when Mr. Dobbs snored too loudly or when my sisters had a farting contest, giggling as if they'd invented it. Even so, I knew I was all right. I let myself fall asleep because at least for that night I wouldn't wake later with a start, feeling that something bigger than me was on my chest or maybe *in* it, taking all the air away, taking too much.

IN THE PARKING LOT of Donut Planet, a giant sugar-dunked cruller spun above the store, looking more like a flying saucer on a lightning rod than anything you might eat. We sat in the car — my sisters and I, Keith and Tanya — while Granny went inside for donut holes and chocolate milk. It was barely light, and we were on our way to the Gospel Lighthouse for Easter service 1973. To save time, Keith and Tanya had spent the night at Granny's, but the plan backfired. We were up past two, talking under our blankets, and Granny, who had the hearing of a prize pointer, was up too, telling us to quit our yammering every hour or so. Now we were tired, cranky, all pushing elbows and knees in the backseat.

After a particularly endless sermon, there was a picnic, complete with egg hunt and enough mayonnaisey potato salad to fill a sedan. We gathered with the other kids in our good clothes, the boys wearing vests and striped clip-on ties, the girls in floppy flowered hats and white gloves bought or saved especially for Easter, put away for the rest of the year. At the preacher's signal, the hunt began with a shriek, though for most of us the best part — waking to Easter baskets filled with hollow chocolate rabbits, marshmallow Peeps and jelly beans, all resting on squeaky plastic grass — was over. That year, we got two baskets, one from

Granny and one from the Clapps. We'd come into the Clapps' kitchen Friday morning to find the baskets sitting on the table where our plates should be. Wrapped in purple cellophane with floppy yellow ribbons, the baskets were bigger than anything we would ever get from Granny. I stared at my basket as if it couldn't possibly be real, but it was. There were the jelly beans I could hold in my hand like change, parceling them out so that by the time I had a red one, I wouldn't quite remember what the last red one had tasted like. Was it cherry or strawberry or that unplaceable *red* flavor, sweet enough to choke on?

The baskets were real, so did that mean something had changed? Would Mrs. Clapp get up from her chair and do something motherly? Hug us, maybe, or say she was sorry? I waited without committing to it, touching the cellophane on my basket gingerly, as if it might give off a shock.

AFTER THE PICNIC, WE started the drive across town toward Keith and Tanya's, past the old airport with its empty blue tower, and neighborhoods dotted with Easter decorations, plastic eggs on strings in the shrubbery and accordioned paper rabbits hippity-hopping in picture windows. Usually we sang gospel songs in the car because that's what Granny liked to hear, but that day we sang "Leader of the Pack" with Keith growling the motorcycle part. We sang "Sherry" and a deafening "If I Had a Hammer" that hit its peak as we rounded the corner onto their street. Then we were silent because parked in the driveway with its tires well onto the lawn was a police squad car. Another car was parked in front of the house, and several officers stood on the porch next to Vera, who for some reason still wore her bathrobe. She drew both hands to her mouth when she saw us drive up and seemed not to know whether to run back into the house or toward our car. Granny looked rattled too. She told us to wait there while she went to talk to Vera, but Keith wouldn't. He crawled over us to get to the door, making a half-sobbing, half-coughing noise as if he somehow knew already what the police were about to tell Granny: Deedee was dead.

There were hours of crying. Keith went into his room and didn't come out. Vera made tea and then forgot to drink it, the water turning bitter and dark around the floating bag. At some point, Granny went to identify Deedee's body, which was found naked on the lawn of a church at five o'clock that morning. Drug overdose, the police said, though Vera insisted it was murder. Deedee had gone out the night before, late, after money she was owed by a friend. She was broke, she said, and wanted to buy the kids Easter baskets. She would see this friend, do her shopping and be back. Vera said it was murder because the friend didn't give Deedee the money she needed for the baskets; he gave her drugs instead. Heroin. And no, it wasn't the first time she had done it, but maybe she was trying to change her life. Maybe this would have been the time for that, this Easter, those baskets for the kids.

Vera wouldn't let it go. Over and over she told us what Deedee had said the night before, what she was wearing, how clean she looked and sober. Granny let Vera talk, but I could tell she didn't agree. She had of Deedee the same opinion she had of our mother: both of them were far too willing to please themselves, regardless of the cost. Some folks could turn over a new leaf, sure, but others just had one leaf, one color, and that was *trouble*.

I knew Granny believed that Deedee had turned our mother on to drugs. In coffee klatches with a few of the more forbidding mother hens at the Gospel Lighthouse, I had heard Granny use the word *hooked,* which for some reason made me think of a werewolf — a vaudeville werewolf with one furry paw around Mom's neck instead of a cane, as he dragged her offstage and into the woods to do dope-fiend things. When we were with her, there were no woods, but I do recall waking up in the back of the car in the middle of the night, alone but for my sleeping sisters: Teresa stretched out beside me on the bench seat, her face gone in the dent of her pillow, Penny down on the floorboards like a little ball of flannel and hair. We were parked in the driveway of a strange house with a porch light so blue and bright it gave even the mailbox and line of trees a radioactive glow. Our mother must have been inside, but there was nothing to do but wait for her to remember us.

As Vera talked over her cold tea and Granny nodded, holding her tongue, I was stuck on two things. The first was what the preacher must have seen when he headed out, at first light, to post the title and times of the sermon on the bulletin board. It was cold and so early. Deedee's body must have been white and ice cold, covered with dew. The second was a certainty flat as a table that if our mom hadn't gotten into Roger's car that day, it could have been *her* on the lawn, her with the tracks up her arm and her photo in the paper for everyone to cluck at, *What a shame.*

For the funeral, we dressed up again in our Easter clothes. Tanya sat in a huddle on Vera's lap, but I couldn't tell if she was sleeping or not. Keith was crying, still or again, and we were too. My sisters and I sat around him on the bench. If we had piled right on him, we wouldn't have been close enough. The organ started up with a slow version of "What a Friend We Have in Jesus," but it was just so much droning to me. I had my mind on my mother, trying to picture where she might be — in a car, a desert motel, a windowless bar with football noises and a stranger next to her saying, *What's your name again, honey?*

That's it, I thought, *that's where she is,* and I sent her a telepathic message: *Stay gone.*

Mrs. Clapp came to pick us up at Granny's after supper. It didn't feel right to go, but it was a Wednesday night and we'd already missed enough school. The radio was on when we got into the Cadillac, and it hit me that something had seriously changed. Because of Deedee, I knew about people dying. I listened for "Tell Laura I Love Her," but it didn't play. WKNG was stuck on love songs, "Kiss an Angel Good Mornin'" and "Baby Don't Get Hooked on Me" and "Stand By Your Man." We pulled into the driveway, and Mrs. Clapp turned the engine off, then got out and began to fuss with the packages in the trunk. My sisters were already headed inside and I knew I should be too, but I didn't want to move. The sad songs were out there, flying through the air toward the radios in cars all over the world and toward me, if I could just sit still and wait for them, bent like an antenna. Reaching. Pining.

WE LEFT THE CLAPPS the way all of our leaving happened —
abruptly and without discussion. This time our social worker came
to school to pick us up. A teacher's aide brought us out to her car,
which was parked and purring in the circle drive marked FOR BUSES
ONLY. Our clothes were in bags, as were a few of the toys we'd
gotten for Christmas a few months before. Mrs. Clapp didn't let us
keep anything the first time we left, so I was surprised to find my
autograph dog with the permanent marker snapped to its collar and
the watch with Minnie and Mickey Mouse ticking up and down on
a seesaw with the seconds. The dog was my favorite toy and doubly
special because Olivia had signed it with eyes in the O and a tongue
hanging crazily. Our new school would be Palo Verde Elementary
on the far west side of Fresno: I wouldn't see Olivia again.

The first time I'd worn my Mickey Mouse watch was Christmas Eve. As my sisters and I watched "Frosty the Snowman," I
lay on my side, supporting my head with my hand. Later, when we
got ready for bed, I'd taken my watch off and saw deep, red
slashes on my wrist. I thought it strange that impressions could be
left and read this way, like a brand or a kind of tattoo. The watch
had been on my wrist for an hour, only an hour. How long would
it take for the marks to go away? How long would other things,
like sweaty fingers or the press of a mouth, have to be held to a

body to leave a mark that would take? I think that's why I decided to tell Mrs. Clapp what her husband was doing — because I thought she knew anyway. She knew because she could read the signs on me and was mad at me for not telling.

The business with Mr. Clapp began soon after we came to them, when I was five, continued for the months before we went to live with Dad and Donna, and picked right up again when that fell apart. One night, after a breakfast-dinner of French toast and sausage links and jiggly fried eggs that I couldn't bring myself to even look at, I walked by Mr. Clapp in the living room, reading his paper as always.

"Hey, Paula," he said, like the song, "why don't you come sit with me?"

I nodded okay and clambered up into his chair. His gray slacks felt as rough as a cat's tongue and familiar. *Had this happened before?* I couldn't remember. Maybe I had just looked at the fabric so many times, at his disembodied legs under the *Fresno Bee*. He scooted me up against him, moving the paper around in front of my body like a screen, and seemed to keep reading, though I was in the way of the words. He didn't say anything, and I didn't say anything. I'm not certain we breathed. My sisters were in the playroom hunched over a half-finished puzzle of Big Ben, Mrs. Clapp spooned leftovers into Tupperware not fifteen feet away in the kitchen, but I couldn't see them. They couldn't see us, or didn't. We were alone in the chair, the house pushing back and away to leave us in our bubble. *The world can be this small,* I thought. Mr. Clapp's forehead loomed like the surface of a planet, his wristwatch ticked like a bird's heart, and there was no other sound but the rub of pages as he turned them.

"Go on now," Mr. Clapp said finally. He helped me off his lap but kept one of my hands, pressing it to his groin hard, like he wanted it to hurt. Then I was away from the chair completely, and his paper flipped back up again.

This happened every night for a week until I couldn't remember another way, couldn't recall how it felt to inhabit all the nights before. At first, he just moved my hand in tight, dry circles on the outside of his slacks, the zipper catching my fingertip like a tooth at the top. Then he unzipped his pants altogether, tugging his underwear down to move my hand in. It scared me, the pained faces he was making and the noises, the rough way he moved my hand. He seemed to forget I was there. Maybe I wasn't in his bubble at all, but my own. Maybe no one was ever *with* anyone else. I began to cry just as he shuddered to a stop, leaving a dribble that looked like Elmer's school glue on his hairless stomach and on my forearm. It was warm and there was a smell — like damp socks and grass cuttings and something else, something sharper. He wiped us both with his shirttail, shoved the shirt back into his slacks, zipped and buttoned and helped me to the carpet, which was still there, somehow, as were the doors and hallways leading to what was real. I went into the playroom and flopped down on the floor with my sisters to lose at Ker Plunk! — all my marbles in the usual avalanche.

I didn't tell my sisters or Mrs. O'Rourke about the chair, or about the times Mr. Clapp trapped me in the hallway or by the fireplace and said, "I've shown you mine, now show me yours." I didn't tell them about how I woke many nights to what seemed to be his shadow in my doorway, a smudge or a stain, a haunting. Was it him? Had he come for me? I blinked and blinked, trying either to make him more clear or less so. Everything had grown so gauzy; I felt like a passenger on a dream train, or like one of those guys on the submarine in *Twenty Thousand Leagues Under the Sea,* the depth sounder pinging with distance. "You're pretty," said Mr. Clapp. "You smell like oranges."

I didn't tell anyone anything until I finally told Mrs. Clapp. She stood at the sink washing vegetables when I came into the kitchen, the sleeves of her burgundy sweater not pushed up, but cuffed neatly past her elbows. She didn't turn around when I started talking, but I kept going anyway, saying what I could to her back. It was hard to get enough breath to speak the words: I was a balloon losing air, hissing myself smaller. I'm surprised she could hear me at all.

I also couldn't stop thinking about what Mrs. Clapp would do when I was finished telling my story. Would she turn around and hit me? Drag me off to my bedroom and make me stay there without food or water? Lock me outside for the duration? I watched her thick shoulders and hips, watched her small, fat feet in their purple pumps. Nothing. She didn't shift her weight, or tap a toe, or clear her throat, even. Her attention stayed on the potatoes, the average, everyday-size potatoes that no one would ever push in a wheelbarrow. Her hands moved under the running water, scrubbing roughly, rinsing spidery roots and dirt nuggets down the drain and away.

The next day, she called Mrs. O'Rourke to say we'd have to be placed elsewhere immediately. She had back problems, chronic, incurable, and needed quiet now, a good long rest. This didn't surprise me at all. I had seen it myself, hadn't I? Her back so painful, so persistently stiff that she couldn't turn to face me: spent balloon, bubble girl, the eight-year-old in her kitchen.

EVERY MORNING OF THE first month we spent at the Fredricksons' was a test. I opened one eye at a time to the wallpaper flowers, hot-pink and purple and raspberry daisies as big and round as dinner plates. Miraculously, they didn't go away. Nothing did — not the room, not my new parents or my Barbie beach house or the banana-seat bicycle with silver-blue streamers on the handlebars. It was as if I'd been born for real, this time as a girl no one would think about leaving or passing along to the next address like a fruitcake. I had a ballerina jewelry box that tinkled softly when I lifted the lid. I had a toy box and a closet full of clothes that Samantha Fredrickson said I could keep, no matter what happened. Sometimes I'd go into the closet and press into the bright row of my new dresses the way my sisters and I liked to do with the racks of clothes at department stores. *But these are mine,* I told myself, fingering the hems and sleeves and buttonholes, nodding so that my face rubbed clean cotton.

The Fredricksons were nice people, maybe the nicest we'd ever known. On our first night in their home, they told us we could call them Mom and Dad if we wanted, only if we were comfortable. Then they took us to Montgomery Ward so we could each pick out a bicycle, brand-new, any one we wanted. Rows and rows of them stood on their kickstands like shiny dominoes. I thought: *If this is the only good thing that happens, it will be enough.*

Samantha Fredrickson was twenty-six and used to be a physical therapist. "Now I'm a mom," she said. "Anyone can be a physical therapist, but I've always wanted to be a mom." She was tall and thin with crimped reddish movie-star hair. Tom was a good inch shorter than his wife and stocky, with a receding hairline and bushy mustache that looked, well, *friendly.* He worked for a company that made desserts in bulk. I don't know what he did exactly, only that he got to bring home whole cartons of cherry and apple turnovers that came out of the oven bubbling, the sugar-dusted crust crisped up perfectly.

Our new mom and dad liked to sit us down in the living room for family talks. "We wanted a baby," Tom Fredrickson said at the very first family meeting. "Sam and I have tried for a baby since we got married, but the doctors say we'll never have one of our own."

Samantha started crying a little then, and I thought about how unfair it was that Samantha, who wanted children so badly, wasn't able to have them, but others who obviously didn't want them and couldn't take care of them popped them out like kittens — people like Louise Spinoza and Aunt Deedee. Like my mother. I went over to where Samantha was sitting on the couch, crouched down and put my head in her lap. I wasn't a baby, but I fit pretty snugly there, I thought, my left ear resting in the space between her knees that was as smooth and pink as the opening to a conch shell. If neither of us moved, would I hear the sea? her heartbeat? mine?

FOR SEVEN MONTHS WE lived with the Fredricksons on Santa Rita in a subdivision that was still going up all around us.

Most of the houses didn't even have yards yet, just plots of lumpy dirt marked with sticks where the patios and front walks would go. Our house wasn't big or small; it looked like all the other houses, and that made me happy. We were like everyone else. The bus dropped us off, and we walked home to find snacks on paper plates, cinnamon graham crackers, cherry turnovers with a lace of singed filling, cheese cut into little triangles. After, we could take our bikes out and go anywhere in the neighborhood. Samantha (and we did call her Mom, shyly at first, testing the word like something hot in a cup) would stand at the door and call out, "Just be back before dinner."

Sometimes we rode over to the model home, which sat open from one to four every day. Kids weren't supposed to go in, but we risked it anyway, looking over our shoulders for the real estate agent as we crept through the sliding glass door in back. Once in, we'd drop down on the living-room carpet, which was plush and springy, pink as an after-dinner mint, and roll back and forth, back and forth until our hair snapped with static. At the breakfast bar, there were padded chrome stools that spun only partway around before jerking back, perfectly pressed hand towels in the bathroom, a glazed bowl of real oranges on the coffee table. In the master bedroom, a round bed was raised up on a round platform, the whole thing covered with blue satin sheets that were so shiny they looked wet. We'd lie on the bed, our heads touching in the center, shoes carefully off the edge, and agree that nothing in the world could be as soft.

One day, the real estate agent came to show the model when we were there, and we had to hide. Teresa rushed into a broom closet, and Penny and I stood as still as possible behind the blinds in the living room. The wife disliked the layout right away — wasn't there a conversation pit advertised? — and the showing was quick. False alarm, no one even came near us.

Afterward, Penny asked if I remembered the time when we

had to hide behind some bushes at Granny's. It was because of Dad. Someone — was it Mom? — took us there and told us that we couldn't make any noise or Dad would hurt us. Did I remember that?

"No," I said.

"I do," said Teresa, out of her closet now. "Dad was really mad or drunk or something." One nut-brown curl had fallen into her eyes, and she swatted at it as if it were a bug.

"Was I there too?" I asked.

"Of course you were, spazola. Where else would you be?" She shrugged.

"Oh, yeah. I remember now. There were bushes, right?"

"Uh-huh," Teresa said, dropping it.

In truth I didn't remember it at all, not a thing, and although I didn't want my sisters to think I knew less than they did about *any*thing, I wasn't at all surprised. There was a lot of stuff I didn't remember, so much, in fact, that I had begun to regard my brain as its own complicated thing — sometimes a doctor, sometimes a drawer, sometimes a deliverer of memories like mail. When something big got lost, I just thought of it as a tonsil and heard the brain-doctor saying, "It has to come out. You won't feel a thing, and later there'll be ice cream."

OUR SECOND FAMILY MEETING was about fire safety. Tom Fredrickson had drawn a map of the house with red circles around all the windows and doors. He showed us where the smoke alarms and fire extinguishers were; he stopped, dropped and rolled.

"If anything happens," Samantha added gravely, "you need to get out of the house as fast as you can. Once you're on the front lawn and safe, run to a neighbor's to call the fire department."

Neither of them said anything about us waking each other up or checking to see if everyone was all right. With fire safety, it was every man for himself, I guessed. I began to cry, just a little at first, but soon I was nearly gagging.

"It's okay, Paula," said Samantha. "You don't need to be afraid. We're just telling you what to do in case something happens. You're going to be okay."

I tried to stop crying long enough to tell her that that wasn't it, that I wasn't afraid for myself. She came to sit beside me and stroked my hair, but I couldn't calm down. I got louder and louder, and she was angry with me suddenly, her patience gone.

"Stop it, now," she said. "You have nothing to be afraid of."

I took one of those deep snotty breaths and stopped. My face was fat and wet. Finally I was able to say, "What about *you?* How will we know you'll be all right? What happens to *you?*"

Although we'd only been at our new placement a few weeks at that point, I was happy to let every good thing about the Fredricksons eclipse every bad thing about the Clapps. We wouldn't go back there, not with Mrs. Clapp's back problems, not with everything that had happened, and they wouldn't come to the house on Santa Rita, which was beginning to feel protected in a magical way, as if it were broad daylight and the Clapps were vampires, as if it were real and the Clapps were make-believe.

Real and Make-Believe was the name of a textbook we were reading in my third-grade class at Palo Verde Elementary. The cover was half purple, half white, with purple lettering in the white space and white lettering in the purple. This reminded me of Gee Gee and Gia, Mrs. Clapp's awful dogs, but even their sniff-sniffing and toenail racket was hushed, dimmed, as if I had already stepped over the purple border into a *realer* real where they couldn't ever follow.

Unfortunately, nothing I had learned in second grade at American Union seemed to follow me either. I was supposed to know how to write in cursive and how to do my times tables, but I didn't. My teacher, Mrs. Just, had long, hard fingernails that she rapped on her desk when she was waiting for a kid to answer a question. *Click click click,* like poodle claws, and I'd lose my concentration, answering that six times six was twelve. Mrs. Just gave me extra math homework and said I should be embarrassed of my education. Still, I was glad I wasn't a boy; she was meaner to boys. She'd come right up behind Chris Curtis while he was scratching Spiderman or the Bat-Signal into his desktop and lift him clear out of his seat, shaking him like a doll.

Since I didn't have a new best friend yet, I spent my lunches in the library. I never knew what book to choose, and so I would sit on the carpet by the fiction shelves, opening one day all the red books, the next day every book with an animal in the title and reading just the first page. After a week of this, the librarian offered to help and I let her. From then on, she recommended things to me. She told me I read better than most sixth-graders, which made me feel a little better about not being able to get through a math test without counting on my fingers.

Part of me would rather have been playing outside with the other kids, but I hated not knowing anyone. On the first day, Mrs. Just assigned Marcy Levesque to show me around, and I thought she might be my friend, but at the morning recess, when she asked me if I needed to go to the rest room, I said, "No thanks, I'm not tired." She thought I was kidding and laughed; then when she realized I didn't know that *rest room* meant *toilet,* she laughed even harder. The library was easier. I liked the way the books smelled, and how after a time, my hands smelled like them, like dust and old paper and other people's stories.

I saw my sisters, of course, in the hallways or playing on the foursquare court at recess, but I didn't talk to them, and they didn't talk to me. We weren't friends at school. We had to make our own way, even if that meant feeling utterly marooned until the bell, when we'd meet at the backstop for our walk home. We'd sit on the grass for a while, dragging bits of stick through ant hills or braiding stems through Penny's hair so it would do a Pippi Long-stocking thing, and reenact our separate days, how Lorrie Vaughn's brother nearly brushed against Teresa when he walked by with his lunch tray and how her face must have looked when she almost absolutely died; how Brian Baker stuck another bean up his nose and had to be taken to the nurse for the prong treatment; how Penny snuck a feel of Mrs. Smith's skirt at story hour because it looked just like a bath towel. Felt like one too.

There were lots of kids in our neighborhood in the hours after school, hanging out on someone's lawn near the bus stop, sailing their Huffy bikes over the railroad tracks as if they were part of a motocross course. They ignored us until one afternoon when we were playing in one of the half-built homes on the edge of the subdivision. Still missing outside walls, the houses were like skeletons, pink insulation puffing out from the slats, Sheetrock dust in drifts on the concrete floors. I was flipping Malibu Barbie off the faucet of a newly installed sunken tub, pretending she was an Olympic-class diver, when a group of kids rode up on bikes. We heard them too late to hide, so we stayed where we were.

The kids started picking through the house. When they reached us, Teresa said, "We're sorry. Is this your fort or some-thing?"

"Naw. You can play here. Anyone can," said the boy with frizzled sandy hair and a blue Dodger's sweatshirt. His name was Marty Spirello, and the girl next to him was his sister, Jana. They lived a few blocks away and rode our bus, though we'd never talked to them before. The other three were Leslie Ferris, Michelle Austin and her brother, Richie. Teresa and Leslie nodded at each other; they were in the same fourth-grade class at Palo Verde Elementary.

Marty pushed his sneaker toe against a brick, shoved it over and said, "Hey, let's all go to the Candy House."

The other kids barked their agreement, but my sisters and I just looked at one another. We didn't know what or where that was, or even if we were invited.

"It's all right," Jana said. "We've been there lots of times." She was pretty, with straight ash-blond hair falling from a perfect center part. Her nose had a bridge of the tiniest freckles, as if someone had poked a felt-tipped marker through the holes of a Band-Aid and then pulled it off. Jana nodded at my Malibu Barbie's orange halter-and-shorts set and said, "I have that one too."

I liked her right away.

We all hopped on our bikes and headed back through the maze of streets with names like *San Miguel* and *Rosa Linda*. The subdivision had a Spanish theme, and all the houses were stucco and ranch style in colors you'd find in the desert: adobe, sand, sage and a deeper green called *high pine* that I thought was closer to *lizard*. Who would choose a lizard-colored house? You'd be surprised.

We crossed a major street and were suddenly out of the neighborhood altogether. The houses lost their sameness and grew bigger as we rode on. One had a driveway you could land a plane on and a front door the size of a car. I'd never seen such houses, wrought-iron gates and columns and green ivy snaking up chimneys. Who needed a fireplace in Fresno, anyway, where winter was a big sock of fog lowered between the end of December and February, when it was seventy degrees again? But I knew the people in these houses didn't have to think about what they needed anymore. Thus: a giant fountain shaped like a peacock and a yard that had, in two huge oak trees, identical playhouses with rope ladders and shuttered windows.

The sidewalk of the Candy House was lined with manicured bonsai trees and rocks that looked as though they'd come from the middle of a volcano. Jana and Marty marched right up to the door and rang the bell, which didn't just ding but played a whole song, one I hadn't heard before. No one came for a minute, and Marty had his hand raised to ring the bell again when the door opened to show a middle-aged woman with hair as stiffly shaped as the bonsai. She said hello and put something into Marty's open hand, then closed the door again. Marty was smiling when he turned around and trotted over to parcel out the goods: See's candy suckers in chocolate and caramel, enough for us each to have two.

"Is that lady someone you know?" Teresa asked.

"Nope," said Marty, slurping back sucker drool. "This kid named Chuck used to live next door to us. He told us about her."

"Where does she get the candy?" I asked. "Do you think she minds?"

"Dunno. I guess if she minded she wouldn't answer the door." Marty peddled off and we followed.

After that, we spent whole afternoons at Marty and Jana's house, swimming in their built-in, playing in the yard or in the garage, where their dad kept his rock-polisher and a whole crate full of rocks that had looked ordinary until he put them into the machine, smoothing their edges, finding their color. Marty and Jana taught us a game called Murder in the Dark that involved everyone hiding in a room with the lights out while the seeker threw butter knives until he found everyone. The key, Jana said, was not to yell out when the knife hit you. I didn't really understand why anyone would make up such a game, but I played anyway, ducking under a bed or pile of clothes with my arms over my head, like in the drills at school, waiting to get clobbered.

Once a week or so, we'd go back to the Candy House. Teresa got brave enough, after a time, to be the bell-ringer, but I always hung back, waited on the walk near a bonsai that looked like a cup without a saucer. I was as happy to get a free sucker or two as any kid there but never quite felt comfortable with the whole situation. I mean, why was the lady in the house giving us candy when she didn't even know us? How did she get to be a Candy Lady, anyhow? And what if she wanted to stop one day? Would she, like Marty had said, simply stop answering her door? Hide in the kitchen while the bell sang once, twice, three times?

All of this had particular resonance for me because I had similar questions about the Fredricksons. From the beginning, when we were strangers, when we could have been anyone at all, they had been doling out free suckers. And what were they getting out of it? A family, I guessed. Tom and Samantha had waited for and wanted a family for a long time, maybe as long as we had. Now there we were, found. Happy. Out on the thin new ledge of happy, and if we fell we might never stop falling.

RIGHT BEFORE SCHOOL LET out for the year, Tom and Samantha began planning a family camping trip to Commodore Lake. We went to Montgomery Ward again, this time to choose a tent and cooking stove and Coleman lantern. Tom got the map out so we could see which mountains we had to cross, how long the drive was.

Fresno is smack-dab in the middle of the San Joaquin Valley, surrounded by mountains. We saw them always — Sierras on one side, the Coast Range on the other, like library lions — but had only driven up into the mountains once, when the Clapps took us to Fish Camp and we played in the snow. Two years had passed since then, but it felt even further away, felt like a distant, miniature version of all of us. Our camping trip with the Fredricksons would happen in July, well past the snowmelt, but Tom said it

would be cool enough at night for campfires and campfire songs
and roasting marshmallows. We might even hear a grizzly bear or
two, or see their footprints, he said.

A month before the end of school, my sisters and I lobbied
for a trial "camp" in the backyard with the new tent and won.
Tom set it up in the center of the yard where the grass was finally
coming in, in patches, like new hair. There was a lot of reading of
the instructions and a little swearing, but finally the tent looked
like it should, a bulgy blue triangle with a mosquito-flap door. We
dragged out blankets and pillows and a grocery sack full of
snacks, then walked the three blocks to fetch Leslie Ferris, who'd
been invited by Teresa to spend the night.

I liked Leslie, but I also thought that if she was a girl, I
couldn't be. She was only a year older but already had breasts.
They'd come up overnight, like dandelions or a sponge cake, and
now had taken over her whole body. She walked like a tank, was
loud and pushy and knew more dirty jokes than anyone of my
acquaintance. On the walk back to our house for the sleepover,
Leslie hugged a Peter Rabbit sleeping bag and told us about a
fight her parents were having over dinner.

"Why do they have to fucking do this?" she said. "They're at
it all the fucking time." Since she was looking down as she talked,
it seemed as if she was addressing the *fuck*s to them, the Peter
Rabbits.

We headed out to the tent right after dinner, a full two hours
before dark. It was fun at first. We did scary faces with flashlights
and ate so many marshmallows I could feel them in my stomach,
squishing fatly together, fusing like cells to become one giant blob
of a marshmallow. Leslie told several versions of her favorite joke
about a character named Johnny Fuckerfast. They all had the
same punch line: Johnny had a girl in a bedroom or closet or
something, and his sister, who didn't know about the girl, yelled

to him that his mother / grandma / teacher was coming. Johnny fuck HER fast. Get it? We laughed at all of them, the snorting, spastic laughter of girls who know they're being bad.

Soon enough it grew dark, and that's when the trouble started. It seemed Leslie knew about space too, not just sex. We scooted partway out of the tent so that we could look up at the sky, and Leslie pointed out constellations and told us how far away the moon was. I knew *light-year* meant how far light traveled in a year, but it got me thinking about years in terms of heaviness, how two years might be dropped side by side from a building or from deep space like a brick and an elephant. That set my mind into a dark enough spiral, but then Leslie started talking about falling stars.

She pointed up at a particularly bright one and said, "It takes so long for the light of that star to reach Earth, it could already have burned out years ago. Or maybe it's not even there at all. Maybe it's falling through space right now."

That does it, I thought. There was no way I was going to stay out there when there were stars the size of Texas, the size of a whole ocean, hurtling through space. And we weren't even in the house but in a little tent held together by string and plastic stakes! I faked a stomachache, fooling no one. "Waaah, waah, wah," Teresa and Leslie called to my back as I headed for the house, my sleeping bag wrapped around my waist like a doughy hula hoop.

It helped a little to think of them pinned under star parts. It helped a little to be in my own bed shepherded by the huge flowers, but not enough. Before I really knew what was happening, I was crying so loud I woke up Tom and Samantha. It was Tom who came into my room and patted my blankets, asking if I knew that most falling stars couldn't survive Earth's atmosphere and disintegrated into nothing but dust. Did I know it was far more likely for us, any of us, to die in plane crashes or automobile accidents?

That set me howling with new ammunition. "Why does anyone have to die anyway? Why can't we just go on like this forever?"

Tom sighed, giving up, and went back to bed.

THERE WAS SOMETHING *WRONG* with me. I was sure of it. Why else would I suddenly be afraid of everything? Not just of big things like fires and falling stars and the dust of falling stars, but everything: crossing the street, lockjaw, botulism, bank robbers, whatever was on the six o'clock news. The earthquake and bomb drills at school were pretend, I knew. The siren would fade off in sixty seconds, and we'd get up, brush our knees off and go back to the spelling test. It wasn't real, but this only started me thinking about when it *might* be. Terrible things happened all the time — earthquakes, tornadoes, terrorists — and how would my desk keep me safe if a big hunk of granite were flying at my head? I couldn't breathe thinking about it.

The math tests, too, were starting to make me crazy. Mrs. Just had started to time us. She set a stopwatch for three minutes, and we had to get as far as we could on the sheet of one hundred multiplication tables. Everyone who finished would get licorice and a chance to compete in the end-of-the-year math competition. A third-grader could win against a sixth-grader, she said. It had happened before. Every time we took the tests, my heart pounded and my face reddened. Numbers floated through the filing cabinet of my brain like dryer lint. I forgot everything I knew.

One week, Mrs. Just came up to me in the middle of a test and said, "Are you all right?" I just said, "Yeah," but she stayed right by my desk, leaned in and said, more quietly, "Do you have to go to the bathroom?" I suddenly realized I had my legs crossed and was rocking back and forth. I didn't even know I was doing it, which, however embarrassing it was, had happened before.

It was like falling into a trance, when I touched myself or crossed my legs and rocked, a still, familiar place that was like the center of a me-size marshmallow, soft and swaddling. It felt good, but more than that, it calmed me down. It made me feel better on the *inside*. I don't know how long I'd been doing it, maybe always. Samantha saw me once and told me to stop. "That's private," she said, so I started hiding behind the couch, where I thought no one would see me. When she found me there, she got very upset and said we had to have a talk. She led me into my room, where we sat on the bed.

"It's not wrong, masturbation," she said. "It's just . . . something people keep to themselves." Her face seemed to be wrestling with itself, eyebrows in a tight vee, her top teeth after the same bit of skin over and over at the side of her mouth.

I had never heard the word *masturbation* before, but told her I wouldn't do it anymore. I would have said anything to stop her worrying. It was too much; *we* were too much, my sisters and I. I could see she didn't know what to do with us. *You're doing fine,* I wanted to tell her, *better than anyone else ever has.* But I didn't say anything, just sat and watched her hands, skitching around on the bedspread, straightening, plucking at hairs and lint and invisible somethings.

SCHOOL ENDED, AND SUMMER opened like a long, good book. In July we took the camping trip, and it was everything we had imagined. We fished in a thread of cold stream, played rummy in the tent, made hot chocolate by boiling water in a tin can held right in the fire. There were jokes about bears stealing our toilet paper, but we never saw one. One night, we heard something that might have been a grizzly but was more likely a big truck or thunder. The air in the mountains smelled different, and food tasted better, even scrambled eggs that browned into lace in the skillet because we had no real butter. All of it was perfect because it wouldn't last. We had two more months with the Fredricksons. Two more free-sucker months and then there was just the bell, ringing on and on, all the way down.

September found us at the last of our family meetings. *The Mod Squad* was on TV with the sound turned off, and I couldn't quite stop watching as Tom told us very slowly that his office was transferring him to San Francisco. Although that was less than two hundred miles away, we were wards of the court and couldn't ever leave Fresno County. We'd have to stay and find other parents. Over Tom's shoulder, the Mod Squad sped in a car toward a double set of railroad tracks and vaulted, with the help of a rise, all the way over. They sailed for a moment without weight or consequence, and then came down hard with a metallic crunch I could see rather than hear.

I felt sad as Samantha and Tom took turns clutching us tightly, but also relieved. Wanting to stay with them was like wanting to live in the model home, or in the Barbie townhouse I coveted because it folded neatly into a suitcase with a handle on top. All the furniture was glued down inside so it didn't go flying when you moved the house. Real things flew and fell into pieces, this much I knew. My sisters and I were real, and the Fredricksons were too, finally, with the crying and hugging, the snotty goodbyes. I could stop cringing, waiting for the bomb to hit, because it was here. Here again, the same bomb, the one I had memorized.

IN THE LINDBERGHS' BEDROOM, there was a space between the waterbed and Hilde's dresser that was exactly big enough for a skinny eight-year-old girl to sidle in, scooch down and believe herself invisible. This is where Penny hid with the blue rotary phone when she called back to the Fredricksons' house to talk to Samantha. This happened not once but several times, and finally Samantha had to phone Hilde and tell her that someone needed to explain to Penny why she couldn't call anymore. We all had to move on. It was for the best.

So, the Fredricksons were still in the house on Santa Rita. Maybe the transfer to San Francisco had fallen through, or maybe there had never been a transfer. They just didn't want us. Or they did want us but just couldn't handle us any longer; we were too much work. After I found out, I couldn't stop thinking about my old room. Had the Fredricksons found the right little girl for it? Was she waking to the wallpaper flowers at the same moment I was waking in my bottom bunk at the Lindberghs' to Tina's obnoxious breathing and the sound of rain that wasn't rain at all, but Hilde watering the lawn and roses and patio and the side of the house — pretty much anything the hose would reach.

At the Lindberghs', I opened my eyes not to hot-pink flowers, but to Tina's blankets, which invariably slid from the top and over the side, making my bunk a cave. A wooly igloo. If it was a school day, I could be still in my igloo until I heard Teresa's alarm calling us all into the bathroom to fight for the sink. On Sundays, Hilde was the alarm, hollering in German until everyone was up and dressed and wet-combed. Then we'd pile into the car and head to church with the Latter Day Saints, which was a big change from Granny's Gospel Lighthouse. The Mormon preacher didn't jump up and down and yell, didn't raise his voice at all, in fact. He talked in a slow, measured way and walked rickety and slow and always kept his skinny hands clasped in front of him. This, coupled with his large bald head, made him look a lot like a praying mantis.

Saturdays at the Lindberghs' were sleep-in days — unless Bub was cooking. He liked to experiment with leftovers and believed anything scrambled with eggs and stuffed into a flour tortilla was a breakfast burrito: pineapple, bacon and black beans, for instance, or creamed corn and cheese sprinkled with pimento that looked like bits of salamander tongue.

"Here, taste this. It's good," he'd say, holding some steaming concoction inches from my face. It would do me no good to crawl back under my pillow: Bub Lindbergh believed in trying everything as a sign of character. If I dismissed frogs' legs, I'd end up wasting my whole life because I wouldn't take chances. I might as well keel over dead right then. Same went for pickled pigs' feet, tripe, the tongue of a steer laid out on a plate like a bumpy pink miniature of Florida. If I made a face, I hadn't really tried it and got another mouthful.

Trying things extended well past food. Once I said I hated the song "MacArthur Park," and Bub let me know I was mistaken. "You can't hate that song," he said, "because it's a parable. Jesus spoke in parables. You don't hate Jesus, do you?"

It was actually the rainy cake lyric I objected to, but I swore to give the song another listen anyway, swore to spend a long summer reading *Think and Grow Rich* because Bub said it was the most useful book ever written, swore to go to the county library to learn about constellations because Bub promised the knowledge would save me if I were ever lost at sea.

BUB REGARDED THE OCEAN (and there was just one, you know, *The Ocean*) with all the mystery and majesty others reserved for Jupiter or Neptune. When he learned, some months after our coming, that my sisters and I had never even seen it, he declared this a "flat-out shame," and we went, piled into the good car one weekend and headed to Morro Bay, where Bub took home movies on an eight-millimeter camera. He directed us to rush into a single portable toilet all together and come out, one by one, looking relieved. We danced in a parking lot like chorus girls, Teresa and Tina bookending our line of four, sassing it up with some hip-wiggling. We ate fried squid and let the spidery tentacles dangle out of our mouths for the folks at home.

Morro Rock was like a giant turd in the sand. There weren't any other rocks around, just the beach, the dunes clumped with ice plant and leaves of sea fig that looked like the stumpy fingers of a green dwarf. There was a fishing pier and fried-fish shacks and a dozen gift shops selling saltwater taffy and crab magnets, ashtrays shaped like happy flounder and seashell frogs playing seashell guitars. Behind the wharf stood a factory or refinery with three towers blinking red. They stuck up into the Morro Bay sky like concrete cigars and made a low and steady foghorn noise. Beyond all of this was The Ocean, opening out toward a skein of pink clouds. It was as big as I had imagined in all my drowning dreams at the Clapps', as big as anything ever.

Tina and Teresa had changed into their two-pieces in the backseat and were ready when Bub took up his camera and told us to run into the water. Too embarrassed to strip down in front of everyone, Penny and I rolled our jeans up past our knees and tugged them higher as we crashed into the white-green surf. The water was so cold it needled my legs and feet, but I didn't care. I stomped and splashed, popping kelp bulbs with my heels. I nearly fell down from trying to watch gulls pine and reel, spilling from the sky like salt. I yelled into the crash of waves, while behind me the blinking towers droned steadily, a noise I swore I could still hear on the drive home, taffy clinging to my teeth, sand dried to a paste between my toes.

That was when I got my first introduction to dream-talking, as the car climbed the snaking Coast Range in full dark.

"Close your eyes and breathe deeply," Bub said. "Breathe in and out, and now you can taste cinnamon at the back of your throat. Cloves. The air is hot and dry on your skin, and when you open your eyes you see sand everywhere. Miles and miles of it, the color of amber."

This was a game and I wanted to play it right, but try as I might, I didn't smell cloves — I smelled shrimp fritters. I heard the hoarse barking of elephant seals and the surf pushing through pylons under the wharf. Under that layer was the car itself moving sickeningly on the curves, Tina and my sisters swaying with their eyes closed, breathing noisily.

"On the horizon," Bub continued, "you can see a smudge of green like a fingerprint. It ripples and shifts like water, like a mirage, but you walk toward it anyway and keep walking, your thirst growing. When you're close enough, you see a cluster of date palms and a glittering pool of water, and a brightly striped tent with camels outside, grazing on straw, drinking deeply from the pool. The flap to the tent is pushed open and standing there is . . . anyone. Whoever you want it to be. Picture that person."

Now he had really thrown me for a loop. It was hard enough to picture the things he spelled right out; now I had to make a choice and see it clearly enough to push it into the scene with the camels — which in my version smelled like the ponies at home — and the palm trees I'd turned into coconut because I knew what those looked like.

Think, Bub would have said if I'd asked for advice. *You have an imagination, use it.* So I squinted hard and conjured a sky as heavy and fragrant as a Persian carpet. The camels were there, smelling of pony and chewing straw like gilded wands. The tent opened slowly, and who was there? Who? He wore poofy Aladdin pants and curly-tipped shoes and a hat like a cotton swab with a tiger's-eye jewel in the center. And his face? From a distance I couldn't tell, but close up, it was Bub, his eyebrows and eagle nose. For an instant, a flash of hard imagining, he was my anyone.

THE OTHER THING BUB liked to do in the car was sing. He was a more-than-passable tenor with a soft spot for doo-wop, early Elvis, Marty Robbins's gunslinger ballads and the Kingston Trio. As soon as he found out Penny and I could carry a tune, he taught us "Lemon Tree" and "Little Sister" and "Smoke Gets in Your Eyes."

"Now, Penny," he'd say, "you be Mary. Paula can be Peter, and I'll be Paul." And off we'd go into "Five Hundred Miles" or "Autumn to May." When Penny and I offered to teach him "I'm a Trampin'," one of the songs we'd learned early from our cousin Keith, Bub made a face and said didn't we know what a tramp was? Didn't we know that no one, not no how, ever got to heaven that way? Penny and I nodded, embarrassed, but continued to sing it privately when we walked home from the bus or roller-skated around Noreen's cul-de-sac with our new foster cousin, Krista, who, even at six, had a throaty Stevie Nicks thing going on. She liked to tie one of her sister Vicky's flannel shirts around her waist as a skirt and flip it back and forth diva style, which inspired me and Penny to go looking for costumes too, like the dusty pink bed jacket at the back of Noreen's closet that made us want to bust into "Que Será, Será" and "Please Don't Eat the Daisies."

Soon, time at Noreen's became one big road show. Penny, Krista and I took turns standing on the picnic table, belting out everything from Tanya Tucker to Nancy Sinatra, while Teresa, who could not sing, judged. Tina acquiesced to be a judge at first too, but then lost her patience. Couldn't we play Horse Ranch? Or the waitress game where she got to be the cook and ding the egg timer while barking things like "Come pick up this order and make it snappy!" When we said no, we wanted to keep singing, she pouted on the lawn. "C'mon, Teresa," she said. "We don't need them." But Teresa didn't budge. Her head had been turned for a time as Tina's "bestest buddy," but that had faded when Tina tried to pit her against us. Now she was ours again. Tina would either have to join us, all of us, or be on her own. "Whatever," Tina said, and stomped one chubby foot. Then she went inside to watch The Show with Hilde and Noreen, who couldn't have been more thrilled. Hilde fell over herself to offer Tina popcorn and Popsicles, a pillow for her feet. Tina declared The Show her show too, selected a favorite female villain, a favorite chair from which to watch the fur fly, and asked Hilde to teach her to knit.

Although I didn't really miss Tina outside (she was way too bossy and confused me because I was used to taking orders from Teresa), I was surprised to see her give up so easily. She'd wanted sisters and ordered us, like shoes from a catalog, to be delivered at her door. Now here we were, and she was inside like an old lady, knitting a blanket for a winter that would never come. Maybe she just couldn't get over the fact that we were one another's sisters first, that she couldn't be the center of attention because our center had already been formed long before we knew her. Or maybe she was jealous because we were encroaching on the space and the people she had owned outright until we came, like Krista. Like Bub.

It is true that my sisters and I fixated on Bub, attached ourselves to him like coral, like urchins, like sea sponges. I had never known any grown-up like him. He had wild ideas, and as soon as one popped into his head, he just had to see if he could make it so. Once, he welded my banana-seat bike to Penny's and then set up a tongue and harness so our hulking Saint Bernard / Labrador dogs could pull us around the block. It worked, by the way. Another time, he decided he wanted a convertible. He walked out to our old orange Subaru with a crayon, drew some rough lines, grabbed up a hacksaw and cut the damned top off. As if that weren't enough, he found some cans of spray paint in the garage and went to town on the car until the whole thing was a swirly purple with a white handlebar mustache between the headlights. He taught us girls to drive on it. The car became our toy, and the five-acre field, with orange cones set up near the stock tank, became our slalom course.

Sometimes Bub's brainstorms had to do with money, like night classes in real estate at Fresno City College or the metal detector that he took along to the beach, embarrassing us, or the John Deere tractor he was going to repair and repaint to sell at auction for a huge profit. "That thing's an antique," he'd insist. "A piece of our history." He might have been right, but for the whole of our stay with the Lindberghs, that history sat out by the tack shed on flat tires, housing entire nations of spiders. Our property was a graveyard of Bub's ideas, like the big hole at the top of the field that he dug one weekend with a borrowed backhoe, saying it was the beginning of a swimming pool he would finish some other time. Some other time never presented itself: the moved earth was soon covered with long grass and weeds and resembled an ancient burial mound I'd seen in a geography book; the top of the mound was the highest point on our land.

Bub was such a good salesman of his ideas — the pool that would feel positively Elysian on sweltering summer days, the pigeons we'd teach to home, the worm farm that would thrive on coffee grounds and potato peels and pay for a few more ponies, maybe even a sailboat — there was no way not to be disappointed when he abandoned them. Still, I found myself getting excited every time. When he read in a magazine that he could buy the plans to build his own forty-foot sailboat from a factory near Hollister, he thought of nothing else for months. We would sell the house and sail around the world. He had it all worked out: Penny and Tina would learn French, I'd learn Italian, Teresa, Spanish. German was covered. We'd cross the Atlantic and spend years skimming conti-nents: Welsh moors, Greek islands blue as jewels, exotic ports in Spain and Turkey and Egypt. Then, who knew, maybe Iceland, New Zealand, Fiji. Because we girls wouldn't yet be finished with school when it came time to push off, we'd take courses through correspondence. This would require self-discipline and diligence, what with all the distractions: chirping porpoises, boat-size sperm whales, manta rays like swift slices of mushroom, sea turtles and swordfish and coral reefs teeming with anemone.

When Bub went on like this, Hilde made a production of clearing her throat, saying, "I'm never going to leave this house."

She meant it too; I could tell. She would rather die in that fat brown fart of a house than have the whole world offered up like a buffet, countries passing through the window in our jib sail like images through a viewfinder. It struck me that there were stayers, who always stayed, whether they should or not, and leavers, who invariably left, no matter what they were leaving, or whom or how or when. Hilde was a stayer; my mother was a leaver. And me and my sisters, which were we? Maybe neither yet, since none of our staying or leaving had ever been up to us. Which was Bub? I wanted to think that he was somewhere in between, that he could sail his boat anywhere and everywhere because he knew how to use an anchor. Knew what it was to *be* an anchor.

To Bub, fear — of change or failure or disappointment — wasn't a reason not to dream. He wanted us girls to plan big — the bigger and broader and less ordinary, the better. Like the time I was filthy rich with diamonds for a day. I found them down by the water tank where Bub had started building a fort for us a few months before. It was going to have real walls and a roof and a rope ladder, but he'd only finished the first stage — a structure that surrounded the well, flat on top, and looked from the house like an odd wooden hat for the water tank's silver head. Littered with scrap lumber and bent nails, the head of a broken hammer, the ground around the water tank waited patiently for Bub's attention.

I went down to the tank to make my own fort, one that needed only to last the afternoon: several two-by-fours set against the tank in a partial tepee. I lay down in the zebra stripes of shade and looked out at the toast-colored grasshoppers sticking to the toast-colored grass. The sun was shrapnel. It glinted hard off the long grass and beetle shells and flecks of mica. Then I saw something else, a nugget the size of a ragged pea shot through with light. I picked it up and felt it sear into the center of my palm like money. It was a diamond; it had to be. I spent the next hour raking through the packed dirt around the tank with the sun boring into the top of my head. In the end, I had a pile of diamonds the size and weight of a robin's egg. I wrapped them in a corner of my T-shirt and carried them up to the house, where I dribbled them into the toe of one of my dress socks, liking the way it reminded me of the pouches of gold that dangled from prospectors' belts in *Paint Your Wagon*. Did staking your claim require a verbal declaration or something in writing? or maybe a flag planted there, like astronauts colonizing the moon?

I decided to say nothing until Bub arrived home from work. After he'd taken off his work boots and washed his hands and face and sat, finally, in his chair, I held the sock up, emptying the diamonds into my palm. "Look," I said. "Look what I found."

He didn't laugh. He didn't ruffle my hair and say, "Those are just quartz, silly." He whistled low through his teeth and asked, "What are you going to do with all your riches?"

SAILING AROUND THE WORLD was going to take some skill, so we practiced on *Bounty,* a superfast racing-class sailboat called a Thistle, which Bub had sold a few of the horses to purchase. We joined the Fresno Yacht Club, took lessons on eight-foot Flippers, learning to find the wind, trim a sail, tack without getting hammered by the boom. We were still too young to crew on *Bounty,* so Bub trained Hilde and Cousin Vicky. While they sailed, we sat on the bank, fished off the dock, pulled up sticker bushes and threw them at one another. There were a handful of Yacht Club boys around during this time, but none like Mike Stebbins. When Mike sailed by in his Flipper, life jacket on but untied, long legs kicked over the side so his Bass deck shoes dangled casually, he had every girl in a half-mile radius nearly falling overboard to check her hair in the reflection of the flat lake. Although Mike Stebbins always protected his nose with a slather of zinc oxide that looked a lot like toothpaste, it didn't matter; he could have spit loogies or burped his way through the alphabet and he still would have been a stone fox.

Unfortunately, Mike took no more notice of my sisters and me than he would a burr stuck to his shoelace, so we were stuck with the second string: Tony Harlan, Pete and Danny Berringer, Todd Olson — boys who *did* spit loogies and burp the alphabet, to no great effect. We were happy enough to have these boys around, though. With all of our parents out in the middle of the lake, well out of earshot and engaged for hours, we were free to get into whatever trouble we could collectively cook up. Sometimes we settled for a floating-dock version of King of the Mountain; sometimes we used our life jackets as sleds and flung ourselves down the side of a canyon made of a pinkish clay that was startlingly slick and only hurt when you slid off your life jacket and had to scrape along the rest of the way with your shorts riding up to give you a world-class wedgie.

On a particularly scorching summer day, a bunch of us climbed a hundred-foot sand hill that sloped gradually down to the lake. One third of the way up, a dirt road was cut into the hill, upon which several cars were parked.

"See that space between the red car and that station wagon?" Pete Berringer said to no one in particular, pointing. "I'll bet you can't roll this rock down the hill, through that gap and into the lake."

We all looked down at the rock he had in mind, a boulder the size of a medicine ball, and then most of us looked away, chicken, which is what Pete had been banking on. Even Teresa had her hands firmly in her pockets and was kicking sand.

"Oh, all right, you sissies. Watch." He squatted to dislodge the rock, then shoved it over a few feet. He knelt down, eyeballing a path as if he was shooting marbles, then sent the rock with a push. It skittered down the hill, gave a few bounces that had us cringing and biting our lips, and then flew right through the gap, landing in the lake with a belly-flop-sounding splash. Pete puffed out his scrawny chest and said, "Hah!"

Hating to be outdone by a boy half her size, Tina stepped up. She put her hands on her jean-shorted hips, leaned all of her weight on one dirty bare foot and said, "You think that's something?" She looked up the hill and spied a boulder that was double the size of Pete's rock, squashed flat on one side. She headed right for it, and we followed. This was getting interesting. By the time we got there, Tina was digging like a dog under the rock, throwing up sand. It started to fall before she was ready, but she gave it a shove anyway, and we all watched with our mouths open as the boulder flew on a diagonal toward the red car and missed it by a hair. "HAH!" Tina said, and blew up at her damp bangs.

After that, Pete and Tina were unstoppable; they threw every rock down that hill they could get their hands on, softball-size or bowling-ball-size, it didn't matter. Danny, who was only eight to Pete's ten, got nervous and tried to stop them by saying he could see the parents sailing back into the harbor, but no one was listening. Pete had his eye on a gigantic specimen near the top of the hill. It was an extraordinary rock, truly, half the size of the red sedan they were half aiming at. Although it should have taken all of us shoving to get it going down the hill, all of us weren't willing to bank on the angle of its fall, and so we watched as Pete and Tina huffed and puffed, sweat staining the armpits of their T-shirts. It wasn't budging.

"C'mon," Pete said to Danny and Tony Harlan. "Get over here, you pussies." Just then, the rock shifted, and shifted again, so that Tina had to skitter over to the side to get out of the way. The descent was spectacular. It took the hill like an elephant on roller skates, veered left for no reason we could see, and blindsided the sedan with enough force to make it shudder.

Tina gave a chipmunk shriek and looked to Pete. We all did. He wasn't the oldest there, but he was the oldest boy. He would know what to feel, what to do, what came next. "Huh," Pete said, shrugging his bony shoulders. "I didn't think it would do that."

A long hour later, when the race was over and all the boats were docked, Bub, Hilde and Pete and Danny's parents stood around the red sedan, clucking and shaking their heads. We thought Pete and Tina were in for a real creaming, but Mr. and

Mrs. Berringer were sensible people who believed in "life lessons." Pete and Tina's punishment would be waiting for the owners of the car to arrive and telling them exactly what had happened. That was part A. Part B was that they would spend the next several years paying off the damage with their allowances. Pete and Tina sat down in the sand and waited for the owners, looking positively green. Two years without allowance meant no *Mad* magazines, no pinball, no Saturday matinees, no popping into a corner store for a bottle of grape soda and an Abba-Zabba bar. Life lessons were expensive. *Was it too late to ask for the creaming?*

MOST SAILBOAT RACES WERE held at Millerton Lake, some twenty miles from our house, but we also took *Bounty* to regattas all over California, Redding to Tamales Bay to San Diego. Our favorite was the Mile-High Regatta at Huntington Lake, where there were always tons of kids on the beach and where the grownups stayed up late singing "Ghost Riders in the Sky" and "Sloop John B." around a campfire. Every year, something terrible happened before or during the trip to Huntington. It was tradition. The first year, Tina ran into a tree and split her head open while we were playing yard games in the dark near the Yacht Club. The second year, our truck blew a rod on the Grade, a section of mountain highway so steep you could see it from our property, cut into the Sierras like a firebreak, like an arched white eyebrow. There was a loud *pling* when the rod blew; then the truck shuddered and stopped dead as a road-killed toad. In time, a nice family came along and offered to drive Bub up to the next town so he could call a tow truck, and fortunately he stopped saying *goddamnitshithellshit* long enough to accept.

Another time, we got all the way to Shaver before disaster

struck, an engine fire this time. Bub saw smoke threading from the hood and pulled the truck over. Leaving the engine running, he got out to raise the hood, and my sisters and I moved up in the camper to look through the cab window. The flames were a foot high, popping and curling. When Bub yelled for us to get out of the camper, my sisters and I fell over one another trying to get through the small door. So much for keeping our cool in emergencies. Bub was hollering and Hilde was hollering. We weren't carrying a fire extinguisher, so Bub shook up several cans of Dr Pepper and shot the carbonated, squiggling streams at the fire.

"The puppies!" Penny screamed suddenly, and we realized we'd left our eight-week-old Saint Bernard / Lab mixes, Ben and Barry, in a cardboard box inside the camper. If the truck exploded, they were goners; we had to save them. Bub was busy with the Dr Pepper and Hilde was busy with her nervous breakdown, so it was up to us girls to rescue them. This was no time for fear. I lunged back through the door like the Bionic Woman, grabbed the big cardboard box holding the puppies and tried to push it through the door. It was too big, though, even when I squished down the sides. I shoved and shoved, whimpering like the puppies. We were doomed. The puppies and I were going to die in the volcano of the camper while Bub screamed *goddamnit* over and over to the fire and my sisters hopped up and down and yelled . . . *what? Take the puppies out of the box?* My brain turned on like a refrigerator light — *out of the box!* — and I handed the puppies through the door just as Bub stopped swearing. The fire was out, the emergency over, and we were saved, all of us. Even if I turned out to be more like Laverne or Shirley than the Bionic Woman, even if Bub was more like, well, Bub, than the cavalry, we were delivered.

AMBER SWENSON MARCHED ACROSS the street and up our dirt driveway and rapped three times fast on the jamb of our open front door. "Yoo-hoo!" she hollered. "Anybody home?"

It was Saturday. Tina and my sisters had gone to the grocery store with Hilde; Bub was out back, swearing under the hood of the Subaru, something to do with a fan belt; I was in the living room watching *Land of the Lost* in my bathing suit. It was 105 degrees, standard fare for a Fresno summer. I got up to see who it was, and my mouth fell clean open.

We hadn't seen much of Amber or her brothers since the star-thistle episode. Throughout the school year, Amber had been in the third-grade classroom next to my fourth-grade one at Jefferson Elementary, but she was easy enough to avoid. She and her brothers rode a different bus than we did, and if I saw Amber in the halls or at recess, I ducked and hightailed it the other way, needing no reminder that the last time I had tried to make friends I'd nearly croaked from blood poisoning. Now she stood in our doorway in white Ditto shorts and a tight-fitting pink T-shirt with kittens batting at a ball of string.

"Hi," she said brightly. "You're Paula, right? I'm Amber."

"Yeah," I said. "Hi." She wasn't packing any obvious ammunition. She didn't have her mean brothers with her. She looked harmless, really, more than harmless with two honey-colored ponytails sticking out from right above her ears. Her shoulders and hips were broad, her waist doughy. Both of my legs together were smaller than one of hers, but Amber didn't seem to be self-conscious of her size. When I invited her into the house, she bounced in like a Superball.

"So," Amber said, looking around at the yarn explosion that was our kitchen; everything but the stove and refrigerator was covered with something Hilde had crocheted. "Do you have any bread?"

"Uh, sure. Yeah." I walked over to the counter and picked up the loaf of Wonder. "Is this okay?"

Every square inch of Amber's face brightened when she saw the red-and-yellow-dotted plastic bag. She sat down at Bub's place at the table. "More than okay." Disposing of the twist tie in a nanosecond, she pulled a slice out and methodically began to tear the crust off, keeping it whole, like an apple peel. Then she crushed the white square in her hands and began working it like a snowball, smaller and rounder. When it was walnut-size, she ate it, popped the whole thing in and chewed happily.

Three slices had been scarfed this way before Amber took a breather. "Okay," she said, leaning back in Bub's chair, "that's yummy. The parents never let us have bread, not the good kind anyway. They say it has too much sugar or something stupid."

"The parents?" It was odd, her putting it that way; not "my mom and dad," not "my parents" but "the" (like Bub's one ocean), as if the world wasn't littered with, lousy with parents.

She lifted her big shoulders toward her ears, lowered them again. "Yeah, the parents. The rents, the parental units."

"Right."

She fished back in the bag and started dismantling another slice. "So, what are you doing tonight?"

"Um, nothing, I guess. Watching TV."

"Why don't you come over to my house for a sleepover?"

My mouth fell open for a second time, but I caught it, closed it and said, "Sure," as casually as I could, considering I was the Superball now. Amber Swenson wasn't a sticker-bush girl at all, but a doughy bread girl, and she had just invited me to my very first sleepover.

"Ask if you want. You can let me know later." She dug a fat, felt-tipped pen from her shorts pocket and wrote her phone number on my palm. As she walked down our driveway toward home, I stood in the doorway, blowing on the numbers, hoping they didn't blur with sweat before Hilde got home.

AMBER WALKED OVER TO get me after dinner, even offered to carry my Raggedy Ann sleeping bag. I knew already that her house was nicer than ours, bigger and better maintained. The Swensons' yard was green and plush, while ours was a singed, weedy thing. They had hired men to come and dig a thirty-foot-long, eight-foot-deep pond in front of their house, with a dock and mature willow trees. Our pond had been one of Bub's projects, self-mixed concrete set with rocks and only big enough for the dogs to sit in there side by side.

The minute Amber led me through the back door, I realized the inside of their house was considerably nicer as well. There were plants everywhere, not sickly yellow avocado shoots, but real plants flourishing in terra-cotta pots. There was art in frames, a glass coffee table perched on a giant, gnarled piece of driftwood, and two fireplaces. Amber's mom was in the kitchen loading the dishwasher. She wore tiny jean shorts, a scoop-neck white T-shirt with the sleeves rolled up and leather sandals. "Hi there," she said, turning around. "I'm Valerie. Welcome." Her shoulder-length brown hair was held back from her face with tortoiseshell combs, and as she readjusted them, I saw that her hands and face were tanned the same coppery brown as her hair.

"We're going to my room," Amber said, ushering me quickly down the hall. She shut her bedroom door behind us and plopped down on one of the two twin beds, both of which were covered with a satiny apricot-colored spread. The walls were papered floor to ceiling with a pattern of dogs and cats standing on their back paws, peering over a wooden fence.

"Your mom sure is pretty," I said, sitting lightly on the edge of the second bed.

"Yeah, whatever."

Before I could insist, one of Amber's brothers flung the door open and shouted, "Hey!" He was tall and wiry with a tumble of hair a shade darker than Amber's. Dark eyes, a sharp nose and thin, pale lips crowded the center of his narrow face, making him look like some kind of bird.

Amber huffed and rolled her eyes. "What do you want, creep?"

"Nothing, supercreep. I just wanted to see what you dragged home." He gave me the once-over, Keds to bangs. When I forced myself to meet his eyes, he barked, "What are you look-ing at?" and stormed out again. The door shuddered.

"That was Ross. Don't worry, he's always like that."

It was hot in Amber's room, so we went outside. Sitting at a wooden table on the patio were Valerie and Amber's dad, Dean. They were sifting through a flat of raisins, plucking out the stems and those that hadn't fully dried yet, talking softly; behind them, the sun, beginning to set, was gauzed over with orangy-pink clouds.

"Hiya, princess," Dean said, waving us over. He was easily twice as large as Valerie, and his voice was gruff, like a sailor's. In fact, he looked a bit like a sailor, a merchant marine, somewhere in between Popeye and Bluto. Like his wife, he was deeply tan, but his features were coarser. His lips were fleshy, and pores were visible on his thick nose. "Who's our guest?" he asked Amber, reaching to the far corner of the table for a highball glass that held some kind of brown liquor on ice.

"This is Paula. She lives across the street with the Lindberghs, but she's not their daughter. She's a foster kid."

Although Amber said this all as cheerfully as if she'd been discussing flavors of ice cream at Baskin Robbins, I colored deeply. How had she come to have this information? Had it been broadcast over the loud speakers at school? Did everyone know?

"Oh. Well, isn't that interesting." Dean tipped the glass back, clinking the cubes, and I noticed his eyelashes were a pale blond, almost white. On the bottom rim of his left eye, right on the lash line, sat a tiny mole. It bobbed when he blinked.

The sliding glass door opened hard and out came Ross and another brother, Bo, who was shorter and shaggier. They walked past us toward the garage, but not before I heard Bo ask Ross, "What's *she* doing here?"

Back in Amber's room, we started a game of backgammon, but I kept forgetting to protect my guys. Soon, four of them sat on the fence, waiting for the right roll.

"You're not very good at this, are you?" Amber said, with the sunniness that seemed to accompany everything she said.

"No, I guess not." I fidgeted with the dice. In the next room, Amber's brothers were having a loud debate about what to do with a dead rabbit they'd found. One — I think it was Ross — wanted to skin it and pick the meat off the bones so they could have a clean skeleton. The other said no, they should save themselves the work and put it in some kind of bag and let it all rot off. Suddenly, I wanted to go home and sleep in my own bed, even if it wasn't technically mine. It was too strange there with the dead-rabbit talk and Mr. Swenson's jiggling mole and all of them knowing I wasn't anyone's real daughter.

"Actually," I said, letting the dice drop flatly to the game board, "I'm not feeling very good. Maybe it was dinner. I don't know. I think I might throw up or something."

"Oh. Well, you can use our bathroom."

"No. I don't want to be sick here. I think I should go."

Amber wasn't happy about my leaving, but she walked me across the street and stood with me at the gate for a minute, one fingernail picking at the white paint on the LINDBERGH ACRES sign. "You'll have to come back sometime," she said. "You know, when you're feeling better."

"Yeah, definitely," I said, and headed up the drive toward the house. I would go back too, I thought, and soon. But right then, I wanted only to lie on the blue-brown shag with my sisters watching TV. Maybe there would be popcorn or root-beer floats. Maybe it would be one of the times Bub and Hilde leg-wrestled over who got to pick the show.

I walked through the front door with a sigh; everything still smelled like pork chops and peas from dinner. The TV was on, just as I thought. It sounded like *The Six Million Dollar Man*. I turned down the hall to put my sleeping bag away and heard someone behind me in the hall. It was Hilde. "Oh," she said, looking down at me as if I were a dirty footprint on her carpet. There was a crease between her eyebrows, and her jaw muscle twitched. "What are *you* doing here?"

FROM THE BEGINNING, HILDE was just as hard to love as Bub was easy. When she wasn't watering her beloved lawn, Hilde huffed around the house, straightening doilies and knickknacks, folding and refolding the kitchen towels. When she wasn't entirely silent, she mumbled, a growly German muttering that sounded like she had a mouth full of marbles. Maybe it was because English wasn't Hilde's first language that she had trouble saying what she meant; I didn't know. She avoided real talk like she avoided traffic on her daily drives to Noreen's. If something made her unhappy, Hilde's response was either subversive or extreme. The subversive bit was easy enough to take, like our fan war. At night I ran a small electric fan because it was the only way I could sleep — everything was quiet in the country, too quiet. Sometime after midnight, Hilde would come in and turn it off. I'd wake up to the absence of noise, wait until I thought I heard Hilde snoring again and then turn it back on. Fall asleep. Wake up when she turned it off. This happened every night for years. We never said a word to each other about it.

Another time, I noticed that Hilde had stopped washing my dishes. After dinner, I went into the kitchen for a glass of water and saw that everything had been cleared and put away except my green bowl with the pyramid of kidney beans at the bottom, my soupspoon, my yellow Holly Hobby glass with a sinking film of milk. They sat next to the sink ready for washing, though the sink was not only empty of water and suds, but scoured with Comet and smelling like a hospital.

Like Mrs. Clapp, Hilde had all these rules, some of which we couldn't possibly know about until it was too late. The time she saw me sitting on the toilet seat with the lid down, for instance, and flipped out, chasing me around the house with a wooden spoon because the little feet on the bottom of the lid would leave marks on the seat. *Can you ruin a toilet seat?*

Hilde also couldn't abide "butting in," which meant trying to interrupt when she was yelling at your sister. One afternoon, Hilde and I were arguing about some stupid thing in the kitchen.

I don't even remember what. I stood at the stove, scrambling eggs for an after-school snack, and she stood behind me. The whole time, I attended to my eggs, not even turning to look at her, and this seemed to make her madder; I could hear it in her voice, like something heavy trying to wheedle through a strainer. Then Penny piped in, sticking up for me. She was sitting a few feet away, doing her homework at the kitchen table. Somehow Penny's butting in was worse than my sassing, because Hilde flew at her, lifting her all the way out of the chair. She had Penny around the neck in a choke hold, and her legs kicked at the table, knocking a cup over, spilling water all over her math book. I couldn't believe it was real, that such a thing was actually happening. Hilde shook Penny like a dog, like a maniac cartoon character shaking a cartoon dog. Little choking noises were coming out of Penny; she couldn't scream, and her face was purpling.

Standing with the spatula in my hand, my eggs singeing on the back burner, I thought, *Hilde could kill her*. But nine-year-old girls didn't get strangled to death for butting in, did they? And if I tried to stop Hilde, then wouldn't I be butting in too? I wondered how far things could go, what could really happen there in the kitchen with *Star Trek* blaring from the living room, the high shrieks of phasers and tricorders and bodies being transported from ship to planet in a confetti of particles.

And then Hilde stopped. She let go, and Penny dropped into the chair with a thud. Penny put her hands up to her neck, holding them there where the red marks pulsed, then she shot me a look: *Why didn't you help me?* Her eyes were glassy. I didn't know what to say, so I turned back to my eggs, gone brown and brittle as cornflakes. I didn't think I was going to be able to get them down, but somehow I did. I sat next to the soggy math book and ate while Penny ran to her room, slamming the door behind her, and Hilde went outside and started watering the lawn, the sunburned, weed-afflicted lawn that no amount of water was going to make right.

ALL YOU HAD TO do was look at Hilde, her mouth in a hard line as if a ruler had slapped it there, arms crossed severely over her heart, to know there was no map, no access, no turnable knob to the door that was her — at least not for me and my sisters. She could be warm — I saw how eagerly she mothered Tina — but I didn't feel any of that directed at me and didn't see any warmth directed at Penny or Teresa. To us, she was a mom-size armadillo, all shell and no shelter — and it made me nuts. I simultaneously wanted her to love me and hated that I cared. I looked to my sisters to see how they were handling the problem of Hilde's impenetrability, but found no help. As far as I could tell, Teresa didn't give Hilde a moment's thought. Maybe it was too late for her to want anything from a mother, all the comings and goings adding leathery layers to her own shell. And Penny, maybe Penny wasn't protected enough. Although she wasn't getting any more affection than Teresa or I, she didn't stop trying to find it, cuddling up to the petrified log of Hilde on the couch after dinner, leaning forward to touch a fuzzy wand of Hilde's hair in the car. And if she couldn't get love from Hilde, then she would take it where she could get it. That's why she called back to the Fredricksons' house, and why she stayed after school every day to help her second-grade teacher, Mrs. Munoz, clap her erasers, following her from one corner of the classroom to another as if Mrs. Munoz had sugar in her pockets instead of chalk nubs.

For Penny, even strangers would do. Once, when she was eight or nine, Penny had an ear infection that kept her up several nights running, the pain pounding and acute, her fever high. Finally, Hilde was forced to miss an afternoon at Noreen's so she could take Penny down to the free clinic, where we received all of our checkups and shots. It was a busy day at the clinic, mid–flu season, and they had no choice but to stand in a line for several hours, Hilde tapping a foot on the dirt-tracked tile, pretending to read an issue of the *Star* (*Lizard Boy Eats Four Pounds of Flies in One Sitting! Bigfoot Stole My Wife!*) as Penny cried loudly. Nearby, an enormous black woman sat in one of the orange plastic chairs next to a gaggle of her own children, all coloring quietly in a ratty copy of the *Storybook Bible*. Penny wailed on; Hilde ignored her pointedly, and finally the big woman had seen enough. She went over to Penny, picked her right up and carried her back to the orange chair. Until the nurse called Penny's name, she lay in the sweet pillow of that woman's lap, rocked and rocked while the woman said, "Baby," over and over to the top of Penny's head.

IN JULY OF 1976, just down the road in Chowchilla, a bus-load of children were kidnapped on the way back from a swim outing. The twenty-six kids and their driver were crowded into two vans, driven around for hours, then ushered into a moving truck that had been buried in a quarry one hundred miles north, near Fremont. After sixteen hours underground, the victims dug themselves out and were safely returned home.

I was almost eleven that year, scrawny as ever with a particularly ugly pair of glasses: angular plastic frames the color of algae. Although I remember hearing about the kidnapping on the news, I was far more interested in the summer Olympics, which had just begun, and in Nadia Comaneci, the Romanian spitfire who was racking up perfect tens in gymnastics. She was fourteen, weighed eighty-six pounds and made everything look easy. She flew, leaped and pranced in her white leotard, playfully flicking her wrists and ankles at the crowd like an organ-grinder's monkey.

That was also the summer we started building Bub's fantasy boat in the backyard. He drove to the factory in Hollister to collect the plans and had me and my sisters out the next weekend, digging postholes for the enormous shed the boat would hatch under. The supplies came in a big delivery truck: prickly swaths of fiberglass, drums of resin and acetone, sheets of one-inch foam that would cover the whalelike skeleton and help construct the hull. Soon, everything outside smelled like fingernail polish. Fiberglass hairs flew in the slightest breeze, burning like nettles when they caught in our clothes.

Fiberglassing was an endless process, the cloth smoothed down, gooped with resin, rolled over and over to get the bubbles out. Then each layer — and there were seven in all — had to air-dry before Bub hit it with the electric sander. I worked in a pair of Bub's coveralls with my roller, humming Barry Manilow (*Oh, Mandy, you came and you gave without taking*), simultaneously pining for and dreading September, when I would start seventh grade at Clark Middle School. Middle school was a big deal, this I had known since the night our baby-sitter Yolanda told us how, when she was a seventh-grader, some eighth-grade boys grabbed her and made her play Truth or Dare on the lawn behind the cafeteria. "You just *have* to go," she said. "If you say no, everyone will think you're a baby."

Everyone *already* thought that. On the last day of sixth grade, my three best friends — Tara Adams, Laurie Carroll and Julie Wilson — had walked me out to my bus and dumped me with ceremony. They'd held a vote — unanimous — and decided that although I'd been fine as an elementary-school friend, they wanted to start fresh at Clark, raise their standards. I just wasn't mature enough. *Have a fun summer,* they'd each written in my yearbook in plump, girly cursive. *Stay sweet.* I climbed on the bus sobbing, committed to hating them forever, but deep down I knew they were right. There was nothing mature about me. I didn't even wear a training bra yet, my period was light-years away, I'd never had a boyfriend and I couldn't read passages of Judy Blume's *Forever . . .* without blushing or giggling or both. Come recess, when all the girls crowded into the bathroom for gossip and quality time with their hair, all I wanted to do was

squat in the sandpit and collect iron with a big magnet I'd borrowed from Bub. I had half a Folgers can filled already and was
ever fascinated by the way the iron flew right out of the sand to
cluster on the magnet like the fur of some alien animal. Still, I
didn't want to be a baby. I wanted to be Nadia Comaneci, to fly
high and stick my landings like a rivet.

In late July, Granny called to say there was going to be a
family reunion at Radio Park, and did we want to go? We hadn't
seen Granny in many months, and although I didn't really want to
go to the reunion, didn't want to scarf down macaroni salad and
baked beans and burned kielbasa while various relatives tried to
pretend it was a wonderful thing that my sisters and I had been
farmed out to foster parents (*and such nice folks, but aren't they
Jehovah's Witnesses or Krishnas or some such thing?*), I did want to
see Granny and felt terrible that so much time had passed since I
had. Keith and Tanya would be there too. My sisters and I were
getting along famously with Cousin Krista, but Keith and Tanya
were real family, much-missed Louskateers. We would go.

Granny came all the way out to the Lindberghs' to pick us
up on the afternoon of the reunion. She looked just the same in
her print dress and peach cotton stockings, and whistled the same
wavery gospel songs while she drove us to the park, though
my sisters and I had the radio going. Once, she leaned over and
adjusted the volume so she could say, "How you girls doing?
Have you been good?" Before we could answer, she launched into
a story about Tanya winning a bumblebee pin for being the best
speller in her whole school. It was just as well, since I didn't know
if Granny meant were we *being* good, or *doing* good. In any case,
so much had happened that if we started telling her about it all,
we might never stop talking.

I felt much the same way when we got to the park and Aunt
Bonnie and Vera and various women from Granny's church (what
were *they* doing there anyway?) started crowding around us, giving

us choking-tight squeezes and asking how we were. I felt embarrassed by the attention, like we'd been dragged out for a "Look at the Orphans" parade. How were we? Did they want us to gush over our new family, or cry, or cough up a secret something? What?

"We're just fine," Teresa said and elbowed me, pointing to a nearby tree where Keith and Tanya swung like spider monkeys.

"Yep, just fine," I agreed, and ran off and up the tree to be free from such prodding, hidden in leaves.

We spent the rest of the day with Keith and Tanya, only coming in from playing when Granny hollered "Lunch!" for the third time. We had fun with them, but I was glad when Granny said it was time to head home. I wanted to be back in my resin-stiff coveralls singing Barry Manilow, but once I was home doing exactly that, I missed Granny and my cousins so much that I felt it in my joints, a rainy ache in my knees and wrists. It was a strangely *between* time. I didn't know which was more my family now, where I was the most home. And that feeling was sort of like the way I knew I didn't want to be a little girl anymore but wasn't quite sure what came next either.

I just wanted to lie down in the middle of the field and not get up. Lie down and wait for grasshoppers to click and light in my hair as if it were dry grass. I thought if I could just lie still enough, long enough, the ants and beetles would forget me. The horses would step over or around me to get to the salt lick. Soon, evening would come, ticking and humming to bring the moon from its hole. I would hear everything with one ear to the ground and one to the sky, the crickets and June bugs; bats careening through scrims of the tiniest insects; a car at some distance, slowing; porch lights hissing on as families settled down to fish sticks and fruit cocktail.

Once, when I had a fever, I wandered out back and lay down on a sheet of plywood. It was Christmas day, and I had woken up feeling like the Michelin Man, puffy under my skin, a hot snowball. Bub's relatives started arriving after breakfast, and soon they were everywhere, hanging their sock feet over the arms of the couches, stuffing their faces with deviled eggs and salami logs and celery smeared with peanut butter. On TV, a giant Bullwinkle bobbed on rope tethers, as fat and silent as my head, which felt packed with seared cotton, so I went outside. The day was cold for Fresno, maybe forty-five degrees, but it felt like a nurse's lily-white hand. The plywood was rough against my cheek and chewed at my red sweater whenever I moved, but it also felt just right. I thought: *The way I am curled is like an ear. My whole body is an ear.* In cowboy movies, the tracker kneels down to find a story made out of sound. That was me, keeping sharp for my future — the rhythm of it like a train or fast horse, some good thing coming from a great distance to make itself mine.

I WAS HALFWAY TO the bus stop before I realized I forgot my gym shorts. It was 7:23 A.M., and I had no choice but to hightail it back to the house, panting because the bus would be rolling up at 7:30, come hell or June, and I was wearing the stupid shoes that I couldn't tie because that year everyone was just knotting the laces at the ends. Through the front door and tiled foyer, I had no choice but to drop to my knees and speed-crawl to my room because Thou Shalt Not Wear Shoes on the Carpet, and crawling was faster than getting my shoes off and on, even though they were knotted, not tied. Panting aside, I was in top form, perhaps a personal best. My bed was there with its blue spread and pillow flat as a sigh, and my sister's bed was there with yesterday's clothes in a wad at the foot, but the gym shorts were nowhere to be found: not where I thought they should be, like in my shorts drawer or at the bottom of my closet, or where I thought they would never be, like under the mattress. It was now 7:26. If I didn't leave right that instant, I wouldn't make it to the bus at all and would have to ask Hilde to drive me. Anytime I asked her to drive me anywhere, she made a face that communicated: *I'd rather shave my legs with a fork.* So I gave up. I speed-crawled back to the foyer and stood to brush the knees of my green Ditto jeans and there she was, eating saltines stacked like a condominium over the kitchen sink.

"Mom, have you seen my gym shorts?"

She looked at me, her face orangy-pink, as unknowable as a squash. She shrugged, crumbs snowing onto her blouse. "I don't wear your gym shorts."

I turned, harrumphing, resigned, and ran to the bus stop as fast as my stupid shoes would carry me. When I got there, half-moons of sweat under my arms, my hair frizzing into pom-poms over my ears, Teresa said, "Didn't you find your shorts?"

"No," I said. "Mom hid them again."

UNDER THE DOG-FOOD bag in the garage, or at the bottom of the trash compactor, or in a cupboard behind crusty cans of furniture polish and bug spray, we'd find our shoes, homework, hairbrushes. Hilde hid food too — corn chips and Tootsie Pops and sugared cereal — which we'd find by following streams of black ants. The hiding was weird, but perhaps no weirder than anything else Hilde did, like putting all of my laundry in the lint-infested crack between the washer and dryer, like never driving or answering the phone after dark, like slapping Teresa ten times in a row because she wouldn't answer a question.

At thirteen, I was no closer to puzzling Hilde out than at nine. I could rant and rave, screaming swearwords, and get no more than a blink from her. Or I could be drying my hands on a dish towel hanging on the oven door and get smacked halfway across the kitchen. Hilde's rules made sense to her, perhaps (tugging on the dish towel would ruin the hinge), but to me they seemed, like her anger, as unnavigable as a field of land mines. One minute everything was fine, then *kablooey*.

I spent a great deal of time thinking about Hilde, thinking about what *she* was thinking and feeling and what, if anything, she wanted from me — but it didn't seem to be doing any good. So I experimented with not thinking. Not feeling. The next time Hilde and I had a fight that escalated, I let her drag me into the garage without a struggle. She told me to stand up against the workbench and I did, steadying my feet into a vee on the concrete. I thought, *I'm one fluid ripple. I'm air.* As Hilde pulled the broom back, her hands gripped the straw so that I heard snapping in the bristles before the handle came down into the soft skin above the back of my knees. I didn't cry out, but *looked* out — past the cobwebby pane, past the roses and lawn into the field where everything was as yellow and textured as a field in a painting. The broom handle bit again, and this time I looked *in*. She wanted me to cry, but I wouldn't cry. I thought, *I am making this happen.* But when it was over, I had gained only the beginnings of bruises that would cover my body, butt to calves, in an ugly, changing rainbow: blue-purple to black-red to yellow-green. I hadn't won anything or shown her anything, and all I felt was empty.

AS CRAZY AS HILDE was and as crazy as she made me feel, by the time I was thirteen, we'd been with the Lindberghs for four years. Their house felt as much like home to me as anything I'd known. I had my room, or half of it, and I could close the door and read in the blue beanbag chair until my brain addled and I believed I could be anyone. I wrote poems about daisies and dandelions and marigolds. Most of my poems had flowers in them because I thought they made excellent metaphors, the whole seed-to-flower thing like the birth of the soul. Leaves or petals could be hands, the flower's center a face, and roots could be so many things. One of my flower poems was about a gardener, weeding, and Penny read it and asked if the gardener stood for our mom. I just said no and went back to work, but later I wondered if she meant Hilde or our real mom, the one we never, ever talked about.

It had been so long since we had seen or even heard from our social worker, my sisters and I began to believe that the Lindberghs were likely it for us, where the marble had stopped on the parent roulette wheel. It was a relief to think we wouldn't have to move again, but was moving the worst thing? What if the perfect mom and dad were still out there somewhere, waiting to make my teenage years a kind of heaven? I wasn't sure I was ready to let go of that fantasy or my habit of going into every restaurant on the lookout for parents, reading the dining room as if *it* were the menu, checking out the couples at the tables around us, paying attention to how they talked to each other, how they talked to their kids, how they held their forks, for christsake. At the slightest sign someone would be good to me, I'd try to glow, making myself over in small, hopeful ways: placing my napkin in a neat triangle on my lap, keeping my elbows well off the table, smiling sweetly even with a mouth full of mashed potatoes, chewing each bite twenty-nine times, *or was it supposed to be thirty-nine?*

What did it mean if Hilde was my last mother, and I didn't know how to get mothering out of her?

ONE NIGHT, HOURS AFTER everyone had gone to bed, I woke up sick. I started crying, and Hilde came in asking what was wrong. "It feels like there are spiders in my stomach," I said. I knew that sounded strange, but it *did* feel like that, like they were crawling around in there, a bunch of them. My sisters made fun of me for being so afraid of spiders, but the thing is, there were billions of them on our property, and not just in the garage: fat tarantulas sunned themselves on the concrete slab out back, daddy longlegs maneuvered along the tiles in the shower. Once, I found a big brown spider on the long curtains over the sliding glass door and knocked it into a jar with a pie plate. It was about the size of a silver dollar, and its back looked furry until I noticed the fur was really hundreds of little spiders stuck there, their bodies folded like gross tiny envelopes waiting to open. Sick. My plan was to suffocate all of them in the jar, so I found a lid, screwed it on and went into my room to do some homework. When I came out for dinner an hour or so later, the jar was gone. I panicked. Was the spider big enough to knock the jar off the counter and roll out the front door like a gerbil on a wheel? No, couldn't be. But where was the jar?

Just then, Tina walked in from the living room and said, "Were you torturing that spider? Poor thing was gonna die in that jar, so I let it loose outside."

It was free? And right outside? I was so pissed at Tina that I wouldn't talk to her for the rest of the day, but the worst thing was lying in bed that night, thinking the mother spider was out there somewhere, plotting her revenge, rallying the other furry, gross spiders to help her chew through the screen and descend on me en masse.

Anyway, I was trying to explain to Hilde about the spider feeling in my stomach when I vomited, partly on the floor next to my bed, partly in the hall as I tried to make it to the bathroom. I stood there holding my barfy nightgown away from my body, and Hilde walked into the hall saying, "Ugh!" She shuttled past me into the kitchen and brought back a plastic bucket and sponge. "You'll just have to clean this up," she said. "I can't do it."

Hilde couldn't abide throw-up. I didn't know anyone who liked it, but Hilde got the shakes if she was within ten feet of barf, making little gagging noises like she was going to be sick too. I felt sorry for myself, there on my knees on the carpet, sponging up my own puke, which was spongy too, and pink. Samantha Fredrickson would never have made me do that, never. She had been a great sick-nurse. Soon after we got the Montgomery Ward bicycles, Penny and I had collided spectacularly on the sidewalk in front of the house. We came down in a knot, legs scraped and caught under pedals, elbows bleeding on the pavement. One of Penny's handlebars had been jammed into my neck, and after Samantha ran out to disentangle us, I was horrified to find I couldn't turn my head at all. All that afternoon I lay on the couch while Samantha administered warm compresses, rubbing my neck and shoulders lightly with her fingertips. It was just a crick, she said, nothing serious, but I needed my rest. I stayed on the couch all night and all the next day, watching television and letting Samantha baby me. *What if the crick doesn't go away?* I thought. *Would that be so bad? I could just stay on the couch and let her rub me and feed me soup through a straw. And if I can't ever turn around? So what? There isn't much back there I want to see.*

I'd been thinking about Samantha Fredrickson so intently, her cool hands, the concerned tilt of her head, I was surprised to find that back in my body on the carpet, the spider sensation in my stomach was completely gone. I washed up, changed into a fresh nightgown and was able to go right to sleep, though Hilde had shut off my fan, of course, of course, when she came in. I felt altogether better when I woke up the next morning, but Hilde said I had the flu and needed to skip school. I could have gone with her to Noreen's if I'd wanted, but I fake-clutched my stomach and said I didn't think I could handle the drive. Noreen's would be monumentally boring, plus I'd never stayed home alone before. After she left, I made pancakes from a box and put them in a bowl with syrup and peanut butter. I ate them on the sofa — strictly verboten — and watched all the morning shows plus *Quincy* and *Emergency*. Somehow it was only eleven, so I ate an orange. It tasted so good I ate another, and another, until the peels were in a huge, pithy pile on the dish towel in my lap and I felt sick again.

When I walked into Bub and Hilde's room, I told myself I was looking for something to soothe my stomach, but instead went right for Hilde's dresser. On the top sat a few pictures of Tina, some Avon perfume bottles, an old hairbrush with gray-green lint in the bristles, Kleenexes. I unscrewed the lid on the perfume bottle shaped like an upside-down lady's fan. It smelled like vanilla, but when I got brave and put a dab on my tongue, I found out it tasted like rat poison.

Right in the center of the dresser top — where a vase and flowers would have gone if Hilde were that type — stood a beauty-shop Barbie, just the head on a pink pedestal, like a wig mannequin that stylists practice on in salons. Barbie's hair was a white-blond flip held back from her face with a pink elastic band. A little pink tray at the front of the pedestal held play makeup: baby lipsticks, blue and violet eye shadows, an eyebrow pencil like a sharp crayon. It killed me that Hilde had such a great toy and kept it for herself. She didn't play with it, of course, but didn't let me or my sisters play with it either. It was hers. When she bought it one day at Thrifty Drug, she said, "It's about time I had a doll." She explained how she never had toys as a kid because her family was so poor after the Second World War. For part of a year, they didn't even have a house, just wandered through different villages begging for potatoes. On one particularly cold night, her baby brother froze to death in his sleep. He was in his mother's arms, but even her body heat wasn't enough. (How about that? Sometimes, not even a mother can save you.) After Hilde told the story, I used to have dreams about him, white and still, a baby angel Popsicle with lips that clinked like something ceramic when I touched them and frozen tines of white eyelashes.

I didn't know what I was looking for in Hilde's dresser, but I couldn't stop looking. My heart knocked hard at the thought of getting caught, even though I knew she'd never come home from Noreen's in the middle of the day. I opened her top drawer and touched her underwear, the D-cup bras that looked like they could hold nuclear missiles. Under a stack of slips, she'd hidden a box of diet cookies, half empty, beneath which was a litter of crumbs like caramel-colored sand. Her bottom drawer was a mishmash of never-used dish towels and handkerchiefs, recipe clippings from magazines, number 2 pencils in cellophane, six-packs of sugar-free gum. In a back corner I saw the top of a peanut-butter jar and thought it might be there to hold change, but no, it was full of peanut butter. The cookies I understood, but a full jar of peanut butter? Did she think we'd all be air-raided, or was she just wanting to keep something for herself since us girls gobbled pretty much everything in the cupboards that was even semi-edible?

Way back under a bag of recycled gift bows, Hilde had tucked some old photographs and a stack of letters. The letters were creased and yellowed, and the handwriting unmistakably Bub's, with surprisingly feminine *l*'s and *m*'s, *y*'s that dipped like the handle of a ladle. They began *Meine Liebchen* and ended with *Ich Liebe Dich,* and were clearly from the time before they were married, when Bub was stationed in Zirndorf. Bub and Hilde liked to tell the story of how they met: Bub was in a café with some of his buddies when he saw Hilde eating alone at a table. He sat down without even introducing himself and began waving his thumb right in front of Hilde's mouth. He held it there, right in the way of her sandwich, so she bit it. She bit it so hard she made him bleed. "He was just so rude," Hilde said and grinned, remembering.

One of the photos in the drawer was of Bub, at twenty-five or so, wearing a ribbed turtleneck and formfitting slacks. His hair was short, slicked on the sides, and so black it lost texture, looked like a wig or like black water suspended above his skin, which was pink-white with a spattering of freckles across his nose. His eyes were dead clear and blue. The one I liked best of Hilde was full-length and taken from a distance. Although light had smudged her face, she was clearly laughing, her mouth wide-open and full of teeth. Her waist was unbelievably narrow, a hand-span cinched with a double-tied sash the color of pomegranates. The photo was black-and-white, but I knew the dress, off the shoulder, crino-lined with seven layers of chiffon. She kept it buried behind the boxy Butterick blouses, the tent dresses with flowers like stalks of broccoli, the polyester number with the lavender panda bears that made us all cringe when she wore it to church.

When I looked at the pomegranate dress, I could see Hilde as a pretty girl with long arms and legs, wearing a heavy cloak with a hood, holding a candle as the whole village walked in a twin-kling line to midnight Mass on Christmas Eve; playing with potato dolls stuck with cloves and leaf hair; running fast along a dirt path that skimmed the forest, wind and speed in her summer dress, her arms stretched like wings or nets to catch whatever might be there.

I felt myself wishing that Hilde herself was as easy to open as her bureau, that I could look into her face as simply as into Bar-bie's rubber one and say, *Why do you hide my gym shorts? What are you thinking when I roll around on the floor, curled like a sow bug so you can't get at anything soft? What are you thinking ever?* I couldn't do this, of course. And even if I could, I might not be able to bear her answers. What if she admitted she never loved me at all or that she wished Penny and Teresa and I were gone, off in someone else's house, eating *their* peanut butter?

I believe it's both a curse and a blessing that we only ever get to see little bits of people — like the opening of a pocket, a shy blue edge or threads in a fringe, but everything else held back. When we were girls, Penny reached over and socked me in the chin. I had made her mad about something, I'm sure, but the point is I didn't think she would do that. I really didn't. She looked shocked too, with a hanging mouth and big eyes, and ran to her room thinking I might chase her. I *couldn't* chase her, though, couldn't even move because she had stunned me. I was rooted there, thinking: *Who was that? My sister I know like my own ten toes, so that girl must be someone else.*

Sometimes I shocked even myself, like when I was eight and called Bub into my room to ask him if he'd think about sending Penny and Teresa back with the social worker. He gave me a sound spanking and told me no good girl would have thoughts like that about her own flesh-and-blood sisters. I sobbed and sobbed, knowing he was right, and still could not stop thinking about how, if I were their only foster child, they might forget and start treating me like I was real.

Sometimes I was shocked to think I knew something, was *certain* about it, and then found I'd gotten it all wrong. Like the time I saw Hilde standing at the stove frying pork chops, one hip stuck out and her hand on it. She had to be mad, standing hard like that, pissy about something or other. But when she turned around, she looked at me calmly. "You have such pretty hair," she said.

Like that.

I WOKE UP HOT, a minus sign seared into my left cheek from the window gasket, my hair sweaty and snarled from blowing out the side of the car like a dog's. After a long sleep, coming back into my body was like swimming through sand, bubbles, my own mysterious particles. I was always a little surprised to find myself intact, as if car sleep was a kind of time travel that might make misplacing an ear or big toe as easy as losing a purse in a rest-stop bathroom.

The car was empty but for me and quiet, parked in front of a general store, the kind with a hitching post out front and a wooden sign that creaked like a porch swing. Inside was cooler but not by much. A metal ceiling fan recycled air that smelled like someone's shoe. IF WE DON'T HAVE IT, YOU DON'T NEED IT boasted a sign near the register, and that might have been true, their stock skimpy and various: four bottles of Aqua Net next to a small Alpo pyramid, cough syrup in sun-bleached cardboard, waxed black shoelaces, beef jerky and cashews and Campbell's cream of mushroom soup, quarter-inch nails and electric-pink pots of salmon eggs.

At the old-fashioned soda fountain counter, my sisters spun on chrome stools while Noreen and Hilde looked on, sure they were going to break something. Hilde had only gotten larger and more nervous over the years. Every time one of my sisters' sneaker toes grazed the glass case, Hilde's face twitched and her hands raced along the edge of her blue-flowered Butterick blouse.

"Well, if it isn't Sleeping Beauty," Bub called out. "Come over here, Miss Poo. I want to show you something."

Bub stood near the back of the store, his shirt stuck to his back and damp through in the middle in a stain the shape of a pork chop. He draped one arm over my shoulder and steered me like a car toward a wall pasted with yellowed postcards and newspaper clippings, photographs of locals holding stringers of trout. What he wanted me to see was a framed five-by-seven of a rabbit sitting placidly on its haunches in a field. Between its velvety ears rested two tiny antlers, nubby and spurred.

"That," said Bub, "is a jackalope. Half antelope, half jackrabbit, very rare. Maybe only a dozen or so have ever been seen." He scratched his nose. "Betcha this picture's worth a hundred dollars."

This was our game. His game, rather. I was fourteen; he'd been my father for five years, and in that time, he'd never lost his pleasure at seeing just how much of any story I would swallow, never lost the surprise of finding that, indeed, I'd take most, if not all, of anything. Once, on a drive into the foothills below the Sierras, we saw horses grazing along unbelievably steep grades. When I asked Bub why they didn't just tumble down the hill, he said that that particular breed of horse was a "kant." Their legs were shorter on one side so they could keep their balance. Left-legged kants could only walk around and around the hill clockwise, and the right-legged kants could only go the other way.

I believed him too. Believed though we had our own horses, twelve of them in all, different breeds and temperaments; though we'd spent I don't know how many Sundays at the livestock auctions without ever coming across a horse with longer legs on one side. Bub grinned and my sisters snickered, and I felt silly — but not so silly that I'd doubt him the next time. Kants and jackalopes and merpeople, these were fine things to think about. Real gold on river bottoms and ten-foot catfish and Sasquatch in the foothills, looking for a wife.

Before we left the general store, each of us was allowed to choose two of the hard candy sticks that filled the many jars along the fountain counter. They came in every possible flavor, barberpole-striped and wrapped in noisy cellophane, a nickel apiece. I picked sarsaparilla twice because Bub said it was an old word we didn't even use anymore.

"It means *root beer*," he said. "But *sarsaparilla* says it better, don't you think?"

I did and was rewarded with a postcard version of the jackalope picture, which I kept safe from stickiness all the way to Uncle Floyd's house, through Delano and back out along a county road, past loping hills, past mesquite and mariposa twisted and bent over like old women trying to wish their feet into water.

FLOYD WAS BUB'S UNCLE on his mother's side and was, according to the aunts, *something else. A hoot. A real firecracker.* When we drove up, he was sitting up on the porch in a big rocker surrounded by stacks of faded newspapers, dusty knots of nails and fishing tackle, empty feed bags, paint cans and several garden tools with rusted heads. Floyd wore jeans with no shirt or shoes, and a huge straw sombrero — bright pink and green and yellow — flopped this way and that on his head. Pinched between his knees was a square bottle of Jack Daniel's. As near as I could tell, he'd been drunk all day.

It was well known but never brought up that Floyd chased women, most notably Bub's sister, Gloria, when she was in her early twenties and married herself. Gloria had managed to wrestle free of Floyd and straighten herself out, and now she was the one sane adult in Bub's whole freakish family. But how had Gloria been led astray in the first place? Why was anyone the way they were? My sisters and I had been left over and over, shuffled all over Fresno County like cards in a bent, sweaty deck, and in a way, we felt we were more normal than any of these cousins or uncles; more normal than Noreen, who chewed tobacco and kept half a box of Kleenex stuffed in her bra and a chain of safety pins attached to everything she wore, just in case; more normal than Tina, who had lived in one house her whole life and still wanted her mother to do everything but tie her shoes for her.

As we climbed out of the car, Floyd called, "Hey," and flicked one of his hands in hello, but didn't stand. "It's too hot to move," he said, and we had to agree. You could have roasted a turkey in Floyd's yard. Several large hardwoods shaded the peeling clapboard house, but they didn't help much. Late-afternoon light busted through to rest on the lawn in patches as big-boned as Floyd's three huge dogs.

Freed from the hot backseat, I realized my green terry-cloth shorts were damp through. When I pulled them away from my legs, the skin underneath felt raw and new. I approached the porch slowly. This was my first time meeting Floyd, and although I tried to glimpse some of the dirty dog in him, except for the sombrero, he looked like any man sitting on a porch to me. The grown-ups grunted hello and pawed one another like circus bears, then went inside. Us girls stayed out to explore Floyd's yard, which looked a lot like our own in terms of clutter. There were piles of scrap lumber and abandoned car parts, and little mounds of leaves and trash waiting for a good burn day. Tina found an old pit for horseshoes, and we played for a while, mainly because the game gave us permission to throw something big and heavy across the yard at one another. This was the reason we liked lawn darts too, and why when we went out shooting pigeons with BB guns, we were much more interested in aiming at the toes of one another's boots than at anything that might fly.

Soon enough it was time for supper. Floyd lived alone, and since his idea of cooking meant opening up a can of pork 'n' beans or slicing potted meat to put on crackers, I was glad we'd brought groceries from the general store for Noreen to prepare: black-eyed peas and beet greens, corn bread and okra and a salty ham hock with skin like a wrinkled pink glove. Everyone drank lemonade except for Floyd, who was still working on his bourbon. I knew enough to know you had to watch out for a drunk, but Floyd seemed to be the good kind, sweet and sloppy, not too loud. His arms swung around when he talked, just missing the lamp.

After supper, the adults started up a dice game, banishing us to Floyd's living room, where the carpet looked to be three completely different shades of dirty. There was no TV, no Sorry, no Sears catalog featuring women in goofy underwear. We looked through Floyd's tackle box for a while, making little pyramids of the lures and sinkers and greasy rubber worms; we read one another's fortunes in the cluster of glass grapes on Floyd's coffee table: *You will befriend a dog with three legs and a flea problem. Beware the Bazooka wrapper that conceals a dirt clod.* At nine o'clock we gave up and went to bed cranky, too bored even to pick a fight. We laid our sleeping bags down so that no one's feet touched anyone else's feet or worse, stuck right in anyone's face. We pinched our eyes and pretended to be asleep, and then, miraculously, we were.

Sometime in the middle of the night, I woke up with my heart thumping the way it does when you can't get your bearings.

Something big floated close to my face, but when I flinched back, I saw it was the couch, scratchy as a dish sponge, inert. Rising up on my elbow, I could see the various lumps of my sisters in their bags and, across the room, Floyd, fast asleep in the living-room chair. Instead of a blanket, he was partially covered by the sombrero, and his mouth was open so wide I could have tossed a nickel in and not hit teeth. He started to snore a little as I watched him, a puppy-dog snore, light and wheezy, but soon got serious about it. His lower lip began to wobble as he blew out, Fred Flintstone style. Just when I was sure he was going to wake the whole house, he woke himself, choking on his own breath. He sat up, blinking, and looked straight at me, or seemed to. It was hard to tell because he didn't say a word, just sat there with his eyes unfixed but pointed in my direction.

Everything was so quiet that I could hear the mantel clock and the small clock over the stove ticking apart, off a bit, competing. My sisters were still except for Penny scritching her feet back and forth against the silky lining of her sleeping bag, one foot cuddling the other. When I looked up again, Floyd's eyes were still open and unmoving. Was it because I didn't have my glasses on that his face looked mild and dreamy, so strangely young that I could almost see why a twenty-year-old Gloria would fall for him all those years ago? It was just us two awake in the whole world. Was Floyd waiting for me to say something? Or did he just want to let the moment be?

"Hi," I ventured quietly, conspiratorially, and at just that moment, he snorted loudly and started up again, rattling away, getting louder with each exhale. He was asleep, sound asleep with his eyes wide-open, like a zombie. Like the living dead with a sombrero. He'd never been there at all.

THE NEXT AFTERNOON, WE all climbed into Floyd's truck — kids and dogs in the back — and went to visit Floyd's new girlfriend, Goldie. She lived in the same town, not ten minutes away, with her own house and yard. When we nosed up the dirt drive, her collie, Maxine, let go a happy yelp and danced up to Floyd's open window. Clearly, Floyd was a favorite. Over near the barn, Goldie stroked a massive red gelding with a currycomb. Seeing us, she fluffed her own hair up with her free fingers, slapped the gelding affectionately on the butt and walked over. She wore a man-size faded-blue Western shirt, tight Levi's and boots, the heels of which lifted dust as she crossed the yard, smiling.

Floyd greeted Goldie by throwing both of his long arms over her shoulders to grab her firmly on the ass. This drew a cluck of appreciation from Bub, snorts of *Well, I never* from Noreen and Hilde and flushes from us girls. Sex, particularly grown-up sex, had us simultaneously baffled and fascinated and grossed out. *Yuck,* I thought, but kept looking.

Goldie was older than Bub and Hilde but younger than Floyd — forty-five or forty-six, I guessed — and was still quite pretty. She had a round, tan face, tired brown eyes and superfine frosted hair I can only call *beige.* Her coral lipstick crept up past one half of her top lip as if she'd put it on without a mirror. Though Goldie had been married before, she was childless.

"This is my baby," she said, rubbing her thumbs behind Maxine's silky ears. "Aren't you my baby? Yessums."

Floyd had been married for some twenty years to Dot, whom everyone still liked. They had three children: John, Michael and Carlynne. John and Mike were in their early twenties and married and talking about starting families. Carlynne was nineteen going on eight. She couldn't read or write her name and got picked up at her house three days a week by one of those miniature school buses and taken to special classes where they taught her to make change and separate lights from darks and plan a menu around the food pyramid. I never knew what to say to Carlynne. When she was in the room, I held my book way up in front of my face, hoping she'd leave me alone.

"What are you reading?" she'd ask, and I'd point to the cover, though I knew this was mean. "Oh," she'd say, walking away. Just that, just "Oh." I do remember one really good day with her though, when she came out to the house to go riding with us. Bub got her settled on my pony, Queenie, because Queenie was hefty for a Shetland and would take Carlynne's weight better than Chip or Velvet or Teddy Bear. It had rained the night before and the fields were still a bit soggy, so we skirted the road for a while, then cut over to the dry ditch.

Usually the ditch was so water-robbed it turned the dirt into parchment paper. Dust would rise up in little poofs from the horse's hooves when we cantered through. That day, though, the rain had stirred the ditch bottom into a soup of mud and manure. When we clicked the ponies into a trot, mud rained up, flecking my glasses so I couldn't see a thing. Carlynne wore glasses too, and I could see she was struggling to stay on, flop-flopping way over to one side, which was never a good thing. We slowed the ponies back to a walk, but Queenie was too fired up. She kicked her rear hooves a little, whinnied and took off like a shot toward home. That was one thing about Queenie, she was barn sour and bitchy, and probably knew before we had left the yard that Carlynne wouldn't be able to rein her in.

Once Queenie broke loose, the rest of the ponies took off after her. We let them because we wanted to help Carlynne, calling out advice at her back — *tell her to whoa, stop kicking your legs, jerk back on the reins* — but Carlynne couldn't even sit up straight the way Queenie was flying through the ditch. They

rounded a tight corner, and then we heard a yelp and a loud *oof*.
When we caught up, we saw Carlynne plopped right down in the
middle of the ditch on her backside, feet straight out, hands back.
She looked so funny there, nearly unrecognizable in her mud
bath, and we shouldn't have laughed but we did. When we finally
hauled her up, we lost it altogether because under her was a
Carlynne-size dent, a perfect impression of her ass.

After several tries, we got Carlynne boosted up on Patches
behind Tina and started for home. We rode for a few minutes
with no noise except the reins slapping a little on the horses'
necks; then Carlynne suddenly popped up with "That was fun." I
thought she was being sarcastic at first — that's certainly how I
would have said it — then it occurred to me that Carlynne didn't
do sarcastic. She wasn't old enough for that and might never be.
Although her body was a woman's, Carlynne was in every other
way a little kid and, like little kids, could say what she thought
straight out and mean it. That made her lucky — lucky and different in a good way, and for that one muddy minute, I was happy to
be jealous of her.

A FEW WEEKS AFTER the visit to Floyd's, we were in the car again, this time to Dos Palos to visit Bub's aunt Birdie and her husband, Lester. They had a little farmhouse on a ditch bank and kept hogs and willful chickens. In their big garden out back, empty bleach jugs spun upside down on poles, the sides slit at increments and bent out like a pinwheel. When a breeze came, the jugs clicked like playing cards in bicycle spokes, keeping, in theory, the rabbits and blackbirds at bay. Noreen stayed at home this trip, but we brought along Cousin Krista for her considerable entertainment value. She'd say anything to anyone and was the one person in Bub's large, peculiar family that we felt absolutely comfortable with. Krista was now twelve to my fourteen, and in the five years we had known her, she'd only gotten more adorable. Her heart-shaped face was buttery with a tan and clear-skinned; even her lashes and eyebrows glinted with sun.

"It's my favorite foster cousin Penny," she shrieked when we picked her up at Gloria's, running to throw her arms around Penny's neck, nearly downing her. "And my other favorite foster cousin," she said, leaving Penny to come and maul me. "My most other favorite foster cousin of all."

When Krista said "foster cousin" it wasn't only *not* an insult, it was a compliment, the best kind of in-joke. She was making fun of the way everyone else acted like they treated us so well and of how grateful we were supposed to be. She could do an absolute dead-on impression of Hilde getting mad and puffy and ridiculous, and had only perfected her Stevie Nicks over the years, tossing her hair, flipping an imaginary skirt: *Thunder only happens when it's raining.*

Krista was the only thing that made a weekend at Birdie and Lester's bearable, where before the breakfast dishes were cleared, everyone was talking about what we should have for lunch. They didn't have a TV, so we played crazy eights and old maid and Chinese checkers on a set missing too many game pieces. Penny didn't want to go outside because she had listened too well when Bub told the story of the time a rooster jumped at his face, trying to spur him, and how he had to whack it with a shovel four or five times before it would die. So we stayed inside. We sprawled on the floor, picking at the nap on the carpet, pretending to have long conversations with our make-believe boyfriends on an old rotary phone that was as heavy as a cast-iron skillet. Finally, Hilde and Birdie got tired of us and told us to go out into the yard, roosters or no.

No doubt about it, Dos Palos was a hole, the land dry and flat, sunbaked to a single pale brown-green color. The sky was thin and white, and the sun was white. Dust devils ripped along the dirt roads, going nowhere, stirring up less than you'd think. The soil pebbled like cornmeal in some places and was so flaky and riddled with cracks in others that you could push a stick in and pop out a thin, flat chunk of earth like a puzzle piece. Underneath, the soil was much darker and slightly moist to the touch, as if it had once known a whole lot of water, was maybe even underwater, a lake bottom or the bed of an enormous river. Now it was just the bones of that, the dry ghost of something better.

We skirted the roosters, which *did* seem to be looking at us with some menace, and headed out to the barn, where Bub and

Lester were getting ready to go fishing on the Delta-Mendota, a man-made canal full of catfish and carp. Once, on a fishing trip there, I caught a sucker fish nearly a foot long. I fought hard for him and was so proud and so attached to the idea of the fish that I carried it around on the stringer for a good part of the afternoon. I named him Harry and told Bub I was going to take him home and put him in the goldfish pond in our yard. He said fine, but why didn't I let him swim around in the bucket until we got ready to go so he didn't dry right out? I did finally put him in some water, but it was too late; he flopped over once and then lay still, floating at a strange angle, his gills popped open and stuck there looking stretched out, like the neck of a cotton T-shirt that would never lay right again.

We lobbied to go with Bub and Lester to the Delta-Mendota, but they said they didn't want us along this time. They *would* help us get set up to fish there, though, along the ditch out front, which was some four feet across and shallow, its brown current tugging at weeds and water bugs.

"Are there really fish in there?" Tina asked. She stood barefoot on the bank in a pair of Bub's cast-off jeans and one of his white undershirts, but it was Hilde's influence that showed in the downturn of Tina's mouth as she looked dubiously at the ditch.

"Sure there're fish," said Lester, "but if I was you, I'd get at those crawdads instead."

He took up five feet of fishing line, tied an old, spent spark plug on the end for a sinker and then wrapped a piece of raw bacon around that. We watched him toss it in and watched the slow list of the line as the water moved around it. There was no hit, no sudden dip indicating a strike, so we were surprised when Lester started drawing the line back in and even more surprised to see the crawdad surface, holding hard to the droopy bacon, looking like a cross between a baby lobster and a bug.

"Now, when you get about twenty of them," said Lester, "that'll be enough supper for *one* of you." He cackled, and he and Bub moved off toward the truck.

Still, we weren't discouraged. We rummaged in the garage for more spark plugs and soon were all sitting on the ditch bank, watching our lines out of habit. We pulled them in together every five minutes, and nearly every time, one of us had caught one, and we argued over who would pull him off and toss him in the bucket.

Within an hour we were bored and let the lines sit. The crawdads could have the bacon. Krista gathered her hair onto her shoulder and picked through it, looking for split ends. "Do you think," she said, addressing a paintbrush-size clump, "that Birdie and Lester have sex?" She sat up straight then, excited by her own question. Her bare toes pushed into a hillock of cornmealy dirt, sending pebbles of it down the bank and into the water with gross little plopping noises.

Birdie and Lester *doing it?* We all got a visual and said, *"Ewww."* Lester was Lester, short and scrawny with wiry tufts of hair sticking up from his head and out of his ears. He had a rare hearing disorder so that sometimes without warning everything came through too loud for him. Talking sounded like screaming, and screaming sounded like the end of the world. He'd actually wince and have to go lie down in the other room with the lights off. Birdie was a sweetheart, but she must have been six feet tall and had long gray-streaked hair hanging halfway down her back. Witch hair. She also sported a hump the size of a softball on her left shoulder under the hair. Birdie and Lester had no children, so it was easy for us to say no, no way, and move on to other combinations. Bub and Hilde. Floyd and Goldie. Uncle Horton and Aunt Lenora. Uncle Jack and anyone who would stand still for a minute. Cousin Randy and various farm animals. *Ewww, ewww. Sick sick sick.*

Birdie and Lester lived so far out of town that no one ever drove by, but there, barreling down the road toward us, was a low-slung blue convertible full of boys. They must have been going sixty, but somehow we saw everything. They were at least seventeen. They wore T-shirts, some without sleeves, and the driver had on yellow sunglasses, the hippie kind, round with metal rims.

Somehow we knew what to do. It didn't matter that we were all under sixteen and wanted breasts more than world peace; that we had stringy hair and were wearing the same cotton shorts we wore last year and the year before. We sat up straight and threw our shoulders back. We crossed our bare legs and tossed our ponytails and let shy smiles work their way across our faces: We were rare. We were lovely. There was nothing like us for fifty miles, and those boys knew it.

When the car was directly in front of us, it hung for a moment, a held frame in our home movie, and then blew by, pulling dust and a highly satisfying, ear-splitting shriek. Krista looked over at us and raised one blond eyebrow like a movie star, but couldn't sustain it. She collapsed into giggles, and we followed, falling over into the dirt, feeling — as surely as a tug on a fishing line — the pure good weight of our possible selves, of everything we could and surely would make happen.

BEFORE FIRST LIGHT THE next morning, Lester nudged us awake in our sleeping bags and told us to get dressed. On the coffee table stood a pile of old overalls, long-sleeved men's work shirts and heavy gloves. "Hurry up, now. We gotta get there before the birds do," he said. To the blackberries, he meant. We were going picking, which apparently called for us to look completely lame. The work shirts were worn to threads in places, so we put them on right over our sleep T-shirts. When we stepped into the overalls, the legs hung so long they puddled at our feet. We rolled and pinned the legs, rolled and pinned the sleeves of the work shirts, and still found it hard to move with all the excess fabric flopping this way and that. Lester came over as I was trying to see over a wad of denim to get my shoes on and said, "Hell, girl, those must be Uncle Hog's."

Hog wasn't his name, but his initials — Horton Oliver Gaines — though I doubt anyone would have thought to call him Hog if he weren't the size of a small house. He made everyone look slight, even his wife, Lenora, who was not a small woman. Horton and Lenora lived in Turlock, which might as well have been Dos Palos or Chowchilla or Parlier or any number of Podunk towns that dotted the San Joaquin Valley, brimming with row houses and migrant shacks, abandoned bowling alleys and roller rinks, fenced-in lots swimming with trash and marked with competing graffiti.

Occasionally, when we were visiting Birdie and Lester, we'd all pile into one of the trucks and go over to Turlock for supper, bringing with us a stringer of fish or side of ribs or chickens for roasting, and Horton always made the same joke: "Thanks much, but what are *y'all* gonna eat?" Horton and Lenora's son, Randy, was a total pervert, always talking about sex, or talking about anything at all in a way that made you *think* he was talking about sex. He was sixteen and still a freshman at Turlock High, held back two different times along the way. His sister, Brenda, had begun her first high school year as well, though you wouldn't know it by looking at her. She'd filled out early and made the most of it, wearing tight cutoffs and tube tops and skimpy cotton halters that showed off her tan midriff. I thought that if I'd had a brother like Randy, I certainly wouldn't be wearing clothes like that, but she seemed to like it. When we all sat out on the lawn, Brenda didn't cross her legs or put them under her, but let them swing open, flashing the small hole near the seam of her shorts where the denim was worn through and you could see her lacy panties.

One day, Randy and Brenda taught us how to flip pocket-knives off the end of our fingers to stick in the dirt. Hilde, Birdie and Lenora were all in the kitchen getting dinner, and if they had happened to look out the window over the sink, they'd surely have seen us and come out hollering. I kept waiting for this, my back to the house, the little red-handled knife balanced for a moment on my index finger before heading ass-over-end to clatter in the dirt. I wanted them to catch us at it too. Then it wouldn't be me to say I didn't want to play anymore because I was scared the knife was going to nick my knee or the fleshy part of my calf going down. But the women never came out, and the game went on.

In a way, picking blackberries was more of a danger than flipping knives. The bramble was an awesome thing, ten or twelve feet high, so that we had to lean ladders against it to get up top, where the berries had gotten full sun and were the sweetest and ripest. Of course the birds knew this too, and though we'd gotten up in the dark and skipped breakfast to get there early, ten or twelve birds circled and dipped as we set the ladders up. Big and noisy, they seemed to want to know how serious we were about sticking around. We lined up as Lester gave us each a galvanized gallon bucket and strict instructions not to come down until the buckets were full. "And don't eat more than you pick," he added.

The sun wasn't bad at first, but by nine o'clock I was beginning to think that, like the birds, the sun was dive-bombing, wishing us ill. I felt combustible in Uncle Hog's overalls; my hands were sweaty and scratched up under the work gloves, which had only been keeping out about half of the thorns. I grew light-headed on my ladder, a combination of no breakfast and heat and the birds, which sounded like traffic, like tire-screeches and blaring horns. They wanted us to leave and I did too, though my bucket was only half full.

I looked down into the bramble and saw, for the first time, the way it knotted then opened up then knotted again, all the way down. It was one thing, wrapping back and forth on itself, knitting hand-size, bird-size, body-size pockets that were laced over with thorns but free in the middle. All the way at the bottom sat a cubby, an oblong cave with a leaf bed. I couldn't move my eyes away from it, thinking that if a deer, or a girl, even, could manage to get down there without harm, could filter and twist, the way light does, through the tangle, she might lie right down in the dark soil and fallen leaves and steal some rest.

THERE WAS A TIME when I paced the kitchen window if Bub was late coming home from work, watching for car lights. By six-thirty I was down at the end of the driveway, sometimes in the middle of the street, offering three months' allowance or my pony, Queenie, or a pair of new Adidas track shoes to God in exchange for Bub's life: *Please, oh please, oh please don't let him die and leave me here alone with Hilde the Nazi.* And then his electric-grape Cadillac would careen fatly around the corner onto our street tinkling Gordon Lightfoot from the eight-track: "The Wreck of the Edmund Fitzgerald." I thought I might fall down from sighed relief: *Thank you, God, thank you, Gordon, thank you, LINDBERGH ACRES sign with your paint flaked nearly away.*

I had considered Bub my most trusted protector ever since I was nine, when our dad — the real one, the one whose name we had — called to say he wanted to pick me and my sisters up and take us out for the day. He was no longer married to Donna, so the visit wouldn't involve her and the kids, just the four of us: a dad and his daughters. It was winter — or as wintry as Fresno gets — so we put tights on under our dresses and wore the coats Hilde had gotten us all to match, furry and blue with hoods. We waited out on the lawn wondering what kind of car he had, what he would look like, if he'd take us to the Fresno Zoo or Storyland or maybe to the place where we could race go-carts.

I both wanted to see him and didn't. He scared me, and not because I remembered the time he got mad at me and my sisters for screaming in the car and told us that we had the drive home to choose whether we wanted to be beaten with a belt or a stick from the yard, but because I didn't know him anymore. He used to call me Bobo and wrap his fingers up in the thick curls on my head, saying, "Thanks for the nice, warm mittens, ma'am." What a strange thing, I thought, that you could unlearn your family. I felt it happening even with Keith and Tanya and Granny, who I'd known always. We visited less and less every year — it seemed there was always some track meet or school event or sleepover to get in the way — and when we did go, it took half a day for my body to relax and remember Granny's things, the smell of her bathroom, the sound of her humming around in the kitchen before breakfast. When we left to go back to the Lindberghs, we all felt sad and told Granny we'd see her soon, but we didn't see her soon, and the process would start again, skipping like a record.

At the arranged time, we waited on the lawn until we were too cold, and then went inside to wait some more. The phone rang, and Bub answered. "Yes," he said, then "No." There was a long pause, a "Yeah, well," and then he hung up.

"That was your dad," he said, turning to us. "He's not coming. I told him he had to stay here if he wanted to see you, or that one of us had to go along if he wanted to take you out somewhere. For supervision, you know, but he didn't want that. He said no. I'm sorry."

I went to my room to take off my dress clothes and ended up on the bed, facedown in my furry coat. I cried some because my dad didn't want to see us enough to come no matter what. I cried some more because I understood that our new dad was trying to keep us safe from our old dad — *should he? was there a reason to?* — and that one might replace the other — *did I want that? would it last?* — and I couldn't begin to puzzle out what any of it meant for me, the middle daughter, the daughter in the middle.

OVER TIME, THINGS WITH Bub shifted, slowly, slowly, so it was difficult to be sure who was changing, him or me. For the first time, I saw our house as others must have seen it, as an eyesore, an embarrassment to the growing neighborhood. Some of our less-diplomatic neighbors called to tell Bub he should clean up the yard, the listing corral, the telephone poles he meant to cut down for firewood, the old cars that lay marooned out by the tack shed waiting to be scrapped out or messed with or hauled to the dump. The pigeon coop swam with pale-blue feathers, its walls and floors painted with dried poop though we hadn't kept birds in years. We didn't keep chickens anymore either, which was unfortunate since the chicken coop had become our family's Dumpster. It was Bub's idea. The garbage cans in the house were lined with paper grocery bags. When full, they got walked out to the coop and just thrown in through the creaky wooden door. When the coop filled, which took most of a year, my sisters and I put on waders and rubber gloves and moved the rancid, rat-stinking, snake-infested rotting-paper-bag mess into the horse trailer so Bub could drive it, in increments, to the Rice Road Dump.

"Why can't we just put the garbage into the horse trailer directly?" I asked Bub one day. "Then drive it to the dump when we need to?"

"Good girl," he said. "That's using your noggin. But we might need the trailer for the horses. This way works fine."

It also started to grate on me that Bub had an answer for absolutely everything. One summer evening, Bub and Hilde drove us up to Millerton Lake for a swim. We balked at this because it was full of nibbling fish and fish poop and slimy grasses, but it was too hot not to want some relief — and if we waited for Bub to build the swimming pool he'd promised, we might die first. On the way back, my sisters and I sat in the back of the truck, towels wrapped around our damp suits. Way off behind us was a speck of something, wasp-size and glinty; as it drew closer, we could see it was a motorcycle coming up fast and loud. The bike was low and silvery green and the guy on it barefoot with cutoff shorts, no shirt and no helmet. As he passed, the slightest lean of his body made his bike sway dramatically into the left lane and back — and soon I couldn't make out anything but a colored blur in the distance of curves and crests. A few minutes later, Bub stopped the truck so we could all get an ice cream cone. He wasn't even fully out of the cab before I heard him say, "That asshole. He's gonna end up wrapped around a telephone pole, just you wait."

We ordered our cones, climbed back into the truck and headed home, the wind hopping over and around the cab, whipping the tips of our hair into melting chocolate. Then, a few miles up the road, Bub was forced to slow for the flashing strobes of the highway patrol. An officer waved us along in the line of cars, and we edged toward what I recognized as the motorcycle, or what was left of it. Thrown well off the road, the bike's front wheel was bent, crushing back on the left exhaust pipe. Red plastic from the taillight lay scattered on the pavement in oddly uniform pieces that looked like hard candy. The guy had been thrown into some fencing, his body held in sagging wire as the paramedics labored to extract him. I had to look away, concentrating on the spot, behind layers of foothills, where I guessed the lake must be, the fish going about their fish business, the cool, scummy water rock-

ing the boat dock like a cradle. I didn't want to see the guy again
or the tinfoil crumple of his bike; I didn't want to turn forward to
the cab to see Bub smiling the mean, tight smile of those who are
right about everything.

⌒

AS WE GREW OLDER, I had the feeling Bub was starting to
see the young women in my sisters and me. One day, as I watched
Penny jump up and down on the carpet in the living room, pretending she was on a trampoline, I noticed her breasts bouncing
under her cotton nightgown. I looked away, embarrassed, and
then noticed Bub was watching Penny too, from the couch, his
eyes locked on her as intently as when he watched Captain Kirk
wrestle an alien or lightly touch the dancing woman with leaf-
green skin. I knew that if I shouted then he wouldn't hear me, and
got a sick feeling in my stomach. He wouldn't look at Penny that
way if she were his real daughter, I was sure of it.

Now, when he tickled us, the sessions lasted a little too long.
I was so conscious of where I stopped and the world began that
whenever Bub's fingertips brushed the area where my breasts
would have been if I'd *had* breasts, I had to remind myself to
breathe. *He couldn't be doing that on purpose, could he?* Like the
nugget of rust that tried to poison me years before, I felt my
doubts about Bub fester. They swam in me, impossible to locate,
contain, flush out, and washed up in dreams. Then, on my four-
teenth birthday, Bub taught me how to kiss. For some reason we
were alone in the house.

"Come here, fats," he said, and tickle-wrestled me to the
floor between the kitchen and living room, directly under the
mounted horns of a bull where, when my sisters and I were eight,
nine, twelve, we jumped as high as we could, trying to touch first

the leather band between the horns, then the hanging S curve, then as far up the right horn toward the tip as possible. It was like playing Pony, except these were our jump shots, no ball; every slightly higher station was evidence that we were growing up, that we could do more, handle more.

"Give me a kiss."

When I pecked him quickly, birdlike, on his thin lips, he said, "No, not like that. You need to learn to kiss like a woman." He tried again, pushing his tongue against my closed mouth. It felt so much like the night crawlers we used as bait for fishing, I didn't know whether to giggle or vomit. What I did was throw him off and run out of the house, down the drive, my bare feet flinching on rocks. I felt flushed and confused. When I got to the gate, I stopped. Where would I go? What would I do? Soon it would be dark, twilight coming on, thick and lavender, the evening sky pressing down like a belly.

Finally, I crossed the street and knocked on the Swenson's door. The kids were all out on an errand, but Valerie was there, so I decided to tell her. She was the most marvelous woman I knew, the kind of mother I'd have chosen if I *had* a choice: patient and tender and beautiful. She gave me oatmeal soap to clear up my acne, taught me how to apply eyeliner without looking like a lemur, to wear nylons instead of panties under tight pants, that contrary to popular belief, brown shoes do not go with every-thing. Valerie was more motherly and compassionate than Hilde had ever been; surely she would understand, give me advice, help.

What she did was tell me a story about her own father com-ing to her in the night when she was a teenager, trying to touch her over her nightclothes. She had two older sisters, and it was the same with them. "Listen," she said, sighing, tired, "Bub's not even blood to you. I'd be more surprised if he *hadn't* tried something with you. He's just a *man,* after all."

I nodded like I believed her and ate the macaroni and cheese she offered me, and the peanut M&M's and the chocolate chip cookies. Finally, when there was nothing left to eat and nothing else to say, I went home to the man who was and wasn't my father, who had three different nicknames for me, who told me I was stupid and told me I was pretty, who taught me to swim by shoving me under, who petted my head when I cried about the dead puppy and said, "I know, I know, I know."

WHEN I WAS FOURTEEN I found, under Teresa's bed, a pair of boy's jeans from a nude Jacuzzi party with a bunch of Future Farmers from Sanger. These were boys with hands like fine-grained sandpaper, slightly sweaty and yellowish. They spit their Skoal into Dr Pepper cans or right out the window onto two-lanes as George Strait sang it sad and too true. One of them wore Wranglers, thirty-two by thirty-six, with a fade mark on the back right pocket as perfect and distinct as the sweat of a highball glass onto a cork coaster. I came upon them as I rooted under Teresa's bed for her diary. The blue spread hid dust motes and carpet smells, a dinner plate with fossilized mustard, one wilted gym sock. The jeans were folded, not balled or stuffed. If not for them, I could have been looking under my own bed: same navy spread with its gold flowers, same matching pillow permanently sleep-creased. The jeans were a blue you'd see through someone else's window. They smelled like asphalt and fresh eggs, and a good six inches swam over my feet when I stood to hold them at my waist. What boy had filled these with his long teenage legs? Had she let him kiss her, or just watch as she kicked her own jeans and panties onto his mother's dark lawn?

At the time I had kissed my own hand, the bathroom mirror, the hinged-open mouth of my compact mirror, my pillow, and once, on a trip to Porterville for new saddles, Cousin Krista. We were lying on an old mattress under the camper shell playing Boyfriend / Girlfriend. I was the boy and on top, pressing and squirming in an imitation of what I'd seen in our small collection of stolen *Penthouse* and *Playboy* magazines. Krista's lips were tight and dry, and we smushed against each other so hard I thought we might hurt ourselves. My sisters were there too, watching I guess. After the game, we went back to stuff we usually did, Penny, Krista and I singing solos, Krista going first and doing Marie Osmond's "Paper Roses," which she *knew* was my secret weapon.

AT FOURTEEN, I COULD string live bait on a hook, gut what I caught, shoot an arrow, a pistol, a rifle that kicked me right back on my skinny butt. When Bub built a mock steer out of scrap lumber, we practiced roping it, then the ponies, then one of our two cows until we could do it right, the lariat slipping wider with each swing, flying flat and true. After that it was boxing moves on the lawn. We bobbed and weaved, faked left, drove right. We learned how to Greco-Roman wrestle as a way of working out arguments. "No sissies in this house," Bub insisted. "No catfights. Take it outside."

I looked like a boy, which didn't much bother me at home. We all looked like boys, more or less: beanpoles with dirty hair, scabby shins, respectably callused bare feet. At school, though, girls crowded the mirror between classes to recurl and respray their hair. They lit contraband matches to soften eyeliner pencils. They separated their mascaraed lashes with toothpicks and bobby pins with the rubber tips bit off. Slouching behind them to get to the stall, I caught myself in the mirror and was horrified. My hair frizzed and hovered. I was curveless, guileless, mascaraless, baffled. I didn't speak teenage girl and couldn't see I wasn't the only one. When I saw my sisters in the halls, they seemed magically transformed to me. We walked together to the bus, and from the bus, and somehow I never noticed, until I saw her four tables away in the lunchroom, that Penny's hair was not only clean but in a perfectly splayed auburn feather; never noticed that Teresa, as she leaned against the lockers talking to some boy, knew not to tuck her plaid shirttails in like the dweebs did. How and when had they lapped me?

I wondered daily how I could catch up, what real transformation would take for me. According to Yolanda, our old babysitter, it was all about boys: first kisses, feel-ups, couple skates at Rollertown. After she told us the infamous Truth or Dare story, I thought about it at least once a week for years, and then it was my turn to move up, *grow* up. During my first week at Clark Middle School, I walked around feeling like I was going to vomit. There was also a pressure in my lower back, way down where the fused bones, when you look at a skeleton, are like a hook or the curved tip of a monkey's tail. I thought the sensation might be a cramp that would sooner or later shift around to my front side and bring on my period, but it didn't. It stayed there, pressing and slightly warm, like the hand of someone steering me toward a dance floor or a lawn or a circle of scared and jeering kids to whom I would be forced to spill my guts.

The Truth or Dare thing never happened though. I didn't get grabbed or dragged or led. In fact, I never even saw a game the whole time I was at Clark. Occasionally I heard stories at great remove about how *this* girl let *that* boy get under her bra on the wrestling mats behind the bleachers at a dance. Sex was *happening,* surely, but not to me. At assemblies, I could hear the words tossed around — *wet, tongue, open, finger, pussy* — like volleyballs careening over my head, smacked hard by someone else on the way to some*where* else.

The closest I had come to having a boyfriend was in fifth

grade when Ruben Estrada kicked a soccer ball into my face, breaking my glasses, and felt so bad about it he let me wear his blue-satin Dodgers jacket for the rest of the day. Although Ruben never had more than five words for me, I always knew, after that day, where he was in any cafeteria, assembly hall, soccer field. I knew his clothes in every combination, his haircuts, his good and bad skin days.

Ruben's longtime steady, Angel Lopez, was very "developed," and featured this by wearing T-shirts two sizes too small. My breasts were subversive. Although I wore a training bra, from a three-pack selected furtively at Sears, there was no sign I would ever have anything to fill it except cotton balls and ankle socks. It was desperately unfair that some of my friends had needed a bra since fifth grade, even before they called all the boys into the gymnasium and all the girls into the cafeteria and showed us separate but equal films about the wonderful changes ahead for our bodies. After the lights were cut and the big floor-to-ceiling curtains drawn, the school nurse stood at the front of the room and used her pointer to outline the plastic model's funnel-shaped bazooms while we snickered. Then there was a film following the journey of a single egg, which looked like a Tic Tac, from the ovary into the uterus. On the way out, we were each handed a pamphlet called *Your Body in Bloom,* which was full of diagrams and featured a full-page vagina that looked cottony and girl-pink. (Is pink a girl color because we wear it on the inside? Are boys blue because of faded jeans that feel nothing like our own?)

Teresa had started her period eons before me. The day after she got it, we were at Aunt Gloria's house, swimming. Gloria had recently remarried, this time (her third) to a tall, bearded and almost entirely silent man named Steven. As far as I could tell, Steven did nothing but sulk and read magazines in a red leather chair in the living room. If he had a job, I didn't know what it was, but Gloria was doing well enough for both of them. She'd gone to night school to get her real estate license (unlike Bub, Gloria actually *finished* the course) and seemed to have a real knack for it. She was able to buy a four-bedroom Spanish-style house in Fresno's toniest neighborhood, on the northeast side, and a cute little Toyota truck that suited her size and spunkiness.

Along with Steven and his moods, the marriage had also brought Gloria a seventeen-year-old stepson named Kenny, who had Shawn Cassidy hair and wore only perfectly faded and fringed Levi cutoffs. Kenny would have been a fox if he weren't an asshole. Luckily, he lived with his mother, the ex–Mrs. Steven-the-slug, so we didn't see Kenny that often, but he was over the day we swam, hanging out under the diving board like the Billy Goats Gruff troll. Everyone was in the pool playing Sharks and Minnows except for Teresa, who sat in a lounge chair slathered in baby oil.

"Why aren't you coming in, Teresa?" Kenny crooned, even though he knew. Everyone knew.

Teresa didn't answer. She sat with her legs crossed on the reclining lawn chair and picked at something on the bottom of her foot. She wore her yellow string bikini with the palm trees and looked good in it. Like me, she was small on top, but she had great legs, runner's legs, and a small waist, her belly concave and lightly fuzzed like a peach. Her hair was growing out that year, the shoulder-length waves acting to soften her sharp nose (Bub called it her "hatchet") and still-broken tooth. I was just thinking that Kenny might think Teresa was pretty, when I heard him call out, "Hey, Teresa, are you on the rag?"

Teresa's chair sat under a kumquat tree that was dropping fruit. *Thup* went a kumquat, soft, overripe.

"Are you afraid you're gonna bleed in the water and get eaten by the shark?" Kenny needled.

Teresa still didn't answer him, but she got up then and walked into the house. The back of her legs were shiny and striped pink from the chair. I couldn't see her face.

᠁

THAT SUMMER, WHEN I'D ride Queenie through the long grasses in the ditch, I often felt someone watching me, a murmuring in the reeds, a play of light that might have been a body, shifting, trailing slightly behind, like an echo. Sometimes I stopped the horse and held myself absolutely still, listening. Sometimes I'd look back over my shoulder, thinking loudly: *I'm ready. Find me soon.*

That summer, the heat was Godzilla, its monster breath visible in flushed waves above any flat surface, the sidewalk or hood of our car, the asphalt that had softened into pudding. Our dogs dug holes along the stucco wall of the house and tried not to move anything but their long eyelashes when the flies settled. Their bellies moved in and out in small hiccups. In the field, the horses rested their thick heads on one another's backs and slept standing up.

Tina, long since resigned to her separateness from my sisters and me, spent her days with Hilde at Noreen's, eating tuna-fish sandwiches and working on a blanket that required you to use a broomstick to hold the crochet stitches. She was also fine-tuning the art of bitching, which was her inheritance after all. I saw her as a mini-Hilde, a paper doll around which Hilde and Noreen would fasten the Butterick blouses and polyester slacks. She was even beginning to look like her mother, her hair cut just below the ears and overpermed into a poodlish explosion, her face rounder and plumper by the day.

Penny played a lot with our neighbor, Jeff Gerber. His parents had a pool and a basement playroom they kept air-conditioned and stocked with Oreo cookies and board games. Jeff had a crush on Penny, which was funny since they looked like they could be brother and sister. They were both small-boned and auburn-haired and freckled, with the same sharply bridged nose. Other than the incest aspect of the crush, I knew why Jeff liked Penny. She had become a pretty adorable teenager with long feathered hair, shiny silver braces and a perky little body. Although she was still skinny, she was also short; that made her *petite*. I was skinny and tall; that made me *gangly*. That made me Olive Oyl. When I stood next to Penny at the bathroom mirror, trying to get my hair to do anything but levitate, I was often struck by the unfairness of it all: she was my younger sister — younger by a whole eleven months, mind you — and she was skunking me.

When Penny wasn't at the Gerbers', she shut herself in her room with Bryan Adams on the boom box and scribbled in the black-and-white-speckled composition pad she used as a diary (in that summer of diaries, of discontented diaries and the discontented reading of diaries). She was in love with a tall, lanky boy named Drew. He had a big haystack of hair he wore right in front, like a retro pompadour, and he made her mixed tapes of the Cars, Duran Duran, Foreigner. In her diary, Penny called Drew her "White Rose" and wrote things like, *If I hear "Cuts Like a Knife" two times before midnight, it means Drew and I will be together for all time.* She would have murdered me if she knew I was reading her diary, but I *wouldn't* have read it if she'd hidden it someplace better than between the squishy mattress and the frame of her waterbed. Duh.

Teresa was sixteen that summer and forever off with her friend Stephanie at someone's pool party or in her room with Rod Stewart throbbing from the turntable. I missed her, though I knew we were all better off when she was gone. Once through the front door, she was Instant Beast — just add water! — pointedly ignoring everyone, slamming doors, thumping against the walls of her bedroom as if she was saying, had always been saying, *This house can't hold me for long!*

And me, I felt itchy in my fingers and way down under the skin of my summer feet. None of the things that usually made me happy felt right, not playing in the Swensons' big pond, riding my bike, or reading the Harlequin novels that Rhonda Snelling's mother passed along by the bagful. I looked at myself in the long bathroom mirror: glasses on, glasses off. Hair forward, back, straight up like a scarecrow. Had I always had this face?

If a big change was coming for me, it was sure taking its sweet time. All I could do was wait. Walk down to the end of the driveway, touch the peeling fence, turn around. Make ice cream floats, then watch them melt to goo in the glass. September glowed in the distance like a firefly, like the only thing worth watching. In September, I would be a sophomore, no longer the bottom of the bottom, the new kid who couldn't find Portable Five or her locker combination. In preparation, I experimented with blusher and tinted lip gloss. I flipped through the phone book for the names of boys in my classes the year before — even the ones I hadn't liked — and wrote them all down on spiral notebook paper, then wadded up the pages and fed them to the trash compactor. At dusk, I sat on the lawn and let myself become a mosquito buffet, feeling, all the while, the house at my back. The brown hulk of it like a rhinoceros, dusty and heavy, huffing like a train.

—⚬—

WHEN I TURNED FIFTEEN and my period was still nowhere in sight, I began to think I was missing parts. I went back to the diagram. There was the vagina, angled toward the spine like a spongy mine shaft, stalks of fallopian tubes arcing away and then toward each other, the ovaries perched like the heads of twin Venus's-flytraps.

A friend of Noreen's had edema. When she visited, she had to sit with her feet on an ottoman as they watched The Show and crocheted afghans that threatened to swallow the furniture. Even up, her legs were like squishy tree trunks, and her feet bulged from the mouths of her brown orthopedic shoes. Once, I watched as she pressed her thumb into the mottled skin near her knee. The

print held in a pocket that took an hour to fill in. When I saw pictures of the vagina after that, I thought of edema — the kind of
skin that could save the shape of what was pressed into it. Skin
with a memory.

I kept waiting for there to be a thing that happened to me
first, a thing I could know first and then hand down to Teresa, but
this seemed less likely with each passing day. I remember the first
time I saw her pubic hair. She must have been thirteen or fourteen
then. We were at Noreen's for the day, and Teresa was in the bathtub for some reason, maybe she was just hot. The lights were out
because Krista and Penny were taking turns trying to call Bloody
Mary from the bathroom mirror. I was sitting on the toilet with
the lid down, playing with Noreen's toilet-paper-roll holder. It
was a ridiculous thing, wooden with a picture of an old outhouse,
a crudely formed change receptacle attached to the bottom and a
poem scrawled with every fifth letter backward or fake-scratched
out: *Moving this inside took most of our dough, pleeze drop in a
nickel before you go.* Teresa was chattering on about something to
no one in particular and soaping her pubic hair. *Wait a minute.
Hold the phones.* She had *hair* there? Had it just sprouted up
overnight, like something vegetable? No, she was way too non-
chalant about it, not even looking down there as she moved the
soap around, pulling her fingers up and through so the hair stood
pointy, like a witch's hat.

Now she was in eleventh grade and I was in tenth, and even
from her school picture, I could catalog the gaps that seemed to
stand for the larger spaces between us: the triangular patch on her
forehead where her bangs swung to each side, the space between
her dark eyes, the dimple pressed into her chin's center, the chip
halving her front tooth. She wore her yellow boat-neck sweater
and picture-day acne, and sometime after that photo was taken —
or was it before, even? — she became the kind of girl who'd strip
down to nothing and wear a boy's jeans home.

◈

"YOU'RE PRETTY," MY FRIEND Mindy said to me one day at lunch, "but you could bring it out more, you know. Maybe wear different clothes. Cut your hair."

"Yes, that's *it*," I nearly sang. I just needed a makeover. The real me, the prettier me, was in there, pinned, trapped, suffocated by the dorky me like a pillow over a face. Mindy told me to buy my pants one size smaller, and then lie flat on the bed to get them zipped up. The hook of a coat hanger in the eye of my zipper would help a lot, she said, and my fingers wouldn't get so raw. If I couldn't get makeup, then I should bite my lips a lot and pooch them out a little. She had read this in a magazine. The other thing was she would cut my terrible hair. We agreed to meet in the half hour before school in one of the lesser-used girls' bathrooms.

"Now don't be nervous," Mindy said as she tucked brown paper towels around the neck of my shirt. "I do this all the time." But the light was bad, and Mindy was skittish with her mother's big fabric scissors. The bell rang before she could finish, and we both looked at the half-done haircut in the mirror with alarm. She had cut me short bangs and had taken four or five inches off of *part* of the bottom so that it now resembled badly hung curtains. I cried through most of homeroom, and for the rest of the day wore the long bit dragged around over my shoulder and bunched up, hoping no one would notice, or if they did, that maybe they would think it was intentional, a punk-rocker thing.

Hilde took me to the cheaper-than-a-real-salon beauty college after school but was mad about it. The cut would cost six dollars, and I was making her miss *Rockford Files*.

"Ridiculous," she muttered as she drove, shaking her head. "If your friend told you to jump off a bridge, would you do it?"

Maybe I would, I thought loudly, but said nothing. I stared out the window, holding the long chunk of hair in my fist, rubbing it a little, like a rabbit's foot.

SOPHOMORE YEAR I LOVED Ruben Estrada, Eric Hobart, Ed Chavoya, the boy who sometimes visited Noreen's next-door neighbor, the boy from Roosevelt High whom I watched run a liquid 800 meters at a regional meet the spring before and Bill Mosher. Mostly Bill Mosher. He wore a red plaid shirt, and his teeth were so white and straight they were like a kind of math. He sat diagonal and left from me in Typing II, and I'd forget to hit return for staring at the tan bridge of his hands on the keyboard.

Somehow, Teresa guessed I loved Bill and started teasing me when he'd run by at track practice. "There goes your *lo-ver!*" she'd call loud enough for everyone to hear. All I could do was blush and swear she was wrong.

She didn't let up, though. In February, after a meet, a Truth or Dare game got started on the darkening bus home. I wasn't anywhere near the action, but heard "Oh, no!" and laughing, and there was Bill Mosher being pushed toward my seat by Teresa and Curtis Cunningham and some others. I felt hot and terrified and thrilled.

"Get her," Curtis hollered, and I knew I was going to be

kissed. In that moment, I didn't care if Bill cringed over it, if he made dramatic spitting gestures after or had a good laugh with his friends about how awkward I was. I wanted the kiss and all the ways it would change me. But Teresa was the one who named the dare. It wasn't a kiss at all; instead, he jabbed his index finger under my armpit, then smelled it.

You'd think I'd have been too embarrassed after that to trail Bill from D building to lunch every day, but I wasn't. I did it for the rest of the school year, close enough behind him so that my hand was the very next one to drag the banister, push the swinging door. I'd follow him to the snack bar and back to the lawn under the amphitheater, so close I could smell his burrito.

Me, I didn't eat lunch and hadn't since seventh grade. We got lunch tickets from the Welfare Department, but I threw them away, every day into the same open can. They were stamped *Free* on the back, and everyone knew only poor families got free tickets — the same families that waited in line downtown for hunks of cheese and powdered milk and baby formula. I didn't want anyone to think I was like those poor people. In fact, I didn't want to be different in any way. If people found out I'd been given away not once, but over and over again, they would feel sorry for me. Easier to lie and say the Lindberghs were my parents and always had been. I could be anyone, really. I could be no one, sitting cross-legged behind the last stack in the library with my bag of corn nuts.

⟶

AFTER LUNCH THERE WAS gym, where I stood in the outfield wearing my heinous blue bloomer jumpsuit, praying for bunts. After gym there was chorus, which I liked, even the *mi mi mi* scales, the five-minute arrangements of "Muskrat Love" and

"Feelin' Groovy." One afternoon, as Mrs. Adams was going over solos with the small group of favored sopranos everyone else called the Screamers, I looked across the room at the alto section to find a heavyset blond girl looking back. Did I know her? Was she in my second-period government class? biology?

When class wrapped up, the blonde pushed along the risers, right toward me. "Hi," she said. "You're Paula, aren't you? I'm Stacey. Do you remember? My mom knows your mom."

"Hilde?"

Her eyebrows came together. "No, Lynette. My mom's Lynette. Your mom's name is Jackie, right?"

"Uh, yeah," I said, all of my blood finding my face.

"Do you remember when you lived with us? How are your sisters? Teresa must go here too. I haven't seen her."

I managed to say yes, that she was a junior, though most of me was up in the filing system, shuffling through names and faces, trying to place her, this Stacey.

"Well," she said, smiling a little and turning away. "Good to see you. Say hi to your sisters for me."

"Yeah, okay. Sure."

I was all the way out by the portables before she clicked in. There was a Stacey, a blond slip of a thing, who had started kindergarten with Teresa. If Stacey was the daughter of Mom's friend Lynette, wouldn't that make Mom's boyfriend Roger her uncle? *Creepy.* It was possible we had lived with Lynette during one of the times our dad was away, but I didn't remember. I did have a clear image, though, of Stacey and Teresa holding hands as they turned down the sidewalk toward the elementary school. There was a Cyclone fence threaded with weeds. Mom raced ahead of them with a camera.

Now I was late for class. Mrs. Weller grimaced as I came to the door, and everyone looked up, even Ruben Estrada, who (oh, cruel, cruel world) sat directly in front of me for the first time since fifth grade. It would be last period too, when my hair had gone through all of its contortions and there was a film on my face from the dirty heat and from where I put my hands to my forehead all the way through geometry.

I slid in, opening my notebook and my Penguin copy of *Julius Caesar*. Mrs. Weller started up with the voices and the hand gestures and the forsooths, but I couldn't follow her. "My mom knows your mom," Stacey had said. Not knew, *knows*. Did they write letters back and forth? Or was she here, in Fresno? The text in front of me blurred sickeningly. My desk felt clammy. I looked up, and there was Ruben's neck — brown, solid and the same, the three small moles under his right ear. Everything spun except Ruben, his collar, his moles, his left ear. His hair was so black and shiny it was nearly blue. It looked slick, oiled. Like if I walked on it, I'd surely fall down and never get up.

FRESNO WINTERS SETTLE IN like a wet shawl. The damp is a shock after so many months of drought, as is the cold. You might walk through a shorn field, soggy socks rubbing inside your shoes, the hem of your jeans growing heavier, and not believe any of it, though your fingers tinge pink, then lavender. Not believe the air can be so like water. It was this kind of day in early December when my sisters and I walked off the bus toward home and bad news. Fog had come down, soaking everything. Penny kicked at the wet grass as she walked, streaking one pant leg to the knee. All along the barbed-wire fencing, bubbles of water rested on the sharp tips, looking like transparent ladybugs, spared somehow, and still.

Though it wasn't yet four o'clock, Bub's car sat in the drive with a cold hood. That's when we knew something was up. We found him in his chair in the living room, the TV off, stroking our dog Barry's big square head — though a dog let on the carpet was as rare as a lunar eclipse. Bub stayed quiet like this until dinner and then told us that Floyd had been killed. Not just killed but murdered, and when he said that, his face twisted, as if the word were too hard to hold in his mouth.

Goldie and Floyd had had a fight, apparently, loud and long, about Christmas, how Floyd wanted to come down to Fresno and spend the holiday with Dot and Carlynne and the boys and their wives. His family. Goldie must have thought that Floyd was going to leave her and go back to them because she went out and bought a little gun. She slit a hole for it in her mattress and kept it there, way down in a nest of batting. One night, after they had made love, she waited until Floyd was asleep, dug out the little gun, held it to his temple and fired. Then she snuggled up right next to him and shot herself the same way. Two weeks passed before they were found. It took that long for a neighbor to figure out he hadn't seen Floyd in a while. The dogs looked hungry too and were whining. When he walked up to the house to see what was going on, he didn't have to knock but once; he could smell the wrongness of the whole thing from the porch. They were both naked, and the sheet had been pushed down to the end of the bed. Nothing was covered up. He saw every terrible thing.

LYING IN BED LATER that night, the house dark and too quiet around me, I wished that Bub had kept most of the story to himself. Over and over, I swallowed hard, as if the images were floating up at the back of my throat instead of deep in my overactive brain. I saw Floyd in his chair, like that night at his house, except this time he wasn't asleep, he was dead, and instead of the sombrero in his lap he held Goldie, or parts of her: her hands, her sad lunatic face.

In the police investigation it came out that Goldie had a long history of manic depression and had even been institutionalized years back. Had Floyd known this? Had Goldie known what she was and what she might do, or was her illness like a shadow or seed that had grown inside her until it was large enough and dark enough to take everything over?

⟲

THE FUNERAL TOOK PLACE in Delano, in a small hillside cemetery. The grown-ups were so quiet they seemed stunned, and the funeral went on for such a long time that we started to wander off, one kid at a time, and they let us. We stayed inside the cemetery gate for a while, my sisters and me, Tina, Krista and Uncle Hog's two kids, Randy and Brenda. As we threaded the rows, I felt more than a little creeped out by how old it all was, how long they'd been gone, these people who weren't even *people* now, just names. *Rupert Rawson. Etta-May Aimes. Mother.*

"Watch where you're walking," Tina said. "You're not supposed to walk on their heads."

But what about the baby graves? How could you tell where the heads were when the markers were the size of a shoe, no room for anything but a first name? *Lydia, Thomas, Jean-Ruth*. One had an etching of a lamb held in a pair of robed and disembodied arms.

It was all too much. A low gate hung open between two hedges, and we went through it, heading away from the parking lot and over a small hill until we couldn't see cars anymore or parents and the only noise was us, wheezing with the climb. It had rained that morning but the wet had burned off, and it was growing hotter by the minute, too hot for December. When we stopped to rest, all the girls shucked their stockings.

"I can see your business," Cousin Randy said, pointing at his sister's loosely crossed legs.

"Oh, hush," Brenda said, and pushed her skirt higher. Her panties were pale green, and along one edge I spied a fringe of dark-blond hair.

I turned away then and pretended to busy myself in the purse I'd worn for the special occasion. It was navy blue with a long strap and snap close. Inside, there wasn't much more than a plastic comb and some Certs and my lip gloss, which I took out and fussed with because I wanted Brenda to see that I owned makeup. It was bubble-gum flavored and brand-new, purchased the week before with nearly all of my measly allowance.

"Hey," said Brenda, "can I have some of that?" She slathered on a thick layer, held the lip gloss for a minute, turning it over in her hand like money, then said, "You know, I'd think about trading with you for it. If you really want."

"What do you have?"

"Jewelry. Real turquoise." She reached into the neck of her blouse and pulled out an owl necklace. Its head was a round stone, blue-green and flecked, and there were two little stones for its feet. I'd never had a necklace before and so traded without thinking. Brenda pocketed the lip gloss and unhooked the chain, handing it to me. The owl rested in my hand in the little pool of its chain. I didn't even want to put it on yet; I just wanted to look at it, my owl, my jewelry. Its ears were tiny silver triangles and there were silver arcs for the wings, which lay back, resting. Its body was a silver oval, empty.

Empty.

I could see right through the belly hole to my hand. When the humiliation came, it came slowly, in a flush that built one realization at a time.

Broken.

Brenda had given me a broken necklace, knowing I was too stupid to notice. Maybe the worst thing about being a sucker was that the believing part didn't last. Now that I'd seen it was no good, I couldn't unsee it, not for a minute, not even long enough to wear the necklace once. The whole world could see it was missing the main part.

A HANDFUL OF MIRACLES in the year of our Lord nineteen hundred and eighty-one: (1) I started my period; (2) a boy actually kissed me. (It was Patrick Allison at the drive-in, and he tried to stick his hands down my pants first. He was gross for that, and I vowed never to speak to him again, but the kiss counted.)

That was the summer before my junior year. Teresa was away, working at a mountain lodge Aunt Gloria had recently purchased on Huntington Lake (that real estate license really *was* paying off), trying to save money for a car. It wasn't a great job — she cleaned rooms for minimum wage and waited tables at the small supper club — but she got to be gone. Before she left, she made it clear she would be way too busy to call or write. Way. She would see us in August.

Somehow August came. On Labor Day weekend, we drove up to the lake to pick Teresa up and bring her home. She shared a small cabin with a girl named Sascha, who was there when we arrived at the resort in the late afternoon. Bub invited Sascha to have dinner with us at the supper club, and she showed us the edge of her Ace-bandage wrapper, telling us the story of how, the week before, she'd driven her car over a cliff and only cracked two ribs on the shifter. It was late at night on mountain roads, and she swerved to avoid a deer. "A baby deer," she clarified. In truth, she was probably drunk but wasn't telling. The car was still drivable, believe it or not. It hit no trees and landed absolutely flat, like some kind of UFO. Sascha said it all happened so slowly she felt as if she was flying more than falling. She wasn't even afraid.

"I've got a surprise for you," Bub said to Teresa while we picked through salads, waiting for the main course. "I found you a car."

Teresa's mouth dropped open to show a wet bit of crouton. If she could have spoken, the word would have been *What* or maybe *What the hell?* It was her money, and she wanted to pick the car herself. Even *I* knew that. If Bub's "surprise" find had been a slick little Fiat, she might have been consolable, but it wasn't. It was a white Opel Cadet, a chunky, graceless grandmother's car that looked a lot like a dumpling.

I tried to meet Teresa's eyes across the table to give her a *That bites* look, but she was shut down, boarded up for the season. Her eyes were mica. I thought Teresa might throw her fork at Bub, but she could never do that and live. She settled for slamming her water glass onto the table and storming out, the screen door clattering behind. I wanted to follow her, but Sascha moved first. She didn't excuse herself, but then again she didn't have to. Bub and Hilde weren't her parents, and besides, she'd proven she could take a bigger fall than most of us have occasion to.

We finished our dinner, baked potatoes and leathery filets, while Bub lectured us about ungrateful kids and how he didn't even have a *bicycle* at her age, et cetera, et cetera, blah blah blah. In between rants, he stuffed his face with forkfuls of potato quivering with sour cream. Like Hilde, he'd been growing larger over the years, but for him, the weight was contained solely in his belly. It butted up against the table now, and as he took a particularly ambitious bite, a glob of sour cream fell bull's-eye. No one pointed it out, not even Hilde, who was slurping up au jus.

After dinner, Bub sent me over to Teresa's cabin to see if she was packed and ready to go. "Knock knock," I said, through the screen door. I could see Sascha on one of the twin beds, smoking, her legs crossed Indian style, her shoes kicked to the floor. I stuck my head into the room. Teresa was on the other bed, lying with one arm behind her head and the other tossed casually in the lap of Gloria's stepson, Kenny, who sat beside her. Kenny? I didn't even know he was up at the lake. Furthermore, Teresa hated his guts — *didn't she?*

"What do you want?" Teresa said, lifting her head slightly. Her hand didn't move from Kenny's lap. Her fingers rested on his mangy leg as if she was his girlfriend or something. As if they owned each other.

"It's time to go home. Dad said to get you."

"Okay, yeah," she said, but her head fell back on the pillow. Sascha blew a curl of smoke. Kenny reached over and put his hand on Teresa's stomach where her halter top had pulled up to show the skin, flat and tanner than I'd ever seen it.

"Okay," she said again, and I waited for her to turn back into someone I knew.

NOW WE HAD DONE it. A ten-dollar bill was missing from Hilde's purse, and one of us took it. It was the only explanation. Ten dollars doesn't just walk off on its own, now does it? First there was a family discussion at the dinner table. Bub stated the case matter-of-factly. Hilde's purse was behind the couch, where she always kept it. It was there with the ten dollars when we went to bed on Friday night; it was there with everything *but* the ten dollars when she checked it in the middle of the day on Saturday. He went around the table, looking closely at us, looking into each of our faces so intently I thought he was trying to see behind the skin.

"Do any of you girls know what happened? This is the place to confess," he said, "right now. You'll be punished, of course, but not as badly as if you lie about it."

He leaned back in his chair and waited. Hilde sat beside him, her arms crossed in that way that said she'd double or triple cross them if she could; she'd latch them like a gate.

I scanned my sisters' faces, watching to see if one of them was about to cough it up, but they were looking at me the same way.

Penny: "It wasn't me."

Tina: "Not me."

Paula: "Hmm-mm."

Teresa: "I don't even know what you're *talk*ing about."

"We're going to get to the bottom of this one way or another," said Bub, looking at us and then into his helping of peas as if the little green heads belonged to members of a jury.

⟜

THE NEXT DAY WAS Sunday, and we drove to church listening to Johnny Cash. Bub sang the words to "Folsom Prison Blues" pointedly, his glances into the rearview like poison darts. On the way home, there was no music whatsoever, to make as much room as possible for the soul spilling that would surely follow the morning's sermon. Nothing.

At home, we were gathered for another talk, this time in the living room.

"Listen," Bub said. "On Saturday night Penny and Paula and Tina all had the flu," (as if we had forgotten the flat ginger ale and saltines, the lying around musing about how gross it would be if we all barfed at the same time) "and Hilde's back was out, remember?" (When Hilde's back went, she slept flat-out, beached in the middle of the living-room floor. She drank out of hospital cups with built-in straws, peed into a yellow plastic bedpan, which Bub had to empty, and generally moaned like she was going to die. Yes, we remembered.) "Any one of you girls in the living room could have gotten up in the middle of the night."

Hilde made a throat-clearing noise that sounded like she was scratching her tonsils with a wooden spoon.

"What honey? Do you have something to say?"

"They were sick."

"Yes, the girls were sick. I just said that."

"They were sick. They wouldn't have gotten up."

"So what, are you saying Teresa must have done it?"

"I'm not saying that." Her voice cracked. (She was saying exactly that.)

"What, then? What?"

"Nothing. I'm not saying anything."

Bub shifted his weight on the sofa and sighed, the sound of patience leaking. "I'm giving you girls until tomorrow night. If you don't have the guts to come to me on your own, I don't want you in my house. There's nothing worse than a liar." He stood up disgustedly and walked down the hall to the master bedroom. Hilde followed, tugging on the hem of her blouse.

"This is so unfair," I said, when their door was shut.

"Yeah, whatever," said Teresa. "They don't think *you* did it." She looked around the living room as if she was thinking about burning it down, then went into the kitchen and got on the phone. Was she calling her friend Stephanie? Sascha? Maybe it was Kenny. I thought about the way Teresa and Kenny had been on her bed in the cabin, their bodies knotted like pipe cleaners. They were having sex, they had to be, but I knew it would never occur to Teresa to share that information with me. Somehow, we'd fallen into ourselves over the years, into privateness and silence. Or maybe we'd always been separate, my bubble and hers and Penny's bobbing side by side through all the homes and harms. Why had I never said anything to my sisters about Mr. Clapp and his chair? He had never called it a secret, but I had made it one anyway.

And what were the odds that Mr. Clapp had targeted me alone? After Becky Bodette left, Teresa was by herself in the back bedroom. How easy it would have been for Mr. Clapp to go to her there. And he had, of course. It was suddenly as clear to me as the puzzle of Kenny and Teresa's bodies on the cabin bed. Teresa was as much a bed-wetter as I was in those years with the Clapps, as nervous and as numb. Was Mr. Clapp the reason she wanted to run away that time?

I wouldn't ask. Just like I wouldn't ask if she had stolen the ten dollars. I went to bed and lay there in the dark while Teresa crouched in the kitchen with the phone. I could hear the murmur, pause, murmur of phone talk, but nothing specific. She could have been confessing. She could have been crying or spitting with rage, ready to walk out the door that very night. How was I to know? I lay as still as I could, straining to make out a single word, and heard only my breath, my busy heart, my listening.

⟶

"I CAN'T TELL YOU how disappointed I am that it's come to this," Bub said the next night after dinner. On the table next to his plate was a sheet of notebook paper folded twice, clipped closed with a ballpoint pen. He placed his right hand on top of the paper like one does a Bible.

"Everyone outside but Penny," he said.

Penny looked alarmed — *did he know something she didn't?* — pinned to her chair like a bug, expecting anything. The rest of us bolted. We threw ourselves onto the lawn, picked at tufts of clover and waited for the verdict. Over in our concrete pond, the dogs were fishing. They crouched down and walked back and forth through the shallow water with their mouths open. When a goldfish swam in, they chomped their teeth together and then swung their big heads to one side. The little fish flew into the grass to shrivel like apricots. You'd think the dogs would have eaten the goldfish, they were carnivores after all, but they seemed more interested in the hunt.

Ten minutes later, Penny came out of the house looking unscarred. We asked her what happened, but she just pointed to

Tina. "Your turn," she said, and then deflated onto the grass. "Sorry. Dad says I have to zip my lip."

All Teresa and I could do was wait — too cruel — while the dogs chomped and flung, chomped and flung. Finally I was up. Bub still sat at the table, with the dishes pushed back and piled all around. He had the notebook paper open and the pen uncapped, and his watch was off and lying next to them.

"Sit down," he said. "This is a lie-detector test. If you're lying I'll know."

He took my hand in his and put two fingers on my wrist at the pulse point. "Did you take the money in Hilde's purse?"

"No," I said. He wasn't looking at me but at the watch. He was counting.

"Do you know who *did* take the money?"

"No."

The Timex ticked on. I could feel my blood under his pressing fingers.

"Did Teresa take the money?"

"No. I don't know."

He wrote something down on the paper and then told me I could go.

The only one left was Teresa, and although I wasn't there for her test, we soon found out she failed miserably. Her pulse raced and raced when Bub asked her the questions. It was so obvious she was the one. I heard her screaming in her room when I came back into the house. She had been grounded for a month and Bub had taken away her ugly-ass dumpling car, the one she didn't want in the first place.

"Let this be a lesson to you," Bub said to Penny and me as we tried to watch *Mork and Mindy* over Teresa's screeching. "Lying is the worst thing you can do. How can I ever trust anything that comes out of her mouth now? Tell me that."

TWO DAYS LATER, WHEN the Avon lady rang the bell to deliver an order, Hilde suddenly "remembered" what happened to the ten dollars. It bought cologne for Bub in a bottle shaped like a roadster, and a cake of green eye shadow. Nobody stole anything.

This should be good, I thought, and waited for the apology that was sure to come, for Hilde's shamed face at the dinner table. But she wasn't sorry, apparently, and Bub wasn't sorry. They didn't take anything back. The Cadet keys made their way back onto Teresa's dresser, and she was wordlessly ungrounded. She didn't even seem mad about it, no madder than usual, anyway. She was as cold as something metal, biding her time in the unlaunched rocket of her room. In two months she would turn eighteen, and in that time, no one would be sorry enough to make her want to stay. No one would speak the true, verifiable fact: a liar is not the worst thing you can be.

WHEN PENNY AND I went to visit our cousin Keith at St. Agnes, we shared an elevator with an orderly who was escorting a metal gurney from the second floor to the ninth, so we got a good long look at him. He wore scrubs the color of smog and paper shoes and was chewing something small — a sliver of toothpick? a button? — that made his mouth do a kisslike twisty thing. Penny met my eyes, rolled hers, and that's all it took. We were hijacked by a fit of snorting. After a minute, we had the sense to turn away from each other and were able to gain a thin composure. Then Penny emitted a postlaugh sigh that was half leaking bicycle tire, half hoot owl, and we were off again, laughing loudly as the orderly glowered. The doors opened with a ding at nine. He tried to exit with a maturity that would shame us, but one rubber wheel stuck in the door crack and the gurney spun sideways like a grocery cart possessed. He started to swear quietly at it, forcing it forward with his weight, and a small blob of drool dropped from his mouth to the silver platter of the gurney.

He drooled!

When the orderly finally got the cart unstuck and rushed away, paper shoes whooshing along the corridor, Penny and I were alone in the elevator, red-faced and wet-eyed, sighing. I looked up at the twinkling numbers and said, "You know we passed our floor, right?"

"Yeah, I know."

⌐❀⌐

KEITH WAS IN INTENSIVE care, having barely survived an electrocution accident. He was a field-worker for the phone company — one of those men who go up in hydraulic lifts to check the lines, tool belts jangling from their hips like giant charm bracelets. Keith was up in the lift when he grabbed hold of a power line that was supposed to be shut off. The voltage traveled through his left arm like blood through a vein, then split, shooting down through both legs and feet, and out the top of his head. The jolt sent him flying right out of the basket and down some twenty feet to the hard ground. His partner had been sitting in the truck for the ordeal, which had taken only seconds, and ran out to find Keith crumpled on the side of the road, looking dead, dead, dead.

"It's a miracle he's still with us," Granny said when she called us at the Lindberghs' to give us the news. Her voice sounded lispy and strange, the *s*'s mushed together wetly. I thought it was because she had been crying, but when I asked, Granny had said no, it was because of the stroke she'd had the month before. *A stroke?* I barely had time to process this when Granny started in about Keith. He'd been in critical condition for several days, but was out of the ICU now and could have a few visitors. It would mean a lot to him, she said, if we girls would go down there.

When I got off the phone, Penny and I sat at the kitchen table for a while, feeling stunned and ashamed. How was it that Granny could be so sick without our even knowing it? When was the last time we'd seen her? Or Keith and Tanya? If we were fifteen and sixteen, Tanya must be thirteen already — could that be? — and Keith nineteen. The last time I remembered going over to Vera's with Granny, Keith had just started eighth grade at Cooper Intermediate. While Granny and Vera did some catching up over weak coffee, we went outside with Tanya's Chinese jump rope and started playing in the driveway. Keith didn't join us in the game, of course — he was way too cool for that — but he sat with us, sprawled on the lawn, tugging at tufts of grass. As I waited for my turn, I plopped down next to Keith and started attacking the grass too, building up a little pile of cuttings between my feet. It wasn't until Keith went to scatter my pile, teasing me, that I noticed his hands. The knuckles were raw and purplish, with nicks and one long scrape on his right ring finger.

"What's that from?" I reached over, happy for an excuse to touch him.

"Fight." He didn't pull away.

"A fight? Someone beat you up?"

"Maybe I did the beating up. Did you ever think of that?"

"No," I said, shaking my head quickly. "You wouldn't. You're too good." I went back to my grass nest, raking up the strays.

"Good, huh?" The smirk was in his voice as well as on his face. I looked up to see his blue eyes narrowing as he studied me like some two-headed thing in a jar.

My blush was tidal, blood moving from my neck to the tips of my ears and back. I couldn't even look at Keith and so pretended to be very interested, suddenly, in the Chinese jump rope game. Tanya was at the part where she had to leap up and come down on both sides of the elastic, pinning them down, but she missed. "Dang," she yelped. "Do-overs."

"No way," Teresa said, stepping out from her side. "My jumps."

Keith stood silently and wandered inside, and we left shortly after that. He came out to the porch with Vera and Tanya, and they all waved us down the street. As we passed the abandoned airport, its runway cracked like an eggshell, every third window of its blue control tower blown out, I thought about that Easter morning when we learned of Deedee's death, how only moments before, we had been singing in Granny's car and Keith the loudest, the best — his voice all angels and atmosphere.

⟶

WHEN TERESA GOT HOME from track practice, Penny and I went into her room together to tell her about Keith. She was still in her running shorts and a gray T-shirt with the neck cut out that said *Wild Woman.* "What?" she said from the floor where she sat cradling her albums in her lap. She owned only five and was as possessive of them as a dog with half a bone, putting them in order, going through them over and over for signs of our tampering.

We told her the part about Granny first, about her lispy voice and how she had said she couldn't drive anymore, that ladies from the Gospel Lighthouse were doing her grocery shopping and coming to pick her up for meetings.

"When did that happen?"

"A few months ago," I said. "July." In July, Teresa had been up at Gloria's resort. That was her excuse, but what about Penny and me? We'd been doing our usual summer thing, spending most of our time over at the Swensons', forgetting the Lindberghs for as long as they would let us. Sometimes Bub would call over there and say, "Come home. Can't you see you've outstayed your welcome?" But that was only once a week or so. In between, we were free, free, free.

Although we hadn't been forgetting Granny for the same reasons, she'd been forgotten nonetheless, pressed into a scrapbook like a newspaper clipping. We didn't think ill of her; we just didn't think of her at all. When I put my mind to it, I could easily picture Granny in her kitchen, whistling as she battered chicken for frying, could see her dark shoes and old-lady stockings and smell her White Shoulders. But these memories were as old as I was. I didn't have any new ones for her, didn't have a context for her in *this* life, which was whizzing forward with crushes and pizza parties and long looks in the mirror to see just what could be done about my hair.

"That's sad," Teresa said, petting the album on top: Rod Stewart in a black leather jumpsuit and boots, his hair looking, well, *electrocuted.*

Penny fidgeted as she described Keith's accident, unclipping and reclipping her silver barrette. "We should go to see him, don't you think?" The question was for both of us, but she was looking at Teresa. "Granny said he would like it."

"Absolutely," I said.

Teresa shrugged. "You guys can go if you want. I'm busy."

"You're busy when?" I asked. "We haven't told you when we're going."

"I'm always busy." She tipped Leather Rod to the side and the album slid out. Holding it gingerly, she blew on it several times, then placed it on the turntable. Lowered the needle. "Tonight's the Night" started up, clearly our sign to leave, but Penny and I couldn't stop looking at her incredulously.

"What?" she finally barked. "What?" She put her hands on her knees and set her chin. "Listen, I just don't want to go. You guys can make up your own minds, but leave me out of it."

⊖

PENNY DRIED HER FACE on her sweater as we left the elevator after our spastic laugh attack. "Do I look normal?" she said, turning her attention to her stick-straight hair.

"No. Do I?"

"Nope."

The sixth floor was tiled in white and a yellow-orange Penny said was technically called "baby shit," you know, in decorator's terms. We wandered around lost for a while, but I wasn't in a hurry. I needed the time to prepare myself for Keith's injuries. Granny had warned us that he looked bad, and though I tried to call up versions of *bad,* the only thing coming in clearly was Keith at eight, feet wide, hands on hips, calling out, "To the Batmobile, Robin!"

Our Hall of Justice was a tangle of rusted car parts and sheet metal in one corner of Granny's backyard. *Now you kids stay away from there,* Granny would warn, shaking a finger. *You'll get lock-jaw! Okay, okay,* we sang back in unison, and headed right for it. In those days, Keith was always Batman and would select a Robin to keep me and my sisters from drawing blood trying to settle it ourselves. Sometimes he picked a number or did Eeny Meeny Miney Moe, but usually he lined us up against the fence, held his chin for a moment, as if deep in thought, then pointed. I pre-ferred this method because it had nothing to do with luck; he was choosing, and when he chose me, the sun seemed to shoot off like a bottle rocket.

Somehow, Penny and I got all the way around to the bank of elevators again before a nurse spotted us and led us to Keith's room. Through the door was a single bed spewing tubes, banked by machines that blinked and hummed. There was no one else in the room, so it had to be him, the exploded thing above the sheet. His head was at least twice its size, a black basketball, burned and hairless.

"Look who's here," said the basketball. "Granny said you might come. Get over here where I can see you." It didn't sound like my Keith, my Batman, but it wouldn't: Keith was a grown-up now.

We sidled nearer, Penny half a step behind me. From where we had stood at the door, it had looked like all of Keith's beautiful white-blond hair was gone, but no. There were still frizzles of it over his ears and in spots along his forehead and the back of his neck, like tufts remaining after a carpet has been ripped out.

Keith watched us expectantly as we approached the bed, and the eyes were his own, wide and sky blue inside the char of his face.

"Hey you," I said, and found myself talking through a wad of my own hair. Without thinking, I had pulled a section around in front of my mouth. I laughed nervously and dropped my hands. "How's it going?"

"Sucky. How does it look like it's going?" The words were hard, but his voice wasn't. "Where's Terry?"

"Teresa," I corrected him. "No one has called her Terry since we were kids."

"She's too good now, huh? Miss Prissy Pants." One heavily bandaged arm pawed the sheet.

"No, that's not it. She just doesn't like Terry." I walked over to the window, where the view was all parking lot. It looked like a board game, one where you could roll dice and maybe end up on the free space.

"Uh-huh. Where is she?"

"At home, studying," Penny piped up, speaking for the first time. "She wanted to come but had this really big test."

"Yeah," I added, "big," but I was thinking, *Who knew Penny was such a great liar?*

"She planning to go to college?" The machine to his left chirped twice and quieted. "I didn't go to college. Guess I wasn't smart enough."

Part of me wanted to say, "Of course you're smart enough. You can do anything." Part of me was having trouble breathing.

Under the hospital sheet, Keith's feet were split and shot, the color of charcoal. (*I'm a trampin', trampin',* we sang in Granny's car. Would they take him to heaven now, or anywhere, those feet?)

Penny and I stayed for twenty minutes or so, long enough to tell him how we were doing in school, about our dogs and the big sailboat in the backyard. It must have sounded to Keith like we were doing okay, better than okay, because he broke in, saying, "Swimming pools. Movie stars."

"What?"

"You know, the *Beverly Hillbillies*. From the theme song."

"It's not like that at all," I said, my hands in my hair again.

"Yeah, right."

I spent the next few minutes sputtering, my face hot, trying to tell Keith he'd gotten it all wrong, that we weren't rich or brainiacs or anything, but it didn't matter. He was convinced that we thought we were better than our family. That we didn't have room for them in our new life.

The thing is, he was right.

We said good-bye, patted what seemed to be a safe part of the sheet and got back on the elevator. I pushed Lobby and looked up. We sank like a dirigible.

"Hey," Penny said, remembering the stupid gurney guy, "did you see how the top of the cart was all smudged, like he'd just gotten rid of a body or something?"

"Yeah. That was weird."

We clicked through the slide show of gross possibilities in our separate heads, happy to be thinking of anything but our sorry-ass selves and what was left of our Batman up on the sixth floor.

"Yeah. Weird."

IN JUNE OF 1982, Teresa graduated from high school. Days later, she walked down the driveway and across the street and moved in with the Swensons. She took the room Amber's brother Ross had had, but since Teresa was so rarely there, the room went unchanged: same lion-print blanket on the waterbed, same lion-print wallpaper. She even left the pyramid of Skoal and Copenhagen cans in the corner, the historical Boone's Farm bottle full of petrified coffee-colored spit. *Sick.*

The distance between the Swensons' door and ours was some two hundred yards, and still, Teresa sightings were rare. She worked shifts at Golden Valley Nursing Home, ran an afternoon register at Carl's Junior and waitressed late nights at Denny's. Her work uniforms were all kept folded, if not clean, in the backseat of her car so she could change and keep moving. Penny and Amber convinced each other that she must be taking speed in order to work as much as she did *and* go out after with whomever she was dating, and so cornered Teresa in the bathroom, on one of the few occasions they found her home, to perform an "intervention." Teresa stared into the sink as they lectured, said, "You must be fucking nuts" when they were through, and then was gone again.

In mid-July, Bub, Hilde and Tina took off on a long vacation, temporarily eclipsing Teresa's disappearing act. They climbed into the purple Cadillac one fine morning and headed all the way to Oklahoma to visit relatives — their relatives, not ours. Although Bub and Hilde had asked Penny and me to come along, they didn't seem surprised when we declined. I couldn't remember the last time we'd taken a trip with them, even to Dos Palos or Turlock. When I was eight, I felt shamed when Aunt Birdie had told Noreen we were "just like family" because I wanted to be the real thing. At sixteen, I was grateful we weren't, that we didn't have to lay claim or genetic connection to Uncle Hog, who made his own head cheese inside the upturned skull of a slaughtered pig, to lecherous Uncle Jack, or poor dead Uncle Floyd, or any of a number of large, fussy great aunts whose crochet needles were as fast as their gossipy tongues.

Sometimes I looked at Tina and wanted to say, "Run. Run far, far away." But it was too late; she *was* her family. Maybe if she had been as pretty as Krista, or as smart and sassy as Aunt Gloria, she might have found her way free. Maybe if my sisters and I hadn't kept ourselves so apart, hadn't pushed Tina away with the same force we used with her parents, she would be standing on the walk with Penny and me, waving happily as the car lurched out of the drive. But we had, and she was stuck — right smack in the middle of Bub and Hilde, right smack in the middle of the backseat with her Seek-a-Word puzzle books and her giant bag of Fritos.

Penny and I watched until the car rounded Bullard, then let out a good loud shriek. Without Bub and Hilde, the house expanded like a lung, rising weightless around us. We drank lemonade so thick with sugar that the granules rained toward the bottom of the jug. We stood with the refrigerator door open, took thirty-minute showers, let the dogs on the carpet. At night I used two fans and took a Popsicle to bed. I strung a dream in which I was a whole family, all by myself: the mother and the father and the baby playing with its toes.

Since Bub and Hilde would be gone for a month, Penny and I decided a little redecorating was more than in order. Into the closet went the Holly Hobby plastic place mats, the skunk figurines, the table lamp in the shape of a rearing horse. We stripped the crocheted toilet-paper-roll holders, the crocheted seat covers, the crocheted toaster cozy. Penny eyed the curtain in Bub and Hilde's bathroom that was really a terry-cloth towel, faded blue-and-gold tulips with a fringed bottom. It was so obviously a towel. What was Hilde thinking? "Chuck it," I said to Penny, and she did.

When we felt the house was as presentable as it was going to get, Penny and I hosted a party. We bought pizza and bad beer and let people come right in with their shoes on. I knew Hilde would have kittens if she saw the trail of dirt that was collecting between the entrance hall and the keg, and therefore felt a pure pleasure standing in the doorway, saying, "Come on in."

"Is it okay to sit up here?" Diane Rodriguez asked from the countertop by the kitchen sink.

"Fine," I said. "Totally fine."

I walked from room to room, touching tabletops and chair arms, leaving my prints everywhere.

SOMEONE'S BROTHER BROUGHT PORNOGRAPHY. I came in from the patio, my glass of gin and lime Kool-Aid sweating into my hand, and found the whole room riveted by this image on the TV screen: a woman, naked, riding a contraption like a bike that swept feathers over her clitoris when the wheels spun. She moaned, pedaling faster. Behind her a man walked by on stilts, his stiff penis waving like an arm. It was *Caligula*. Everyone in the living room was laughing but transfixed, reminding me of the time at the bus stop when the Abels were having their pigs slaughtered. As our bus pulled up, the hog had just been split from neck to crotch. Strung up by her back hooves, she swung like a pendulum. Her entrails swam into a huge barrel. The bus waited, doors open, red lights flashing to stop traffic, but we just stood there. We were frozen with watching. The driver was too. "Ugh, that's dis*gus*ting!" kids cried, craning for a clearer view, pushing at the windows.

The morning after the party, I woke up late. My teeth felt thick and knitted. Walking into Bub and Hilde's room, I saw the waterbed was rumpled, sheets everywhere. On Hilde's dresser, the Vaseline jar was open and the shape of a hard dick was pressed into the jelly. Someone had *fucked* the Vaseline! And then what? I thought of a woman in the movie, on her knees with her butt in the air — the way babies sometimes rock themselves to sleep. Then I thought of our new neighbor, Jacy Curry, sloshing around on my parents' bed with a boy, any boy, petroleum rubbing off of him onto the blue plastic mattress.

JACY'S LEGS BEGAN AT her ears. They were as pale as her scuffed Keds, but she got away with it. "A tan would age me," she said, tossing her fine chin. She was fifteen. When I looked at my own legs, skim milk curdling at the knees, I knew I would pay and pay later for thighs tawny or butter-colored now. *Now* required a currency that mostly vexed me.

Unfortunately Jacy had come to live with the Swenson family for several months — her solution to the problem of her mother's sudden transfer to Kansas City — and so I submitted to daily reminders of her desirability. Not only was Jacy beautiful, she got to live at the Swensons', in her own room, like she belonged there.

Valerie's husband, Dean, had recently left her for one of the waitresses at the restaurant they co-owned — a shock to everyone but the waitress. Craig and Ross, the two oldest sons, had moved into apartments of their own, and though their rooms were quickly filled with Teresa and Jacy, the house felt, to Valerie, like a drawer upturned and shaken. She was most like herself when it was filled with long legs and voices, and we were only too happy to oblige. Once the newness of being at the Lindberghs' with Bub, Hilde and Tina gone wore off, we found we were happier spending our nights at the Swensons'. We'd camp on the lawn in sleeping bags until the sun and heavy dew would force us into the living room, where we'd sleep until eleven, our heads under the coffee table.

That was the summer we were obsessed with *The Rocky Horror Picture Show* album. We wanted to look like Susan Sarandon in white panties but would settle for singing all the songs and learning how to do "The Time Warp" with drag-queen drama. Dressed in her baby-dolls and dancing on her mattress, Amber would sing, "*I've been making a man with blond hair and a tan.*"

"*And he's good for relieving my tension!*" I'd belt back, gyrating my skinny hips for all I was worth.

Amber had been wearing the same pink baby-doll nightgown for six years. Rubbed sheer in places, it had turned brownish, the bow at her neck floppy and chewed-looking. When Amber was wearing the nightie, there was no way to avoid her breasts, the physical fact of them. She was enormous, and had been approaching it incrementally since we were nine. There seemed to be no stopping her. All summer she wore tight white saddle-backed shorts with either a half-shirt with *Dallas Cowboys* bowed across her chest (once a guy said, leeringly, *Nice team*) or a scoop-neck pink T-shirt with iron-on bunnies and baby ducks.

"Don't believe a guy when he says he doesn't like big tits," Amber counseled. "They all do. They go right for them. Like radar."

When I insisted my boyfriend, Mark, liked them small, she snorted and sashayed out of the room, her breasts broadcasting their signal to a planet of predictable men.

Truth be told, I wasn't sure she was wrong. I wasn't sure of anything where sex was concerned. Mark was my first real boyfriend, and I still wasn't quite sure how I had secured him — after all, my last memorable physical contact with a boy had been Bill Mosher's finger in my sweaty armpit. As mysterious as the whole thing was, I was part of a couple now, free to revel in all that it entailed — writing Mark's name in all my notebooks, on my fingertips, on the knees of my jeans; getting escorted to the door of my U.S. government class after lunch; and the nightly phone calls, which, though we had nearly nothing to say, we couldn't seem to end (*you hang up first; no, you hang up first; no, you*).

Mark was gorgeous, with navy-blue eyes, a curly halo of sand-colored hair and lovely runner's legs. The baffling thing was he thought I was gorgeous too, and told me so. I remember going to the mirror after a date one night to see if it could possibly be true, and it was. I was beautiful, and yet I could still see, in my sixteen-year-old face, the scrawny, needful girl Noreen had turned to one night, saying, "I'll tell you what, child, you're the ugliest thing I've ever seen." She said it flatly and without malice because she had been thinking it, I suppose, and because it was true. Both were. I was ugly *and* I was beautiful. Somehow, the two didn't cross each other out in me. I felt them both, just as I felt, sometimes in the same instant, that sex was something wonderful and horrific.

I liked tongue-kissing Mark under the Swensons' willow tree, his silky shorts moving under my hands like blue milk. But light touching invariably moved on to rattled breathing and mysterious dampness. More puzzling were my own responses. My body arched toward his hands and lips on its own, possessed. I felt warm and liquid in an instant. And, just as suddenly and beyond my control, I'd flinch, pulling back.

"Sweetie, sweetie. It's okay," Mark would say. "I'm not going to hurt you."

I knew that. I also knew something different, something older. My body remembered other times and intentions, remembered Mr. Clapp's planetary forehead and newsprint-stained hands — and it didn't matter if I could see Mark's face above me go soft with worry. In my body, I was being stung (icy and hot at the same time). Crushed. I flailed and pushed him away, and he let me, getting up then, confused. Kicking stones, he'd walk back to his car and drive away noisily. I'd cry and stop, cry and stop. I'd call Mark to say I was sorry, but couldn't explain anything — not to him, not to myself.

❧

ONE AFTERNOON DURING MY senior year, Jacy walked right into the Swensons' bathroom as I was using it and began pacing in front of the long mirror, considering her jawline. Even on the avocado shag, she walked from her hips, like a dancer. I tried to pee quietly, gracefully.

"Travis is *cute*," she said to her reflection. "Sure. But he's too inex*peri*enced. The one time we did it, he *or*gasmed in, like, two minutes. And I wasn't even *mov*ing."

This ticking off of her meager choices is what Jacy seemed to do best, cataloging, adding or subtracting penciled stars for tropical-colored condoms or Old Spice deodorant. She kept a neat record of her conquests in a green spiral notebook: first name, last name — if available — date, location, merit. That summer at the Swensons', she was on line fifty-nine, the Australian foreign-exchange student she followed to the bathroom at Rhonda Snelling's yard party. The bathroom was so tiny she had to stand up, her rear pressed to cold porcelain, left knee pinched against the wall.

I was seventeen and not a virgin, having "done it" precisely five times, always with the same boy. I didn't need a spiral notebook. Mark was fervently Presbyterian, complete with an enormous colored poster of John 3:16 on the closet door opposite his bed. *For Gōd so loved the world.* We started dating in March of my junior year. The first three months were sweetly repressed: sweaty hand-holding and near-miss kissing. We'd lean into each other at the movies, our breath bitter with Raisinettes. We nuzzled like nervous pigeons until the first full kiss, which was like a revelation. *That he gave his only begotten Son.* Then we couldn't stop kissing. We were inventing it.

We squirmed and panted, fully clothed, in the furrows of the orchard near my house. I'd come home smelling of almonds, soft earth burned into the back of my skirt. This went on and on. When we finally did it on the sofa in his family's living room, I was so surprised to actually find him between my legs, I couldn't muster the sense not to scream. He pressed a cushion against my mouth, stopping it like a bottle.

From that time on, Mark and I were a sexual catastrophe. If he was ready, I was crying; if I was ready, he was feeling guilty and ashamed, saying, "No, we shouldn't. It's not right."

I knew it happened other ways for other girls. There was a whole continuum, from Amber guarding her cherry like it was gold-plated to Jacy throwing it at anyone in pants, to Tina, who had been trying to woo a boyfriend with sex since eighth grade. There was a lean black boy in Tina's class at Clark named Stanley Vargas. Stanley had a fantastic orange-tipped Afro that he liked to comb with a giant pick while leaning against the lockers watching the "talent" walk by. He whistled at Tina one day as she headed to our bus, and that was it; she would have Stanley if she had to tackle him first. They were a hot item for exactly four days, wearing each other's dark hickies like badges, and then Stanley had to be moving on. Nothing Tina could do could change his mind, not wearing a sequined tube top and short shorts, not flirting loudly with his friends, not offering to go "behind the bleachers" with him, which meant various kinds of wrestling on the big blue mats that were stored there, at the back of the gym.

Tina's virginity seemed not to carry any significance for her. She dispensed with it as quickly as possible and with as little ceremony as possible when she was fourteen, with Pete Berringer, who was twelve at the time. This happened in the back of our camper, headed toward some sailing event while both sets of parents sat up in the cab, singing cheerfully along to Kenny Rogers: *Oh, Ru-u-by, don't take your love to town*. Tina didn't even have a crush on Pete; she just wanted to know what it felt like. And once she knew, she wanted to feel it again, with boys who mattered. This only became difficult when Tina wanted the boys who were beautiful. She was just average, like the rest of us. Thick through the neck and arms, Tina could bench-press a hundred pounds, which impressed the boys in the weight room, but not the way she wanted. Her hair was never right (probably because she let Hilde and Noreen cut and perm it), her eyes were small and squinty, and her lips were so thin she couldn't wear lip gloss without it crawling toward her nose. I would have been terrified to chase the boys she chased — the pole vaulters and water polo players and defensive linemen — but she wasn't me.

After Stanley, there was Carlos; after Carlos there was Alan, a diver who wore tight red Speedo swim trunks. Alan had big shoulders, a narrow waist and hips, and was so good-looking he could have had any girl in school, and did, the cheerleaders and pep-squad girls and gymnasts with their pert ponytails. Tina seemed not to know Alan was out of her league and chased and chased him, handing him thick love letters in pink envelopes through the Cyclone fence by the pool — and finally they had a "date," in someone's garage during a keg party, which was about as subtle as behind the bleachers. After that, she thought they were steady; he thought nothing at all.

Still, Tina wasn't giving up, no matter how pointedly Alan ignored her. Once I watched her trail him all the way from the door of the boys' locker room to the buses. She called his name and said, "Wait up," but he wouldn't even turn around. She was like a puppy at his heels, and it reminded me of the way Penny used to fawn over her second-grade teacher, Mrs. Munoz, desperate for one specific smile. They were either very brave or very stupid, I didn't know which.

Tina climbed onto the bus, spotted me and came to sit down. "Do you think Alan likes me?" she said. "I mean, really *likes* me?"

THE FOLLOWING SUMMER, I was back in the Swensons'
bathroom with Jacy. Like the year before, she stalked the mirror
and sighed — but now she had something to sigh about. Jacy was
pregnant, though she preferred the term *infected*. She placed her
hand — nails perfectly buffed and lacquered — on her flat
abdomen. "Parasite," she huffed, turning profile, a police lineup
of one. She thought the infector might be her friend Russell,
whom she had gift-screwed on his birthday, but this seemed inci-
dental. At Planned Parenthood they told her to wait three weeks
before the procedure, to make sure the embryo wasn't too small
and therefore missable. In the meantime, she lolled from plaid
sofa to patio to beanbag chair with nineteenth-century paleness
and melodrama. She threw a hand up, dismissing dinner, and
slunk off for a bath.

When the time came, Penny went to the clinic with Jacy for
moral support. She waited with a stack of *Reader's Digest*s,
increasing her word power while Jacy was off behind a curtain,
extracting herself from the parasite, growing more separate from
us than ever. Three hours later, Jacy left the clinic with a paper
packet of tetracycline in one hand, a wad of Trojans in the other.
Back at the Swensons', she led us into the bathroom, shucked

her shorts and sat down on the toilet. Pressed to her underwear was the biggest maxipad I'd ever seen, soaked through with Jacy's blood. *Oxygenated,* I remembered from biology. Blood was never that bright inside the body.

"I'm cured," Jacy said, smiling.

⟝

SOON AFTER JACY WAS parasite-free, our neighbor, Kevin Stringer, had a pool party. A Santa Ana wind blew that day, hot as a furnace, singed with chlorine and briquettes. I was trying to nap on the diving board but couldn't get comfortable. My suit had dried to my body, pinching under my arms and at my hipbones, and the board felt like a stucco crucifix. Someone to my left whooped out "Marco!" but the voices answering "Polo!" were as muffled and distant as pings in a pop can. I hadn't eaten all day, and my head buzzed, a hive. I was enjoying this feeling of hollow-ness; my bones felt closer to themselves, more private somehow.

Just as I started to twitch into a sweaty sleep, someone found the stereo. Supertramp began to pulse from Kevin's bedroom window: *Good-bye, stranger, it's been nice. Hope you find your paradise.* We had this album memorized. When Valerie processed the lyrics of this song in particular, she worried that, in the sing-ing, Amber was mourning her lost innocence. She needn't have. Amber's innocence was firmly intact. Like her breasts, Amber's virginity preceded her into a room, a pink flag with its own grav-ity. She'd give it up for love, she insisted, but since none of us knew what that was, she might as well have been saying she'd give it up for Jesus or space aliens.

Jacy thought Amber *was* a space alien. "What's so *precious* about your pussy?" she challenged. "Do you want to *die* a nun or something?"

I looked up from the board, blinking against a red, red sun, to see Jacy straddling Kevin's shoulders. They were playing chicken with Amber and her brother Bo, but Amber's weight kept Bo toppling over backward, water flooding his nose. Jacy did a victory wiggle, shaking her bikinied butt. She hadn't slept with Kevin yet and was clearly working it. I was more worried about Rhonda Snelling, who had slipped out the side gate, some twenty minutes before, with Teresa's boyfriend. Although Brian was relatively new on the scene — they'd been dating a few months — I knew Teresa really liked him. When she brought him around for the *Caligula* party, her hair was in sausage curls and she was laughing with one hand over her chipped tooth, the way she did when she wanted to be pretty. Now Rhonda was likely to ruin everything. Her predatory interest in other people's boyfriends was legendary. When Wendy Prather confessed her crush on a boy she worked with at Foster's Freeze, it wasn't a week before Rhonda was in the shop in red pedal pushers and a tank top, licking her strawberry cone obscenely.

The sun moved through its stations, and finally it was five o'clock. I tucked my towel saronglike and left the swim party without saying anything because I didn't want anyone to tease me about my date. Then, walking the half a mile of hot asphalt between the Stringers' house and ours, it occurred to me that this wasn't a date at all, but its opposite. With Bub, Hilde and Tina in Dos Palos for the weekend and Penny still at the Stringers', the place was temporarily all mine. Mark would come to my door. I'd put on a sundress and set the table with three sizes of forks, grilled steak, scalloped potatoes, a green salad. I knew I was playing house, but how often did I feel I really *had* a house? Bub and Hilde took up all the space when they were around, all the oxygen; they filled the furniture like rising dough. Nothing was mine except my clothes. Although we'd lived with the Lindberghs for nine years, I didn't own anything that wouldn't fit in a Hefty bag. For one night, though, I could act otherwise. "This is my table,"

I said out loud to the kitchen rinsed with evening light. "My nap-kin, my knee, my sunburn, my salt, my spoon."

FIVE WEEKS LATER, I stood back as Jacy considered the shelf full of pregnancy tests. They were all in pastel shades, baby colors, a cardboard quilt.

"This one says it doesn't matter what time of day you take it," she said, pointing to a pale pink box. She held up one with yellow flowers. "This one has two. You know, in case you fuck up and don't get your pee right on it or something."

I said fine to the twin-pack and handed over two weeks' allowance to the clerk, who raised an eyebrow but took my money.

Both tests came up negative. I stood in the bathroom, wait-ing for the thin pink line, but the tiny boxes stayed white. I held one in each hand and stared at them for five minutes, then shoved them under my bed behind a haystack of dirty clothes, knowing Hilde wouldn't think twice about rooting around in a Dumpster, let alone my room, for clues of my certain delinquency. Once, she found a film of white powder on the bathroom countertop. Sure it was cocaine, she swept it into a baggie and took it to Noreen's house for verification. Turns out it was a mixture of baking soda and salt Teresa had been using to whiten her teeth. The white boxes of her teeth.

For two weeks I waited for my period. Every time I went to the bathroom, I checked my underwear. The slightest spot would do. Finally, I asked Rhonda Snelling to go to Planned Parenthood with me. She'd been twice before, once for a pregnancy scare of her own and once to have venereal warts burned off. In the car, she patted my hand like a mother might.

A woman at the front desk handed me a plastic cup and sent me off to the bathroom. The room was small with cool beige tiles climbing each wall and, near the sink, a metal box like a secret door. I was supposed to put my cup of urine in the box and close the door; someone from the other side would come along and retrieve it. It was all very *Get Smart,* and I couldn't help wondering if alarms would sound, red lights bleating from fixtures, if I opened the little door at the same time as the nurse or technician and we saw each other or our hands touched.

This never happened because I couldn't pee. I turned on the fan. I ran the water — first cold then warm on my fingertips, like the slumber-party game. I paced, my underwear down around my socks, trying to draw the pee down. It was up there, I could feel it like a small fist, clenched and willful. *I've been in here too long,* I thought. *The nurses must be starting to worry I've drowned in the sink or fashioned a noose out of toilet paper. Soon a clutch of them will gather at the door like white hens, all politeness, tapping lightly:* Miss, are you all right?

I would have been all right if I had been able to pee or stop thinking about time, which was dry and incalculable. I wanted to poke my head through the metal box and talk to someone on the other side. I considered waving my empty cup like a white flag or crawling out of the box, using it as an escape hatch. Hours lurched by, perhaps weeks, and finally there was no recourse. I slithered out of the bathroom and along one wall, aggressively avoiding the woman at the reception desk. If she said a word to me I'd die, I was sure of it, but no, she was busy handing a plastic cup to another girl. Rhonda still sat in the waiting area but wasn't happy about it. She shot me a brutal look from her slate-blue chair: *What the hell is* wrong *with you?* Minutes later I made her pull into a gas station. I had to pee so bad I was cramping.

When I finally knew, I was in the exam room of a gynecologist who could easily have been my grandfather, though I'd never had a grandfather. I chose him randomly from the phone book, starting from the back of the list of practitioners, and though his hands were like hippopotamus hide, I knew I'd chosen well. When I told him I didn't think I could pee, he only nodded, asking me to lie back on the padded table in my paper gown. With one hand on my lower belly, one hand inside me, he judged the fundus: ten weeks, maybe eleven. He helped me up then and asked, with a tenderness that leveled me, "Is there someone you can talk to?"

—◇—

LABOR DAY 1983. I rode low on Sky Harbor Drive in Bub's poppy-colored GT, taking the corners like a professional. Heat wavered from the asphalt like pure sound. I passed gnarls of mesquite, acacia, fig — all an ashy, survivalist green — headed for the cove where Rhonda, Bo, Amber, Jacy and my sisters had gone to escape Fresno's 115 degrees. I was dying for a swim too — wanted nothing more than to wade into the lake and feel my pink heat hiss away — though the woman at the clinic told me swimming after the procedure could lead to infection.

When I got there, the entrance barrier was closed and twisted with yellow-and-black police tape. *How odd.* I parked next to Bo's truck and walked down to the water in my cutoffs and one of Teresa's cast-off Hawaiian-print shirts, my sandals kicking up a dust as parched and pale as flour.

"Hey," Amber called out from the middle of the cove, treading dingy water. "I thought you had to work."

I shook my head and settled next to Rhonda on a worn blanket. It only took her five minutes to tell me Teresa wasn't speaking to her and hadn't since the Stringers' pool party, when she slept with Brian.

"I don't think Teresa and I can be friends anymore," Rhonda said slowly, thoughtfully, not caring that Teresa was some ten feet away on another blanket. "She blames me for everything, but it was Brian's idea. If he likes her so much, why was he screwing me?" She adjusted the halter of her turquoise suit. "I mean, how happy can he *be?*"

No one knew anything about why the police tape was there, but Rhonda led me down the sloped bank and around the shore to show me the flowers, maybe fifty or more white lilies, the kind mothers get on Easter, washed up on the sand. The stalks were soggy and bent, the petals laced with algae and drying foam.

"Weird," said Rhonda, nudging a stem with her bare toe.

I didn't think about telling Rhonda about the abortion. I hadn't told anyone but Mark. He went with me, drove me home after and heated me a can of mushroom soup — trying to make up, I wagered, for how flat he'd been when I told him about the pregnancy. I'd gone to find him at work, asking him to take a walk with me. We were halfway down a city block when I spit it out. He changed course, veered right over to a cash machine, withdrew two hundred and fifty dollars and handed it to me. End of conversation.

Strange: I'd always felt competitive with my sisters, wanting to have experiences neither of them had known, but now that I had done just that, I didn't want to share. I wanted to keep it close, feel lonely with it. Out in a life raft. Under a tablecloth. Up with the contrails, wispy as breath.

In the middle of the cove, Amber's brother Bo splashed around a buoy that looked like a giant head. The water grew green with rising silt and looked thick enough to walk on. I suddenly wanted to take one giant step away from Rhonda and then another, skirting the lily-infested shoreline or maybe going right over the cove like a rippling green carpet. I'd pause to put a hand on Bo's head and the white buoy's head, and then I'd keep on, water to sand to cockleburs until I was over the first hill. Maybe there'd be a cave to sleep in and sun-dried berries to eat. Maybe I'd learn to make fire.

I moved toward Bo and felt the cove water like pollywogs kissing my shins. The sand under my feet was like a living sponge.

"Yo, dork," Rhonda called. "Your *clothes?*"

I kept walking, the waterline at the waist of my shorts, the neck of my bright, borrowed shirt, my chin. I took a gulp of air and ducked, going under.

Three days later, I was lying on my bed, trying to force a nap, when Amber Swenson called. "You *have* to read the newspaper," she said. "*Now.*" So I got off the phone and rifled through the trash to find the *Fresno Bee*. At the bottom of the front page was a picture of the man whose body had floated up at Sky Harbor. He died in a waterskiing accident right outside the cove, and although they searched and searched, they only found his ski and the rope severed by the boat's motor. Finally, the family had a memorial service at the cove. That's what all those flowers were for.

I walked over to Amber's, and she met me in the middle of the road. We stood there looking at each other's tennis shoes. It was too freaky to talk about. We *swam* in that water, kicking up silt and algae, stirring the water into a murky soup. What if he had floated to the surface — that stranger, that father — while we were there?

What if every terrible thing pushed down finds a way up again?

ELEANOR PIERCE WORE BLUE deck shoes without socks and a snap-up-the-front housedress that hung from her shoulders like a sheet from a clothesline.

"Gotta go," she said to whichever nurse tried to hand her a toothbrush or tie her shoes. "Gotta go."

For breakfast, Eleanor took a biscuit or paper cup of peaches for a stiff-paced walk, up to the nurse's station and back, circling the TV room until her left elbow was raw from the wall. To shower Eleanor I had to pin her shoulders against the tile with my forearm and hose her down with my free hand. "Gotta go," she said, gritting her teeth, pushing her body up and against me so hard I nearly lost my balance. Her gray eyes looked past me at Out, at There. She fought like a drowning dog until I gave up and let her go ripping out of the shower-room door and down the hall, buck naked, her soggy deck shoes making frog noises on the linoleum.

This was my very first job, as a nursing assistant in a convalescent hospital, and it required me to do horrible things for people who were dying too slowly: give enemas and tub baths to sixty-year-old men; rinse bedpans and emesis basins and drain catheter bags full of lemony pee. Within a month, I had my fingers in a patient's leg, swabbing a bedsore so deep I could see a gleam of bone. Within a year, I was brushing a dead woman's hair.

My friends had clean jobs at water parks and ice cream parlors. They wore red visors and name tags and said, "Would you like some fries with that?" For a time, I wanted to be a nurse, but I had the nursing home job mainly because on the morning of my eighteenth birthday, Bub told me I was an adult and needed to start earning my keep, pulling my own weight. He said this in the Father voice, the This Will Be a Good Lesson voice, and I knew I had the day to prove my industry. One of Teresa's many jobs was as a caregiver at a nursing home in Ashland making three dollars an hour, which was a lot more than Burger King paid. I could do that, I thought, and I would get to wear those cute white shoes with tights.

PULLING MY OWN WEIGHT at the nursing home began with me going in to fill out an application in my seersucker skirt and tan flats with tassels. It wasn't a hospital at all, which surprised me, but a converted old house with a broad porch and worn shingles. The parking lot was divided from the street by a weight-sensing gate, though the administrator who handed me my paperwork assured me it wasn't technically a locked facility — they just wanted to make sure no one wandered into traffic. I had only been sitting in the office a few minutes when one of the potential wanderers wandered in, a woman named Virginia who was wearing her Cross Your Heart bra over her clothes. She made a beeline for me in cotton slippers that lisped along the tile, her lavender slacks a deeper shade at her crotch where she'd wet herself. She took the chair next to me and leaned in so close I could smell orange juice on her breath, could see dandruff like flecks of wax matting her hair. The administrator peered at me from over her computer monitor, and I knew this was the real interview, how I responded to Virginia, who kept repeating her name over and over, changing the inflection until it sounded like a complicated sentence containing everything she needed to say. I wanted to put down my clipboard and walk out, but that would mean I couldn't report back to Bub and Hilde that I had gotten a job, couldn't go to the dinner table that night pulling my own weight. So I looked right into Virginia's wacky gray eyes, smiled and said, "Hello," the way I imagined a cheerleader/candy striper would.

"Virginia," she said. "Liver, liver, liver."

"That's right," I said, nodding, and she settled back into her chair, beaming like it was Christmas and she was getting liver. My first shift started at seven the next morning. I wore a white zip-up-the-front nurse's dress and stockings and squeaky white shoes that would never be clean again. At my ten-thirty break, I met Teresa in the nurses' lounge, and she toasted me with a paper cup of coffee. "Do you hate it yet?" she said, offering half of a stale donut. When I shrugged, she said, "I'll ask you again at two."

MOST DAYS I TOOK care of the eight ladies in rooms 215 and 217. Eleanor was hell on shower days, but otherwise wasn't a problem. She spun her circuit just outside the perimeter of my attention. Five of my eight weren't even ambulatory. Vertie, for instance, just got shifted from her bed to the diaper-lined vinyl chair right next to it. I wrapped a restraint around her waist, then through slats on the back of the chair, double-tying it like I would a big gym shoe. If she weren't restrained, she'd have keeled right over onto her forehead. Her body had become its own knot — her legs crossed so tightly and completely that it was a struggle to even get slacks on her.

Vertie's husband came to visit on Saturdays and stayed through dinner, pulling up a chair to spoon-feed her pureed squash. He'd read to her from *Good Housekeeping* and rub her papery hand. Vertie was the only one of my ladies who was obviously married. The rest didn't seem to have families at all, or none I'd seen. We never knew, though; someone might show up, so on weekends we were supposed to dress every patient in their best whatever, give their dentures a good soak and scrub and put makeup on the ladies. We all carried lipstick for this purpose — along with thermometers, plastic gloves and blood-pressure cuffs — thumb-size lipsticks from Avon in the tackiest pinks and corals. Thin skin tears if you press too firmly, so we just dashed a little lipstick in the general area of their cheekbones. Most of them looked like transvestites in the makeup, but we talked it up, shouting: "You look so pretty today, Mrs. Escobedo! You're a vision! A dream!"

Across from Vertie in 217 was Beatrice, who was mean enough to have been lonely her whole life. She dressed and fed herself and wouldn't have been any work at all if she had ever shut up. She fired up monologues the way the chain-smokers in the rec room did filterless Luckies.

"Blood vessels and corpuscles and knee joints," she'd say, over and over again — and with such bile she was nearly spitting it. Or: "Extra-long, extra-thick, extra-wide sheets from JC Penney, *not* Montgomery Ward, JC Penney."

Beatrice directed most of her attention at Ruthie, who occupied the bed to her right. Ruthie could not have been less present in the world. She was as quiet as a book in a lap, and yet Beatrice was tormented by her. Tormented because she could cuss and spit, could do a burlesque show in front of Ruthie, and get no response. Ruthie was as cool as a stone in water, a calm that was craziness, surely, and deeply private, but Beatrice took it personally. Beatrice wanted to make Ruthie cry. She couldn't even get her to blink.

Like it or not, I understood this dynamic. It reminded me of Hilde and myself. I don't know when I decided she didn't love me, or love me enough, anyway (*what would be enough?*). I wasn't her real daughter, and if she thought about me at all, it was to wish I were long gone. If I couldn't make her love me, I would make her hate me. I prodded and poked, raised my voice, called her names, went too far until she snapped and reached for the nearest thing: a shoe, spatula, cutting board. If she was seething, then I had made her feel something.

And what did Hilde want from me? I couldn't guess, and I couldn't stop pushing, pulling. It seemed we were locked that way, like binary stars, spinning and spinning, always at the same distance. By the time I was eighteen, we were nearly nothing to each other. When she spoke to me it was to say, "Don't stand with the refrigerator door open"; "Don't track dirt"; "Don't let those flies in." I only spoke back when I absolutely had to. This wasn't difficult since I was so busy, taking afternoon and evening classes at Fresno City College, waking up at 5 A.M. to do homework before my seven-to-three shift at the nursing home. I was almost never home, and when I was, things were quiet between us, as quiet as something dead, which was and wasn't what I had wanted all along.

One day, I came home from work in the late afternoon to find Hilde napping on the couch. She was huffing like a warthog in the heat and had her cotton housedress pulled up nearly to her underwear. I could see the fine, long hairs on her thighs, the moles and pockmarks that were always hidden beneath one of her ugly muumuus. Sweat pearled on her nose and upper lip. How strange to see her this way, completely unguarded. *Has she seen me this way? Has she stood over my bed while I dreamed? Has she ever seen me at all?* As I stood there, a fly landed on one of Hilde's hands, but she didn't move. And what, I thought, if I put my hand on hers? Would she wake up then? Would she cringe? Cry? Gather me in her arms? *I never touch her,* said a fly voice inside. *She never touches me.*

⟶

IT WAS AGAINST EVERY rule to read patients' charts, but we did it anyway, sneaking behind the swinging door of the nurse's station when the RNs were out on med rounds. I always felt a little sickened by what I read, like how Mary — a woman who dragged one leg behind her like a piece of cordwood, whose larynx was so ratcheted by gravel in a motorcycle accident she could only make deep growls and screeches — gave birth to a little girl while in another institution. The father was some orderly or security guard, no one knew who, maybe not even Mary herself. Eddie V. had undergone a lobotomy. Esther Feinstein had been administered so many rounds of electric shock therapy that she literally foamed at the mouth. I began to understand that everyone had a sad story. There was no end to them.

Several months after I started working at the home, one of the veteran girls took a vacation, and I was shifted on the schedule to cover her usual assignment: five huge men, all needing daily tub baths. Most patients got two showers a week, which were easy enough. The shower chairs were toilet seats on metal frames with wheels. We simply transferred the nonambulatory patients to the chair, threw a sheet over them backward and wheeled them down the hall to the shower room. Tubs, on the other hand, required lifting a sometimes two-hundred-pound man — who might as well have been a bag of gravel — into the low-slung bath. Out was infinitely harder, of course, because the gravel bag would be slick with soap.

One tub a day was manageable; five seemed impossible, especially since they all had to be finished before the lunch cart arrived. My first day on the new assignment, I worked like a dog and still only got three done on time. The nurse bringing Ned's lunch found him still in bed, his gown soaked through and cold. I thought she was going to chew me out but instead she sent Berry, one of the more experienced nursing assistants, to help me after the trays had been cleared. Berry weighed maybe a hundred and ten pounds, but she lifted as efficiently as a backhoe. She helped me lower Ned into the tub and left me to the scrubbing, the lifting and lathering of his thick arms and legs. I knew I was supposed to wash Ned's penis, but was squeamish about it. I'd never seen an uncircumcised penis before: it looked like one of those cave fish that live without light or eyes. I swatted at it with my washcloth and called the bath done. By the time I got Ned back into the chair and wheeled him down to his room, Berry had made all of the beds. Each of the other four men sat straight and clean in their wheelchairs with lab robes tucked behind their hips. When I tried to thank her, she shrugged it off.

"It's a shit job," she said, and strode off toward the break room and her cigarette.

What I liked about Berry: when she was up to her elbows in some patient's nasty linen, she could laugh about it, her face saying *Look at my life. Can you believe this, can you even fucking believe it?* Once, when I was on my afternoon break with Teresa and some of the other girls, Berry walked into the room with her arm around Andy, a patient who lived upstairs with most of the other ambulatory men. Andy was sweet and harmless and nutty as a squirrel. He spent his afternoons plotting with his roommate Albert about how they were going to make a break for it, right out the gate to hop a train to Reno. Berry stood there, gave Andy's shoulder an elaborate squeeze and said, with perfect gravity, "Mom, Dad, Andy and I are getting married." Andy grinned beneath the brim of his John Deere cap, his hair tufting from the sides like spring weeds.

Berry was fastidious about her cigarettes. She never lit one unless she could finish it, and when she got down to the filter, she stabbed the butt against the ashtray or asphalt or upturned sole of her shoe. She wore her waist-length strawberry-blond hair in a low ponytail. *Stoner hair,* I might have said in high school, and she did remind me of the girls who cut classes to hang out in the parking lot of the Circle K drinking rum-diluted Coke in huge paper cups, their boyfriends draped over their shoulders or hanging from the back pockets of their tight jeans. Berry used charcoal to line the inside rim of her lower lids, something else those stoner girls did, but her skin was so fair it made her look a little like a witch, dark and hard and knowing.

Because I knew she'd laugh her ass off, I wrote a song about the aftermath of laxative day and left it paper-clipped to the back of Berry's time card. We decided the tune should be "Roll Out the Barrel" because Tuesday-night shit detail involved hosing out the linen from four or five garbage cans. The smell could have killed a cat. We wrote another song together, in the parking lot on our breaks. This one was to the tune of "Do Your Ears Hang Low?" and was called "Is Your Penis Circumcised?" Every time we got to the "Is the foreskin smooth or scaly?" part, we cracked up and had to start over. We laughed so hard we bent low and held our sides; we laughed so hard we cried.

⟲

ONE OF MY TUB-MEN was Sam Barnum, a collapsed house of a man. He was huge, maybe six foot three or more, and his long legs jutted wildly from even the largest wheelchair. When I first

saw Sam, I couldn't stop staring at his forehead, which featured a
dent the size of a Rubik's Cube and impossibly deep. *Where is the
brain matter that used to be there?* I wanted to ask, but it was just
me and Sam in the room, and he was drooling juice from breakfast. Sam didn't scare me so much as make me sad. I learned from
his chart that he tried to blow his head off with a shotgun some
ten years before. Because his forehead was sweaty, the muzzle
slipped as the gun discharged. A large portion of his frontal lobe
was dislodged, but he lived. The left side of his body, including
his face, was heavy and slack, unreachable by motor impulse. His
speech slurred like a lifelong alcoholic's. When his wife and
teenage son came to visit once a month, he said to them what he
said to us all, "Kill me. Please, kill me."

There were too many sad stories at the home; they were
starting to wash over me. As I got better at my shit job, I was also
growing numb — a blessing, I suppose. Without it, I'd probably
have snapped and ended up wearing a gazillion shirts or washing
my hands until they came off in the sink. A lot of girls there
couldn't turn the mess off in their heads and had to do it in their
bodies. Lyla and Bernadette, two sisters from Micronesia, chewed
coca leaves like gum; some smoked reefer out behind the laundry
room on breaks; some poured sour mash into their thermoses.
Then there was the other kind, those who had been there so long
that nothing fazed them, not emesis like potting soil urping out of
a patient's mouth, not Roland banging the emergency door like a
drum with the arm that wasn't blown to smithereens in some war,
not the noises that escaped the dead when we prepared them for
their families or the coroner.

Lupe was one of the oldest of the veteran girls and must
have been pushing fifty. I was impressed, thinking she must be
strong to still do the lifting and bathing. But she didn't do any of
her work, I soon learned — not the baths, the denture-brushing,
nothing. She ran a wet comb over her patients' heads, sprayed a

little air freshener in the rooms and took a two-hour lunch break. Even before I knew Lupe ignored her patients and let them fester in their own smells, I hated her guts. She was a foster parent — I'd heard her talking about it at break to a woman named Raylene who called all her patients her "babies." There I was, microwaving chicken noodle soup, trying to act like I wasn't listening while Lupe went on about it, selling the idea to Raylene as if it were a piece of questionable real estate. "It's easy," she said, "not bad at all, and you can't beat the money." Her husband wanted to buy a hot tub, and if they took in one more foster kid, they'd probably be able to swing it.

The microwave whined and spun my bowl, which had gone volcanic, salty broth bubbling over the sides, adhering to the ceramic like a chicken-colored membrane. I had ruined it, cooked it to death. There was nothing to do but chuck the whole thing, bowl and all, into the trash — or dump it over Lupe's head to watch the noodles burn worm tracks down her face and swim in her ears. That was the other way to go.

I chose the trash and a long spell in the closet where we kept the underwear of patients who had died or been transferred, or whose families simply forgot to label their clothes. Floor to ceiling, there were shelves of disintegrating camisoles, no-elastic granny panties and sad, stained Jockey shorts. I sat in there with the homeless underwear and thought about what Lupe had said, and what it meant for the foster kids she had at home who were surely clueless about their role in the family. And what about my sisters and me? Had the Spinozas been hoping to pave their drive with welfare checks? Is that how Bub helped pay for his endless projects and toys? Maybe so. It certainly was more plausible than philanthropy. And what about the Clapps, who clearly had plenty? We wouldn't have been useful even as pin money, so what, then? Why were we there? As fresh meat? Something for Mrs. Clapp to wrap in plastic? Something for Mr. Clapp to do with his evenings?

Break was over, but I sat for a while longer. I let myself imagine, in pointed detail, a horrible disease that would make Lupe lose her teeth and hair and grow oozing warts on her lips; imagined how long it would take her to bleed to death if I went at her spleen with a spoon. And then I got up and went to work.

AFTER BERRY AND I both shifted to nights, we slid into a routine of sneaking cookies and Kool-Aid from the med room and going down to Jerry Kovitch's private room to watch *Star Search* on his twenty-seven-inch TV. Berry wasn't working the night I found Eleanor Pierce in the med room. It was late, maybe ten o'clock, and all the patients were down. I made my rounds slowly, walking past folded wheelchairs, pleasantly aware of how quiet even my own steps were. I decided that even though Berry wasn't around, I'd steal some juice and head to Jerry's room, maybe watch the news — but when I went to punch in the combination on the med room's locked door, I saw it was already open. Eleanor was in there, cross-legged on the floor with a box of Vanilla Wafers in her lap.

"Hey there," she said, "got any cocoa? Ovaltine will do. Got any Ovaltine?"

This wasn't the Eleanor I had to wrangle into the shower. She was lucid. Present. She sat in the glow of the open refrigerator with a face so unlined and eyes so impossibly clear she could have been any age: a young woman, a girl.

"We don't have cocoa, Eleanor, or Ovaltine," I said. "I'm sorry." I handed her a paper cup of juice and sat down opposite her, crossing my legs too. She began to talk and didn't stop for a long time.

"Do you know the sound a train makes?" she asked. "One really far away? I like that sound. That might be my favorite sound."

She said, "When a black widow spider bites you, your thumb can swell up like a melon."

She said, "My son is dead."

I just listened. Eleanor's voice was like a bobber on a flat lake, that still and even. I listened and leaned into the words she had been saving for years or forever. We sat in refrigerator light, and she talked and talked, blessing me.

∽◌◦◦◌∼

I WAS NINETEEN YEARS old when I left the Lindberghs, ending nearly eleven years with them, nearly fifteen years of shuttling between foster homes like a water bug between floating leaves and garbage. Finally, I belonged to myself. In one of his finer moments, Bub forked over $500.00 for the deposit on a house Teresa and I wanted to rent over by Fresno City College. He called it a loan, but we both knew he'd never see it again. How could I have paid him back? I earned $3.10 an hour at the nursing home, drove a $900.00 car with a battery that leaked a pork-rind smell and was probably slowly poisoning me, had no car insurance, no medical insurance, no bank account. The smallest thing could have ruined me — a fender bender or broken leg — and yet I was happy. I oozed happy, leaked happy like the car battery leaked pork rind. As I drove to my new house in my piece-of-shit car, Katrina and the Waves came on the radio. She was walking on sunshine and so was I. I turned the volume all the way up.

Even with Bub's $500.00, Teresa and I couldn't afford the house, so we scoured the *Fresno Bee* for a roommate and found Val. He held a real job as a mechanic, though you'd never have known it. His fingernails were pristine, and he shaved twice a day and walked in a cloud of Polo cologne. The best thing about Val was his furniture, nice stuff that matched. He moved in and spent the first weekend arranging and rearranging his things, the throw pillows, the framed prints of Monet's watery gardens, the ceramic vases filled with cattails.

When everything was set and settled, we threw a huge party. Teresa had made the guest list, and because I didn't know anyone, for the first hour I walked around my own house feeling like a bellhop, carrying bits of overheard conversations from room to room, other people's talk itching along my fingertips. Most of the minglers were guys who had gone to San Joaquin Memorial with Teresa's new boyfriend, Marcus. They wore vividly striped cotton shirts with the collars flipped up, carried plastic cups of beer to one another from the keg in the kitchen and said "Hey, man" every five seconds. Apart from me, Teresa and our mutual friend Stephanie, who we'd known since middle school, there were no girls at all at the party until Penny showed up with Amber Swenson and Diane Rodriguez. I realized that even though they were still in high school, they were more like me than anyone else there, both thrilled and embarrassed to be at a grown-up party. No one's parents would come home. Anything could happen. *Ack*.

The four of us moved in a clot over to the liquor table, all of us in pegged jeans and flats and V-neck sweaters worn backward. We mixed vodka and sour mix right in the red Popov bottle, shook and poured. Within an hour, everything had loosened and blurred; within two, I stood puking in the bushes outside next to Penny, who was also puking, but we agreed, wiping our faces as we came back inside, that it was a great party. The best.

Toward the end of the night, I found myself in a serious conversation with Teresa and Stephanie about the sad state of my sex life. I'd had one boyfriend, Mark (on the God squad), and a short dating stint with a guy in my speech class who cheated on me immediately, on New Year's Eve, when I was home with killer cramps. Two lovers in nineteen years: how embarrassing for me.

"See that guy over there?" Teresa tossed her head in the direction of one of the collar-flippers, a shaggy blond with full Mick Jagger lips. Half sitting, half reclining on the stairs with his eyes closed, he held a full cup of beer on the verge of spilling. "That's Matt," she said. "He's really experienced. You should sleep with him."

"Okay," I said, and did.

                                   ☙

I HAD MY SISTER back. She'd called me up one day when I still lived with the Lindberghs and asked if I wanted to take in a movie. Afterward, we had coffee and gelatinous pie at Denny's, and I knew, from the easy way she talked to me, that in her mind I was no longer one of them, the enemy family. She could share pie with me, and information. I wasn't sure what had changed about me — and didn't want to ask her in case she changed her mind — but when we left the Denny's parking lot in our separate cars, I found I could still feel the gift of her trust, small and solid as a sugar packet or a book of matches in my hip pocket.

By the time we moved into the College Street house with Val, Teresa and I were closer than ever before. We wore the same clothes and shoes, ran with the same friends, worked the same shifts at the nursing home, took the same classes at FCC. On payday, we drove to the check-cashing place, put rent in a kitchen drawer, prepared to spend the rest. This involved warm beer and hot rollers and the Bangles or Motels at a deafening pitch on the stereo. Stephanie would come over and iron her clothes in her underwear and do the trick where she blow-dried her hair and sprayed it at the same time, forming perfectly rigid wings above each ear. There was never enough money for groceries, but there was money for the Scoreboard, a sports bar/dance club in Ashland. Stephanie had a crush on a waiter there, and we slipped him 100 percent tips to bring us Singapore slings and furry whiskey sours and baskets of French fries, the only almost-vegetable we ate those days.

Months passed like this before Val moved out suddenly, leaving us no furniture except the beds upstairs. Downstairs was so vacant that we could have bowled in there. When winter came, Teresa and I sat over the heating grate and listened to KERA on the clock radio (the stereo was Val's too, as fate would have it). Dinner was canned chili or soup or oatmeal in a big wooden bowl on the floor between us. We dropped classes and pounds, found we could live on fifteen dollars a month for staple items at Safeway — raisin bran, potatoes, Campbell's tomato soup, bananas — plus a little more for emergency hangover food on mornings when we had to be at work, giving tub baths and brushing breakfast-caked dentures only hours after we'd fallen into our spinning beds.

Still, astonishing things happened.

1. One Saturday morning at the hospital, Teresa and I were in Cordelia Danke's room flipping rubber bands at each other and watching a *Berenstain Bears* episode on her TV. It was a slow, warm day, with ribs of sun on the blinds, and I felt like singing something. Nothing but "La Cucaracha" came to mind, so I sang that quietly as I made Cordelia's bed. Teresa began to sing too and kicked up the volume. Walking over to where Cordelia sat like a stone in her wheelchair, Teresa took her hands and serenaded her, filling in the parts she didn't know with rousing da-dah's.

Cordelia was one of our favorites, though she didn't speak, walk or feed herself. Senile dementia was her diagnosis, but that was a catchall on three-fourths of the patients' charts; it didn't mean anything. No one really knew why Cordelia stopped functioning. She was old, but so were lots of people out in the world, driving cars, baby-sitting their grandchildren. Cordelia was old, but that day, Teresa was singing vibrantly to her about cockroaches, and her face woke up. She began to sing back, mumbling at first. Teresa and I were shocked into silence, but Cordelia went on without us, her voice louder and clearer by the second. She knew the words Teresa didn't. Her song grew so passionate, some of the other nursing assistants came in, and the shift RN and the director. The family was called. Within two weeks, Cordelia was up and walking the halls, going into the dining hall for her dinner, choosing her own clothes. After that, no one could tell us that music was not a powerful thing.

2. On another day, Teresa and I took separate cars to work because she had to meet Marcus right after. We left at the same time, but I made a light she didn't and lost her. Halfway through passing out the breakfast trays, I realized I hadn't seen her yet and hurried to the time clock to see if she'd punched in. Nope. Something had happened to her, I was sure of it; it was the only explanation. I went to the shift supervisor, a bitter pill of a nurse named Catherine Birch, and asked her if I could leave for half an hour to go out looking for my sister. She couldn't spare me, she said, and besides, Teresa was likely just blowing off the shift. It happened all the time; I should just go back to work. When I insisted I had to leave, she insisted I had to stay, and finally I ran out in tears. So what if I lost my skanky job? This was my sister.

Before I'd even driven a mile up the road, I saw Teresa walking against traffic, her white jumper spotted with blood. Her tights were ripped, and her knees and legs looked banged up. She'd totaled her car not five minutes from home and had been hobbling to get to me ever since. We hugged like people who had saved each other, which was true. Had always been true.

3. Spring found us in lawn chairs, working on tans in our

ratty backyard. You only had to say the word *sun* around Teresa and she was brown as a berry, but I had only two shades — pink and red. It wasn't fair. REO Speedwagon rattled from our cheap boom box: *Heard it from a friend who heard it from a friend who heard it from another you been messin' around.* When it came time to flip the tape, I flipped over too, to burn my top half.

"I don't suppose you'd go get me a glass of water?" Teresa whined. "Please, please, please, my darlingest most wonderful sibling." Her hands clasped, she swooned.

I got up, play grumbling, and when I came back out with the water, fully intending to dump it on her, she sat holding a blow flower, examining it gently.

"Oh my God," she said, looking at the globe of fine spires like it was a halo around the Virgin. She reached over to pick one of the dandelions near her chair, held it in her other hand and said, "Dandelions are blow flowers, and blow flowers are dandelions."

This should have been funny, but it wasn't; it was a revelation. We'd both lived a score of years without knowing the stages of this flower or weed, without knowing that things can change into other lovely things and stay rooted. We laughed and looked at each other in amazement; then she offered the flower up to me: make a wish.

4. Our mother came back.

WHEN FRIENDS ASKED ABOUT the business with our mother, I tended to use forms of the word *meet,* as if for the first time. I called her by her first name, Jackie, and said we were meeting her for dinner when she arrived in town. She might come by the apartment. She might stay a few days. We were playing it by ear. Frankly, I thought the whole reunion thing was bizarre. My sisters and I were finally adults, finally to the place where we didn't need a mother, real or otherwise, and there she was. Talk about bad timing.

A lengthy letter explained why Jackie chose to reach out to us after so much time. Her mother had died recently of emphysema, leaving her money expressly for the trip to California to visit us. She was coming with two friends from Michigan, where she now lived with her husband, Mike. Her girlfriends had never been to the West Coast before; after Fresno they would drive out to LA to see the ocean and Disneyland. I looked but found no clear clues to her in the letter: she seemed polite, not too eager or sobby, and her handwriting was neat and even. It occurred to me that since I remembered so little of her, pretty much any woman of a certain age could show up at the restaurant saying she was our mother and I would have to believe her. In that way, it was like a game show: Name That Mother, Tic Tac Mother.

In the weeks that preceded her visit, my sisters and I talked at length and declared it would be okay. A-OK, in fact. She would come, we'd show her our photo albums and track awards, the litter of kittens we had named after brands of perfume. We would introduce her to our friends and boyfriends, and she'd see how fine we were doing, how very well off we were, considering, and leave feeling less guilty or whatever. Our life together would go on as usual.

At the time, the three of us were living in a townhouse in Ashland. We had only been there for two months, but things were going smoothly. Teresa and I lost the College Street house right as Penny graduated from Ashland High, so we all joined up together, naturally. There was no real adjustment to be made; in fact, we found living together as adults even easier than as children. Without parents to try and wrangle love or attention from (or ignore or hide from), without fear, uncertainty and obligation, days were distilled, simple. It was just us, and *us* we knew like breathing.

The restaurant we chose for the meeting was the Acapulco, a pink monstrosity on Blackstone where waiters in sombreros served gooey platters of California-Mex. When Jackie arrived, there was a round of awkward hugging, stuttered hellos. She looked nice enough, a lady in her early forties with a poof of dark-brown hair and large, square-rimmed glasses. Her cotton turquoise pants and matching blouse with sailboats looked out of place in Fresno, but then, she didn't live in Fresno; she lived in Michigan, the state that looked, on our Rand-McNally map, like a green mitten sandwiched between two blue snowballs.

We sat down, ordered distractedly, and picked at the shards of tortilla chips in a wooden bowl while Jackie talked. I thought she might wait until we'd gotten through our first round of frozen margaritas, but no, she launched right into the nostalgia — how

Penny never crawled but scooted around on her backside, rubbing a bald spot on her head; how Teresa was always a little helper
in the kitchen, could do dishes and cook spaghetti at five; how
after I was weaned I would steal Penny's bottle out of her crib and
hide in the closet with it. When she'd find me, I'd deny it, holding
the bottle all the while, fat tears dripping from my fat cheeks.

The food arrived, big, messy plates of it. I dabbed at my
puddle of refried pintos with my fork and thought how quickly
everything had become like those beans, a brown, indiscernible
ooze.

She was back.

She was back, and that made her leaving absolutely unavoid-
able. We had to think about it again, all of our earliest questions
crooked like fingers to drag us down the rabbit hole: *Did she leave
because of something we did? Were we bad? Did we deserve it?* I
didn't want the rabbit hole. I didn't want any of it. Memory lane
was a sucker punch; I preferred the brain doctor: *Close your eyes
and count backward from one hundred. You won't feel a thing.*

Suddenly Jackie was crying, sobbing into her enchiladas,
saying how sorry she was. She never wanted to go away, but she
had to. Our dad — she called him Frank — would have killed
her. He threatened her, saying just how he'd do it, his hands on
her throat. She didn't have a choice, did she? He'd have done it
too, we had to believe her.

I didn't know what to think. Did our dad have it in him to
kill her or anyone? How was I to know? I hadn't seen him since I
was six years old, hadn't talked to him since I was fifteen and he
called us out of the blue at the Lindberghs'. Unfortunately, I had
beat Penny in a race to the phone, and so I was the one to hear
his voice — soft, quavering, disturbing — as he talked about his
release from a rehab clinic. "I'm an alcoholic," he said. "And I've
made some mistakes. I can admit that now." He was married

again, to a woman named Zoe, and they were expecting a child. Then, quite abruptly, he said, "You were always my favorite. I used to call you Bobo. You were my little Bobo . . . do you remember that?"

I did remember. I hung up the phone.

"Who was that?" Penny asked. She had opened the refrigerator and was swinging her weight against the door in the precise way that drove Hilde around the bend.

"Wrong number."

⟡

"DON'T GET ME WRONG," Jackie said, "I know it's too late for me to be your mother the way I would have liked. But I really want to get to know you, be your friend. And I want to help you if you'll let me." She paused, took a substantial hit from her margarita, and then said, "You girls are working so hard to finish school. It might make things easier for you to come to Michigan and stay with us. All you'd have to pay for is tuition. You could save some money."

The table fell silent. Penny traced wet circles on the side of her water glass. Teresa tore at the cocktail napkin that said *Arriba! Arriba!* in hot-pink cursive. And our mother? I didn't dare look over to see what expression she wore after making such an offer. She was either remarkably courageous to open herself this way, knowing we would shut her down and rightly so, or she was completely clueless and really thought we might say yes. It's not that it wasn't a nice thing for her to do. It was, and even slightly tempting for practical reasons. Teresa and I were both trying to carry fifteen credits at Fresno City College and working full-time at the nursing home; Penny clerked in a video store and would start classes at Fresno State in the fall. We were making our bills every month, but barely, and it was exhausting to think about money and just how many things could go wrong and level us. That said, we would be crazy to leave California to live with an absolute stranger who was arguably the reason for every bad thing that had ever happened to us. Crazy to uproot ourselves just so she could work out this whole mother-guilt thing. And if my sisters were speechless, unable to respond, then I would speak for all of us. Wasn't I the friendly one, after all? I formed the words *No, thank you,* but before they could leave my mouth, I heard Teresa say, "Wow. What a great idea. I just might take you up on that."

In the end, money wasn't the reason Teresa moved to Michigan — a guy was. Her boyfriend, Marcus, had been messing with her head, making her think she didn't want to be alive if she couldn't have him. I never liked Marcus. He drove an aphid-green Porsche 914 and was always sneering, like a mean dog or a rock star. His face was the kind you look at and know it's either stone ugly or devastatingly handsome, not anywhere in between. Marcus worked construction, and before he dumped her, Teresa would go to his house every day at 6 A.M. to make his lunch because he told her once that she built a good sandwich. What she had for him was that dreadful kind of love where you lose yourself absolutely, going all the way in without leaving a bread-crumb trail; where each day brings on worry like an avalanche because you're sure he's going to leave you — why wouldn't he? Even you have left you.

When the breakup ax finally fell, Teresa couldn't stop showing up at Marcus's door in the middle of the night asking why. One night, she walked in without knocking to find him in bed with Rhonda Snelling. Too stunned to be embarrassed, Marcus got up and started wrestling with Teresa, trying to get her out the door. Adrenaline had her pushing back hard, and suddenly they were at the second-story window, Teresa teetering on the sill, screaming and gouging at his face with her fingernails. When it struck them both how close they were to ending up in the newspaper the next day, Marcus backed off; Teresa stood up, directed a long, lethal look at Rhonda, who was still in bed, damselesque, the sheet pulled up to her collarbones, and left in tears.

Somehow, it didn't help Teresa to know that Rhonda was a tremendous slut, the kind of girl who only believes she's beautiful when she hears it from someone else's boyfriend. In high school, there was no one in our circle who hadn't lost at least one boyfriend to Rhonda. This was different, though. Teresa thought she would marry Marcus and couldn't, in fact, see herself separate from him. What would she do now? Who would she be if not his girlfriend, his sandwich-builder?

Before she had time to answer those questions, Marcus and Rhonda showed up at our apartment. They didn't have the nerve to come to the door and so let the car idle in our cul-de-sac until I went out to meet them. Leaning against the hood of Marcus's aphid-green car, they grinned like maniacs.

"What are you doing in January?" Rhonda asked, fanning her left hand dramatically. There sat the diamond on its thin band, slight as a tear.

TERESA'S DECISION TO MOVE was so quick and final that I swore I heard a clicking noise — *off* — and suddenly she could breathe again. Although there were still several months before her flight to Michigan, in every respect but physically, she was gone. Michigan provided the perfect escape hatch, granting her thousands of miles between herself and the happy couple, and the fantasy of living where no one knew her, where the potential for reinvention was as bottomless as the Great Lakes she'd be living between.

While Teresa busied herself with new hope and shopping for a proper winter coat, I threw myself into denial. At first, not talking about her leaving worked well enough: we went on as before, playing our Tears for Fears album so loud there wasn't room for anything else in our ears or between them, eating pasta right out of the saucepan over the kitchen sink, borrowing each other's clothes and leaving them in heaps on the bathroom floor. Then Penny dropped *her* bomb. She was moving in with David Watkins, her new boyfriend and the man who, until a few months earlier, was her speech and debate teacher at Ashland High. It was quite a scandal, really; she was nineteen and he, her first lover, thirty-four. They set up house with frightening speed, first in a little cottage in the middle of an apple orchard behind the school, then in a tract house with a swimming pool and two-car garage. He bought her a Honda station wagon big enough to hold all three of their dogs; he bought her a washer and dryer.

How else to see it? My family was dissolving. I realized how misguided I had been to feel, for a decade or more, so separate from my sisters. They were there, in every home, in all the kitchens and cars and front yards. Every time I had to endure a sleepless first night in another new room, I *could,* because a few feet away, or behind a thin wall, my sisters were curled, scritching their feet just like I was, saying the tired thread of a prayer that Granny had taught us as soon as we could talk. The world had happened to us simultaneously. Now there would just be me, and who was that anyway?

I found myself losing patience with everything: buttons on my shirt, the paper-towel dispenser, strands of hair in the bathroom sink. Everything was too hard, too stupid. I yelled and screamed at pretty much anyone, even the patients at work. I threw toothpaste and face powder and shoes that wouldn't untie. I said such horrible things to our friend Stephanie when she woke me up too early one morning, that she didn't want to stay over anymore on the trundle bed in my room, talking about boys we might stalk together. And then one day, I went too far and told Teresa, who was recovering from a surgical procedure on her cervix, that I hoped she would get cancer and die. I actually said that. The words hung in the air between us like an ugly bubble.

She left the room.

She left the state.

I was left there without her, hoping she understood, somehow — could intuit like those sets of twins I'd read about who invented a language known only to them, or who needed no language at all — that in losing her I was losing a foot, arm, heart chamber, an anchor, an every goddamned thing.

IT TOOK A WHILE, but Teresa started to send postcards from Michigan, letters with crude drawings of cows and deer and her new boyfriend, Braun: the local wildlife. She never mentioned the way things had been between us before she left, and I didn't either. I just saved her letters and sent back my own as if nothing had ever been breached, nothing lost.

Teresa seemed to be doing well. She had her own room at Jackie and Mike's, regular meals that featured steak and pork chops (I was still on the Campbell's-soup diet), and the use of their little red Ford pickup. Her classes in sports medicine at Ferris State College were clicking right along, and then there was Braun, a tall, blond Wisconsin boy she'd met at a dance club called the Alibi, where the carpet was purported to be tacky with beer and where people regularly peed in the bathroom sinks rather than wait in line. Pretty romantic. After that, she somehow found out Braun's class schedule and always happened to be walking the other way until she wore him down and he asked her out properly. During late-night phone calls, when I asked her what living with Jackie was like, she always said, "Fine. No problem." I couldn't imagine how it could be anything but complicated with all that history, all those questions — and they hardly knew each other — but Teresa wasn't like me. She was the tough-skinned one, the turtle girl. She didn't look at anything too closely, didn't ask questions she didn't want to know the answers to. Teresa probably didn't have a single expectation of Jackie, and so would never be disappointed. I started to think moving was the right thing, at least for her.

On the home front, Penny and David were still doing the nonmarital-bliss thing. Sometimes I'd go over to their house and do their dishes for ten dollars because they were busy and because, frankly, I needed it. Money was so tight that I'd sometimes steal food from one of my roommates, Mara, who received welfare checks. At twenty, Mara was unmarried with no job, no education, no prospects and a two-year-old son. It was hard to feel too bad for her, though, since all she ever did was sit around on the sofa watching soaps, ordering in pizza and Chinese noodles, leaving the leftovers to congeal in Styrofoam on the coffee table. When I'd take a can of soup from her side of the pantry and eat it cold, right out of the can, I couldn't help thinking about all those free-lunch tickets I threw away in high school, and I almost laughed, thinking of how I wouldn't give much thought to digging through garbage for them now.

One rainy day, I got rear-ended, banging up my Civic, and then got slapped with a fine because I'd been driving without insurance. I couldn't afford the repair work, couldn't afford the five-hundred-dollar fine or the insurance I now had to buy or else. Things were getting desperate. On top of all that, I learned my boyfriend Matt — yep, the experienced sex-smith Teresa had urged me to sleep with at that long-ago party — was screwing half the women in San Francisco, where he lived and went to school. He begged me not to break up with him, swearing he'd be faithful, and managed something approximate for about two months, then caved. He was addicted to sex, he said; it drove him, against his will, to strip clubs and nude beaches and skeezy bars where he picked up middle-aged married women and talked them out to his car. He thought the only possible treatment was saltpeter — hey, it worked for the army! — and a promise from me to be patient with his "illness." I broke up with him in his car while Mick Jagger called out to Angie. Matt cried and said he'd kill himself. He even took out the little knife he kept hidden in his glove box and held it to his wrists, but I was dead to it all. I was already gone, already peering out the window of the 727 that would take me to Detroit, trying to breathe cold clouds. As soon as I realized I could go, could step out of and away from Fresno as if it were a pair of spent shoes, I couldn't stop thinking about it. I called Teresa, and the next thing I knew I had a plane ticket waiting in the mailbox. It wasn't for good, I insisted to Teresa and myself, just for a few months, just long enough to clear my head, and then I would come home.

ON MY LAST FULL day in Fresno, I drove out to Bub and Hilde's to borrow a suitcase for the trip. I pulled up the long drive to the house and felt myself growing younger, smaller, less twenty-one than fourteen or twelve or eight, all the hot, gone years flying into my open mouth like dust. The field had fallen to foxtail and star thistle, and the electric fencing sagged so low in places that Patches, the one horse not sold off, was able to walk over it onto the lawn. He still came right into the house too; in fact, Tina had called me a few months before to recount how Patches had walked into the foyer when everyone was outside, busy with something, and then kept going, through the kitchen and into the living room, where he stood in front of the TV and took a long, horse-size piss, a half-gallon or more of it foaming on the blue-brown shag. All those years of Hilde protecting the carpet from shoes and food and the dogs, and Patches had pranced right in. There was some poetry in that.

I stopped my car in front of the abandoned fishpond and opened my door to two hundred pounds of happy dog. By the time I stood at the open front door, my fingers were damp and my jeans were covered with the dogs' short, fine hair. Bub and Hilde shouted me in, and we stood in the kitchen for a while, sipping warm red Kool-Aid out of plastic cups. They wanted to know how my classes at City College were going and if I still had that nice boyfriend; Bub pinched at my waistline and hips calling me Fats and Little Heifer, though I was barely a size five.

I found the house eerily unchanged. The place mats on the table were the plastic ones from our family trip to the London Bridge in Lake Havasu, Arizona, when I was ten? twelve? Fingerprints smudged the ancient yellow wall phone and the handle on the refrigerator, and I wondered briefly if I could find mine there too. I think I expected to feel angry, being back in that house, the same adolescent seething I never knew what to do with, but what came, instead, was a tingling in my fingers and toes and lips, the way hypothermia begins. I stared into the linoleum's gold and avocado swirls until they began to tilt, sickeningly, and then looked up into Hilde's face, alien as ever, completely unreadable. I needed to *go*.

The suitcase was in the tack shed at the back of the yard, next to the peeling tractor and defunct mustached Subaru, and Bub's half-built boat, which looked like it hadn't been touched in a good long while. Although the lock on the shed door was rusty, it gave with several firm yanks. Light rushed in, falling over Queenie's old saddle, stirrups looped stiffly around the horn. A string of bridles hung along one wall, their bits caulked with dried grass and horse slobber. I was so lost in the smells, sweet and loamy and bitter, that I didn't hear the wasps until it was too late. They came at me in an angry, humming arrow. The first sting jangled between my shoulder blades, the second behind my right ear, and I was sent stumbling toward the house. I heard myself screaming, but it sounded too far off and muffled to be me, and the word I heard again and again was *Mom!* I fell onto the patio, scraping my knees, the wasps around my head like an unforgiving rain. Hilde found me there. She pulled me inside, stood with me until I quieted, then helped me off with my shirt.

"Kneel down," she said, and I did, right there on the carpet, in front of the TV and horse light, while apparitions of every childhood dinner rivered in from the empty kitchen. I crouched with my arms crossed, flinching as Hilde rubbed a camphor-soaked cotton swab on my back.

"That hurts, doesn't it? I'm sorry."

Half an hour later, Bub and Hilde stood in the mouth of the front door and watched me leave. I waved once, backing away.

I never saw them again.

ON FEBRUARY 1, 1987, I arrived in Detroit — to snow. Teresa, Jackie and her husband, Mike, met me at the gate, and we ran through a flurry to get to Mike's Chevy Blazer, them in parkas, me in my thin jeans and penny loafers. As we made our way toward the freeway, Mike concentrating on road signs and Jackie fiddling with the radio and the heat controls, Teresa and I sat close in the backseat. She looked well. Her punk, longer-on-one-side haircut had grown out and softened, and her face was rounder.

"You've gained some weight," I said.

"I know, I know. It's a rule here. The Michigan Snow Cow rule: get fat or freeze. Just wait, it'll happen to you too."

"What about those shoes?" I said, pointing to her boots, which were puffy and trimmed with ratty-looking fake fur. "Will those happen to me?"

"Shut up," she said, laughing. "They're not even mine; they're Mom's."

Mom's. It slid out of her mouth so easily. Would I gain that like ten pounds? Like a pair of furry shoes?

"Hey, girls, are you hungry?" This from Mike, who had spotted a Taco Bell and was quickly changing lanes to get to it. He was quiet and decisive, I could tell, a military-looking man with short slicked hair parted deeply to the left and a trimmed caterpillar mustache. Although Mike had been born and raised on a farm in northern Michigan, he met our mother in Arizona. What either of them was doing there, I couldn't glean. They skirted my questions like pros, cohorts, divulging only little pieces of things. They'd been married thirteen years and had come to live in Michigan after Mike's great-aunt had fallen ill. Mike had one grown son from his first marriage, but he was a screw-up, the kind who only called home late at night, wanting money. I didn't ask Jackie what had happened to Roger, and I didn't ask if she'd ever spoken to our dad again. Maybe I was a cohort too, blinking away the hard questions like *Why didn't you come back for us earlier?* Thirteen years meant I was only eight when Mike and Jackie got together. We had just gotten to the Lindberghs then; we weren't even half-grown.

Mike passed back giant Pepsis and paper-wrapped burritos, and we got back on the highway, where strip malls and cineplexes soon gave way to fields of corn that had been harvested and shorn down to the nubs. Ice-covered, grizzled. On the road, snow swirled like a liquid, burying the lane markers, and I wondered how Mike kept the Blazer steady. He didn't seem the least bit fazed, wasn't even bothering to keep both hands on the wheel, in fact. He was an expert, I assumed, Macho Snow Guy. I had seen snow maybe five times in my life. The first time was with the Clapps, when they took us on a day-trip to a town called Fish Camp to visit a family friend. It was past New Year's, but the little town still had its Christmas decorations up, weepy garlands and string lights, fat Santas waving from sleighs. Over it all, snow sat heavily. Wet and dirty, it bowed the roofs of houses and car tops and turned the sides of the narrow, curving road into peppered slush. I must have been six, then, or seven. My sisters and I didn't have boots or gloves and so wore sneakers and two pairs of socks on each hand. We parked near a meadow, and Mrs. Clapp told us we could go out and play, they would wait in the car.

We were thrilled. The snow in the open field was still clean, like sugar on a table, like something that would catch you if you fell at it. We left the warm car and ran into the meadow, lurching like cats in the rain, our sneakers punching through the icy crust and catching at the toes. It was harder than I thought, colder too. When I tried to form snowballs, my hand-socks quickly soaked through, the wet coming at my fingers like a row of little teeth. My feet were wet too, and cumbersome.

"Come on," I called out to Teresa and Penny. They were maybe twenty feet away, hunched over and scooping snow through their open legs like dogs digging in dirt, but they didn't seem to hear me. I wanted to go back to the car and get warm, but knew Mrs. Clapp would be mean about it, gloating — here she'd given us this chance to have fun and I'd wasted it. Why did she even *try?* So I stayed put. It wasn't so bad. My fingers were barely tingling at all. If I stood there long enough, maybe I wouldn't feel anything, cold climbing from my hands to my elbows to my neck until I wore it like a tinkling ornament.

I must have been shivering a little because Jackie poked her head through the gap between the seats of the Blazer and said, "Are you warm enough, Paula? I could turn the heat back up."

"No, no, I'm fine. I'm good," I said, turning back to the gone corn. That's when Teresa reached over and put her hand on my leg. "I'm glad you're here," she said, whispering it like it was just for us, a snowball passed between mittens.

"Yep," I said. "Me too."

⟜

FINDING A JOB IN Michigan was harder than I thought. Elk Grove, the town Jackie and Mike lived in, had fewer people in it than the high school I'd gone to. Downtown was all of two streets and a stoplight. There were three bars in addition to the Moose Lodge, one drugstore, Ace Hardware, a Pizza Hut and several gas station / convenience stores that sold videos and camouflage clothing as well as beer singles and lottery tickets. Unless I wanted to bag groceries at the IGA or work at the Yoplait factory in a hairnet and paper shoes, I was better off twelve miles away in Big Rapids, which was home to a technical college and contained, therefore, all the expected fast-food places, as well as JC Penney's, Kmart and a four-screen movie theater. I ended up at Domino's Pizza as a delivery babe making $3.50 an hour plus mileage. Granted, giving sponge baths and enemas at the nursing home hadn't been glamorous, but I didn't feel I had taken much of a step up delivering pizza to frat houses and keg parties. And worse, small-town Michigan was nowhere. Cold nowhere at that.

Two things were good in those days: I shared a closet with Teresa again, and I had unlimited access to fatty foods. Jackie and Mike kept a freezer full of red meat and cooked everything in the deep fryer. Every day during my first three months in Michigan ended with a root-beer float. I gained my Snow Cow pounds plus a few more. Teresa was busy with school and Braun, but several nights a week we hung out together in our shared room, her studying and me reading in bed in flannel pajamas and three pairs of socks. Sometimes she set me up with one of Braun's friends and we'd all go to the Alibi together, and sometimes she and I would just get into the truck and drive into Big Rapids for soft-serve ice cream, even though it was fifteen degrees outside.

I slowly grew more comfortable around Jackie and Mike, but I didn't know quite what to think of their lifestyle. Jackie worked as a computer technician at a factory that made lumber-saw parts, and Mike did something with quality control for a Chrysler plant. They left the house before seven each morning and would meet downtown at five-thirty for "just one." Sometime between nine-thirty and eleven they'd come in drunk, microwave something in Tupperware, then head to bed. Get up and do it again. I guess I thought having two "daughters" in the house would slow them down so they'd stay at home more, but it didn't. I felt hurt by this but wasn't sure why. I hadn't moved to Michigan to have a mother again, but for free room and board, and I was getting that. What was missing? Why did it sting that Jackie wasn't making any effort to get to know me? That I didn't know much more about her than I had that first night in the Mexican restaurant?

One day, when Jackie called me from work to ask if I'd throw on some chops or make lasagna, I snapped and said, "Why? You'll just end up drinking your dinner as usual." She hung up with a clatter, and I stared at the phone for a long minute, wondering what I'd started. Hours later, I heard the door and soon Mike was standing at the mouth of the room I shared with Teresa. His eyes were glassy, and he leaned against the doorframe slightly.

"Who the hell do you think you are," he said thickly, "talking to your mother like that? Don't you know what she's done for you?"

"No," I said. "I guess I don't." I had my flannel pajamas on and tugged at the thread on a loose button.

"Well, if you don't, let me tell you. Every year we were married I knew when you girls' birthdays were. Not because she told me, but because she would cry and cry on those days. Cry and cry." He was getting into it now, moved himself, his voice thick and choked-sounding. "She never forgot you, not for one day. Don't you think she deserves some respect for that?"

Mike stood silent for a moment, letting his words sink in, and then stumbled out and down the hall. Perhaps an hour later I heard Jackie's car pull into the garage. I waited for her to come down the hall and speak her mind as he had, but she didn't. I heard her running the tap, then the rattle of the aspirin bottle over the sink, then her bedroom door clicking quietly closed.

DON'T ASK ME HOW — I still shake my head at it, wondering — but my three-month head-clearing trip to Michigan turned into years. I earned three degrees, married one of my professors with breakneck speed, had a child within a year and quickly filed for a divorce. My son's birth showed me that although I'd had countless mothers, I didn't know anything about *mothering,* how joyful and transformative and complicated and staggeringly difficult it can be.

I moved often (my record is five times in little more than a year), first via Hefty bag, with everything I owned stuffed into my tired Plymouth Sundance, later in U-Haul trailers, singing along to top-forty country with my son, Connor, and his cat, Zero, beside me on the bench seat. With each move I felt myself growing farther from the homes and people I wanted to forget, but also further from being the kind of woman who knew how to find a place or a person worth sticking around for.

I've lived in Dallas, Phoenix, Ann Arbor, rural Vermont, but never again in California. I do visit every few years when I get particularly lonely for yellow hills dotted with scrub oak. If you take the Pacheco Pass from San Francisco into the Valley, you can stop at Casa de Fruta, where avocados are still five for a dollar, then head down and down, past the marigold farm that flashes electric orange through the curves, past the dramatic bluff where an Indian princess is said to have flung herself to her death for love. When you hit Highway 99, the land flattens into a table offering up fields and farm stands, weed-choked sloughs. Palm trees jut from the horizon like a misplaced dream. Trucks hurtle by full of tomatoes, pistachios, plums, blowing the oleander in the median into a flurry.

This is where I'm from.

Just last summer, I visited Fresno for the first time in eight years. I took a shortcut to the Lindberghs' house, trusting memory, and still found the street. Of course, the house was smaller, the driveway shorter by half, the willow gone entirely. After her parents' deaths, Tina and her husband took over as proprietors. They bought several new horses, changed the fence lines, added some new trees, but most things haven't changed. The John Deere tractor was still standing, a gray mass by the woodpile, every trace of red long spent. Bub's fantasy boat lay abandoned in the backyard like the skeleton of Moby Dick. I got out of my rental car, stood on the shoulder of the road and let myself be haunted. I didn't go up to the house; it came to me, like the dust and pollen and silky fibers of milkweed. Like all the days I was a daughter there. I fished my camera out of the car, took one picture, then another. August had bleached the sky to eggshells, the orchards to straw, the house to a daub of clay. Nothing and everything was the same. Nothing and everything was enough.

Driving north again, I found myself thinking about the evenings — lovely, plum-colored, hypnotically still — when I was a teenager. I'd ride my bike around and around our long block, just to be out of the house and alone. Sometimes, everything was so hushed I could hear a world of crickets in the long grasses, the wind ticking through my tires as I coasted, seeing just how long I could keep my bike upright and moving without pedaling. The phone lines hummed twenty feet up, and a breeze hummed in my ears and there was another humming too that might have been me. Might have been my own signal, parsed and plangent, as indelible as kite string — an SOS sent out past the thirsty air and the fences threaded with weeds and the tentative stars, of all the things I wanted and could not say.

THERE'S A BONNIE WITH my father's last name in the Fresno phone book. I check every year or so in the big row of phone books in the public library of whatever city I'm living in. Just this month I found a Franklin. Not Frank, as he was called when we were kids, but it might be our father. Might be. There's no listing for Cousin Keith, but Tanya is there. I won't call her, but I like knowing she's there, and thinking that perhaps her brain doctor has let her keep a memory of me and my sisters in our blue dresses at Deedee's funeral, or singing "If I Had a Hammer" in Granny's car, or kicking high on the swings in Radio Park. I check the book for the Clapps too, and the Spinozas and the Fredricksons, though I have never found them. They seem to have vanished — but then again, so have I.

Whenever I'm in Fresno, which isn't often, I look for Granny's mint-green box of a house, winding through streets in what feels to be the right part of town, casing neighborhoods like some kind of thief. Penny insists they tore it down years ago to put in a strip mall, but I'll keep looking. If I could see her stoop again, the patch of concrete where Keith spray-painted his name in loopy cursive, the trumpet creeper or pile of rusted car parts or the child-size hole in her back fence, maybe I'd forgive myself —

or come closer, anyhow — for not knowing the month or even the year Granny died.

Hilde Lindbergh died of cancer near Christmas of 1993. Several months before, she'd called to say she'd heard I was pregnant and wanted to send a gift package: a pastel baby blanket she and Tina had worked on together, three pairs of tiny embroidered socks, some used T-shirts they'd found at a yard sale. I couldn't have been more shocked. We hadn't spoken since the day I borrowed the suitcase, and frankly, I had a hard time imagining Hilde giving me the slightest thought, let alone shopping for yarn, thumbing through baby socks at Kmart, wondering what colors I might like. As she asked questions about my new professor husband and congratulated me on the pregnancy, it was hard for me to stay focused. Her voice, still thickly accented, was dragging me back to where I knew she stood, in front of the kitchen window, the yellow phone's receiver disappearing under her chin. It was February, and the field would be green, the grass long and damp in the morning hours.

This was my opportunity to really talk to her, ask her the questions I had carried with me through every change of address, but I couldn't. I felt as mute as a shoe, muter still when she cleared her throat loudly and told me how ill she'd been the year before. "There was fluid around my heart," she said. "It was touch and go for a while." *Maybe she was gripping the phone then? The worn back of the kitchen chair? Maybe her eyes were closed for a half a minute against the light?* She went on to say the doctors had also gone in to remove tumors in her throat, and that she'd had a double radical mastectomy. What I thought was: *I wonder who will save her.* And then, like a small, petulant echo: *Why do I care?*

Bub died two years after Hilde when a massive embolism exploded in his brain, sending him crashing through a glass coffee table. With both of their deaths, I felt stricken and confused. If they had each lived several more years, would I have seen or talked to them again? Likely not, and yet I am still haunted by both of them. The Lindberghs weren't our family and couldn't be the parents we needed them to be, but we did *belong* to each other, and we belonged to those five dry acres. That was my home, more than any place before or since, and if I didn't know I loved it then, every cobwebby eave and crack in the sidewalk and patch of cockleburs, it was only because I couldn't.

Now I'm in Wisconsin, where there's a phenomenon called windchill and the tallest thing on the horizon is a grain silo, but Teresa is here. It's why I came, and why I've stayed so far. She lives minutes away with her husband, Braun — the same guy she began dating within months of moving to Michigan — and their two sons. Like me, she put herself through school and is now a physician's assistant, as supercompetent with her patients as she is with her kids, a mop, a roast. Penny is married as well. After several near misses with older men — like that first boyfriend with whom she set up early home — she declared she wouldn't date anyone who didn't know who Duran Duran was. She stuck to that, and six years ago married Josh, who is her age and adores her. They live in Jacksonville, Florida, where it's hot and wet and crawling with things that'd be only too happy to eat them alive. Penny and I talk several mornings a week while her kids holler in the background, painting the walls with cookie and pestering the dog.

Our mother is still in Michigan, though she divorced Mike long ago and has moved on to husband number five, an easy-tempered, bearish guy named Bart who builds a good fire and likes to putter in the garage and work with heavy equipment. On holidays, we all converge in Madison, drink too much red wine and fight over how long to cook the pork. Teresa's in high-efficiency mode for these affairs, planning the menus and mealtimes and sleeping arrangements. We all just nod and try to stay out of her way. Penny loves holidays because she still likes to be taken care of, brought a second piece of pie, a light blanket, her slippers. She cuddles up to Mom on the couch as they look through the Williams-Sonoma catalog. They get along fine. Penny always was the one who could ask for mothering and find a way to get it. Teresa has a workable relationship with our mother too, and credits the fact that she doesn't expect too much: "She's just human, you know."

And me and my mother? We're still figuring that out. She was there at my wedding, such as it was, and she was there when my son was born, but mostly I feel I know nothing about her. Sometimes, after a few glasses of wine, she'll divulge something about her girlhood in Washington. That's how I learned her own mother ran off when she was nine, leaving her to be raised first by her father, then in an orphanage, then by her older sister, and that they were reacquainted years later. She never speaks of her first two marriages before my father, or the many years she was away at the movies. We never talk about her leaving or what we've lost. I'm thirty-six this year, which means she's been back for sixteen years, exactly as long as she was gone. What have we learned during that time? What can we expect from each other? What can we still risk wanting, knowing, saying out loud? At Thanksgiving, I looked across the room and saw my son on my mother's lap, saw her press the side of her face against his, whisper something low and tender. I didn't look away; I didn't move toward them either. *What can we be to each other?* I don't know. The future is placeless, faceless, open as the backseat of a car heading anywhere at all. The past is a plastic garbage bag between my feet, hot air through a window. My sisters are with me.

ACKNOWLEDGMENTS

I AM DEEPLY INDEBTED to the Corporation of Yaddo, the MacDowell Colony and the National Endowment for the Arts for much-needed support and the gift of time. For early encouragement and advice, I thank Judy Sobeloff, Ted Genoways, Rick Field, Charlie Baxter and Terence Mickey. Thanks to the members of the Harmony Bar Writers' Collective, and especially Steve Kantrowitz for absolute confidence when I most needed it. Big thanks and big love to the many friends who read, advised, abided, talked me down from various ledges and distracted me with Ping-Pong: Margaret Price, Glori Simmons, Lori Keene, Sharon Walker, Brad Bedortha, Pam and Doug O'Hara, Kenny Cook, Jamie Diamond, Sarah Messer, Jonathan Lethem, Bruce Smith, Harry Bauld and Michael Schwartz.

I feel lucky to have found such a good home for the book at Little, Brown and grateful to have the faith, enthusiasm and considerable talents of Reagan Arthur, Emily Salkin Takoudes, Alison Vandenberg, Shannon Langone, Laura Quinn, Alex Kanfer, Andrea Chapin, Kristin Lang and Leigh Feldman. Finally, heartfelt thanks to Sandra Eugster for patience and compassion; to my son, Connor, for his fine mind and heart; and to Robin Messing for getting me through all the drafts and dark days, and for being my hero.

ABOUT THE AUTHOR

PAULA MCLAIN received her M.F.A. in poetry from the University of Michigan in 1996. Her poems have appeared in numerous literary journals and in the anthology *American Poetry: The Next Generation*. Her first book of poetry, *Less of Her*, was published in 1999. She lives in Ohio and is currently a teacher of poetry in the low-residency M.F.A. program at New England College.

LIKE FAMILY

GROWING UP IN OTHER PEOPLE'S HOUSES

A Memoir

~∞∞~

PAULA McLAIN

A Reading Group Guide

A conversation with Paula McLain

Like Family reaches all the way back to when you were only five years old. How did you go about tapping into your childhood memories to write the book?

In early drafts, I avoided dealing with the very young stuff because I was afraid I couldn't really get there, that those stories would be thin — but in the end it was easier than I thought. The details were there, available to me. In traumatic situations, children often protect themselves by stepping outside their bodies and viewing things happening as someone not involved, as a spectator. So you see, from the earliest, I was getting great training as a writer. I was a voyeur, quietly noticing everything, cataloging details, filing images away.

How did your skills as a poet play into your use of language in the memoir?

I love language, the sounds of words and what words can do. This served me in a surprising way as I was writing the memoir. Because I was very focused on and attentive to language and to building the book with one good, tight sentence at a time, one striking or lyrical image at a time, I could forget that I was writing about my life and revealing sensitive material. If I had been less aware of the art of writing, I might very well have shut down and not been able to finish the project.

Considering your difficult and at times painful personal history, why did you choose to write a memoir instead of finding solace in a novel? Did you have reservations about writing about the abuse that you and your sisters experienced?

I did try to write my story as fiction very early on, years ago, when I was still in graduate school, but it just wasn't coming together that way. I kept running into dead ends. I didn't know why then, but now I think that even though I was terrified (am terrified still) of exposing many of these memories and exposing myself at large, I wanted to own my experience. Claim it. Fiction would have provided a nice, safe out, but I believe I was ready to stop hiding from and denying the facts of my life.

When you were younger, it seemed that you had a strong bond with your foster father Bub. How did his betrayal affect you?

Out of all the foster fathers, Bub left the strongest impression, and not only because we were with the Lindberghs the longest. He was such a puzzle, a dreamer, a big talker, and full of a strange poetry, actually. He stole my heart, and, frankly, I didn't know I still had one to steal. When I was a teenager and saw his flaws fully, I was devastated. I thought finally I had found a father, the real thing, someone I could trust and be safe with. When he betrayed me, a door slammed shut. I realize now that he was doing the best he could, that he loved me as much as he was capable of under the circumstances. But I'm still having trouble budging that door.

It is clear in Like Family *that your relationship with your sisters was impenetrable. Can you speak directly to what your sisters meant to you as you were growing up together, and what your relationship with them is like now?*

I think children are islands. I felt very alone in my childhood and shared my feelings about what was happening to me, to us, with no one. But my sisters never left me. This meant everything then and means everything now. They're my family. Things and people come and go, terrible things happen, but what I have with my sisters is, yes, impenetrable. We have this shared history, which we do talk about now. And when we do, I understand that, although I felt alone as a child, I wasn't.

How do your sisters feel about Like Family? *How were your personal experiences different from those of your sisters?*

My sisters have been very supportive of the book all the way along, and proud of me for undertaking the project. I'm deeply grateful for this, particularly since I know they would never have elected to be revealed in such a way. Both of them have said that reading certain passages — even from the distance of twenty-some years, and with the additional buffer that the telling was *my* version of events, not their own — was like reliving memories, experiencing them and the attendant pain and disappointment afresh. Being aware of their feelings has caused me some unease. My sisters have their own versions of our childhood, as well as their own strategies for dealing with the fallout. My sense is that they both feel more comfortable with the past behind them, or at least at a manageable distance from themselves. While I respect this, I'm more inclined to agree with Faulkner, who said, "The past is never dead. It's not even past."

What is your relationship like with your birth parents today?

I have no relationship with my birth father. I don't know where he is or even if he's still living. The last time I spoke to him was on the phone when I was fifteen. Hearing his voice was like being struck by lightning. I couldn't handle it then; I hung up on him. I'm not sure I'm any more ready to handle it now.

I do have a relationship with my mother and have since she came back when I was twenty. It's a complicated relationship, as you might imagine. I don't know if I can trust her or even if I want to try. I don't know that I want her to know me, because that would make me vulnerable to her again. People often ask, "Do you forgive her?" I'm not there yet. For thirty-plus years, I've blamed myself for her leaving and everything that followed. I'm still trying to forgive myself.

There are a number of instances in Like Family *in which it appears that foster parents are exploiting the system. Do you think that this is common? Has the situation for foster children changed since you were young? Do you have ideas about how the system could be changed to make things easier for the children?*

I don't know how common it is for foster parents to exploit the system; I only know my experience. Right now, I'm reading a memoir written by a longtime foster parent that presents another side. In it, the foster parent is a saintly, selfless figure, the one safe oasis in a sea of abusive birth parents and overworked social workers. I'm sure it is this way in some cases, but I didn't know any oases. I knew frying pans and fires.

Since I've left the system, I think things have only gotten worse. There are more kids needing care and fewer parents willing to give it, and no easy answers about how to improve the system. I do think prospective foster parents need to receive more specific and extensive training/education (standard training is thirty hours) to prepare them for the children, often quite troubled, entering their homes. I think there should be more extensive screening for foster parents to weed out the less-than-committed or the possibly exploitive, but I also know how hard foster parents are to come by, and that sometimes even a family who will take a child strictly for the money will be a safer placement for that child than an abusive situation at home. Which brings us right back to frying pans and fires.

How do you define family?

I spent most of my childhood fantasizing about what finding the perfect family — or having them finally find me — would mean. It seemed to me then that family meant permanence — a solid and unshakable connection. Something that couldn't be reversed, erased, dissolved by disappointment or betrayal or the signing away of responsibility. By that definition, I had the ideal family all along, in the bond with my sisters. Our connection wasn't and isn't perfect, of course, because we're not perfect. But it is constant; I trust it absolutely. I have also been lucky enough to find friends along the way who are, essentially, family — in that we love and sustain and know one another in deep and abiding ways. Robert Frost wrote, "Home is the place where, when you have to go there, they have to take you in." I think I once would have said that about family, hoping against hope that I would finally stick somewhere and stay, and belong beyond all doubt or evidence to the contrary. Now I would say, rather, that our real families — the people with whom we share the richest, most dynamic, most nurturing connections — we choose for ourselves.

Questions and topics for discussion

1. Paula and her sisters are abandoned by their parents at a very tender age, and yet their bond as sisters remains unshakable. In what ways is the sisters' relationship fortified by the breakup of their family?

2. How does Bub's ultimate betrayal change Paula's perspective? Is Bub a bad man, or merely human?

3. Paula and her sisters are shuttled from one house to another during their formative years, each time with the hope that they'll finally settle comfortably — but nearly every family they join suffers from its own problems. What does this suggest about the meaning or ideal of family?

4. Penny and Teresa are able to welcome their mother back into their lives with relative ease. Paula, by contrast, remains unsure. Why? Is it an issue of forgiveness or is it something else that makes Paula hold back?

5. When Paula hears from Hilde during her pregnancy, she's shocked. And yet she says, "The Lindberghs weren't our family and couldn't be the parents we needed them to be, but we did *belong* to each other" (page 259). What does Paula mean by this?

6. Each of the three McLain sisters has a strong personality. What particular traits do you attribute to each? How do you think their respective attitudes helped one another? Hurt one another?

7. There are two epigraphs at the beginning of the memoir, one from an Emily Dickinson poem and the other from a Neil Young song. Why do you think the author chose these quotes? What does each say about Paula's story?

8. Is *Like Family* an indictment of the foster care system?

9. Paula's "head clearing" trip to Michigan stretches into several years — she stays long enough to earn a degree, to marry, and to have a child. Then she begins to move all over the country, relocating in turn to several different states, but she never again returns to California. Why do you think Paula doesn't settle in one place? Why does she avoid California?

10. Do Paula and her sisters merely survive their childhood, or do they thrive despite its horrors and instability?

Paula McLain's suggestions for further reading

This Boy's Life by Tobias Wolff

The Boys of My Youth by Jo Ann Beard

Borrowed Finery by Paula Fox

Fierce Attachments by Vivian Gornick

Survival Stories: Memoirs of Crisis, edited by Kathryn Rhett

The Lost Children of Wilder: The Epic Struggle to Change Foster Care by Nina Bernstein

The Heart Knows Something Different: Teenage Voices from the Foster Care System, edited by Al Desetta

The Heart Is a Lonely Hunter and *The Member of the Wedding* by Carson McCullers

My Antonia by Willa Cather

A Tree Grows in Brooklyn by Betty Smith

Housekeeping by Marilynne Robinson

Cruddy and *One Thousand Demons* by Lynda Barry

Cat's Eye by Margaret Atwood

The Virgin Suicides by Jeffrey Eugenides

Sula by Toni Morrison

Who Will Run the Frog Hospital? by Lorrie Moore

Their Eyes Were Watching God by Zora Neale Hurston

Black Tickets by Jayne Anne Phillips

They Came Like Swallows and *So Long, See You Tomorrow* by William Maxwell

The Tiny One by Eliza Minot

Ellen Foster by Kaye Gibbons

The Unwanted: A Memoir of a Childhood
by Kien Nguyen

"Vivid and compelling. . . . A gripping, emotionally raw story. . . . Kien's story deserves a place with the best memoirs of immigration and exile." — Richard C. Kagan, *Minneapolis Star Tribune*

"A painfully evocative memoir. . . . A remarkable tale of survival at all costs." — Julie K. L. Dam, *People*

The Hacienda
by Lisa St. Aubin de Terán

"A beautiful memoir. . . . Lisa St. Aubin de Terán changed from a shy girl into a strong woman from these experiences; she pays them powerful respect, and offers a distinctive and elegant lesson to the reader." — Carolyn See, *Washington Post*

"Seductive. . . . The story of a nightmare marriage, as well as a regretful evocation of a beloved lost world. . . . *The Hacienda* is a transfixing performance." — Michael Upchurch, *New York Times Book Review*

Back Bay Books
Available wherever books are sold